Up and Running with C++

Springer
London
Berlin
Heidelberg
New York
Barcelona
Budapest
Hong Kong
Milan
Paris
Santa Clara
Singapore
Tokyo

Jan Graba

Up and Running with C++

 Springer

Jan Graba
School of Computing and Mathematics
University of Huddersfield
Huddersfield
HD1 3DH

ISBN 3-540-76234-5 Springer-Verlag Berlin Heidelberg New York

British Library Cataloguing in Publication Data
Graba, Jan
  Up and running with C++
  1.C++ (Computer program language) 2.Object-oriented
  programming (Computer science)
  I.Title
  005.1'33
  ISBN 3540762345

Library of Congress Cataloging-in-Publication Data
A catalog record for this book is available from the Library of Congress

Typesetting: camera ready by author
Printed and bound at the Athenaeum Press Ltd., Gateshead, Tyne and Wear
34/3830-543210 Printed on acid-free paper

Contents

Contents

Chapter 1   The Fundamentals of Object Orientation

Aims

- To make the reader aware of some of the major historical contributions to the development of object orientation.
- To introduce the terminology commonly associated with object orientation.
- To make the reader aware of the perceived benefits of object orientation and thereby instil an appreciation of its importance as an approach to the development of software.

1.1   Brief Background

The first OOPL (Object-Orientated Programming Language) was Simula, a language intended primarily for use in process simulation. Though the introduction of Simula dates back to 1967, the principles of object orientation which it embodied did not really begin to achieve prominence until the early 1980s. It was in 1980 that the other major OOPL, Smalltalk, appeared. Like Simula, it has had a great influence on the OOPLs which followed it. Of greater significance in the popularising of object orientation at this time, though, was the development of C++ by Bjarne Stroustrup of Bell Laboratories in the USA. This language was a considerably extended and enhanced version of the popular structured programming language C, which itself had appeared ten years earlier. Since C++ was developed from a more traditional structured language, it is a 'hybrid' language, rather than a pure OOPL. (The author states this simply as a fact, not as an indication that C++ is in some way inferior to those languages which are pure OOPLs.)

Since the early 1980s, the popularity of object orientation as an approach to the development of software has increased enormously, notably in establishing GUIs (Graphical User Interfaces) as the standard means of communicating with computers. It seems certain that this popularity will continue for at least the next few years. Beyond that, of course, it is very risky to predict anything in computing, but, for the time being at least, nobody involved in the development of software can afford to ignore the influence of object orientation.

1.2   Basic Concepts and Terminology

The term 'object orientation' embraces several distinct concepts and involves some specialised terminology with which it is necessary to become familiar before exploring the implementation of those concepts in C++. This section is intended to provide the necessary explanation of such terminology.

1.2.1   Objects

One fundamental issue which must be addressed at the outset is what is meant by the term **object** (in the context of Object-Orientated Programming). Loosely speaking, an object could be defined as *a software representation of a real-world physical object or real-world concept*. For example, software representations of an aeroplane (a physical object) and of a person's employment details (a concept) would both be objects under such a definition.

However, this definition describes an object solely in terms of nouns ('things') and might be taken to imply that an object is made up solely of data. This is not so. An object also contains **functions** (or **methods**) which are associated with the entity which is being modelled by software. For example, an aeroplane object might contain methods such as TakeOff, ChangeSpeed, LiftFlaps, Land, etc. Thus, a more accurate description of an object might be provided by the following simple equation :

$$\text{Object} = \text{Data} + \text{Methods}$$

Such 'wrapping up' of associated data and methods is called **encapsulation** and is one of the fundamental concepts of object orientation. As will be seen later, it is this encapsulation which protects an object's data from the outside world and so leads to fewer bugs (in theory, at least). By contrast, structured programming keeps data and operations largely separate (though looser binding/encapsulation of data and operations may be achieved via routines, units, modules and other such features).

1.2.2   Object-Orientated Programming (OOP)

Essentially, this is the use of objects to model real-world situations/problems. Objects of the same type belong to the same **class**. They are **instances** or **instantiations** of the class. For most practical purposes, a class in OOP may be regarded as equivalent to a **type** in structured programming. Just as we declare variables of a type in structured programming, so we declare objects of a class in OOP. One of OOP's foremost characteristics is **data abstraction**, a feature allowing programmers to define their own **abstract data types** (ADTs or classes). This means that a programmer may create his/her own application-specific types (either simple types or class types) which will fit the requirements of a given programming application more closely that the inbuilt types. These types hide the internal details of data and processing and present only the *behaviour* of an object to the outside world. Of course, structured languages such as Pascal also have the facility to create new types, but it is much less flexible in these languages, since the types created contain *data only*, and not methods.

1.2.3   Inheritance

In many object-orientated programs, a class will not exist in isolation, but will be part of a **hierarchy** of classes, with each of the lower classes (the **derived** classes) **inheriting** data and methods from one of the higher classes (a **base** class).

<u>Example</u>

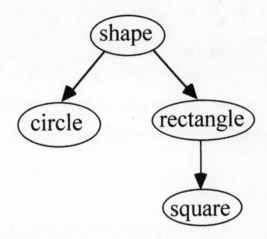

[For some reason, most texts show the arrows in the opposite direction, but the author feels that this is counter-intuitive.]

In this example, classes *circle* and *rectangle* inherit the data and methods of class *shape* (and will have extra members specific to themselves), while *square* inherits members directly from *rectangle* (and, indirectly, from *shape*). *Shape* is a base class, *circle* and *square* are derived classes and *rectangle* is both a derived class and a base class.

The fundamental reason for having hierarchies of classes is to avoid code duplication. If several different categories of object have members in common, then the common members should be isolated and placed in a base class, where they occur just once. For instance, in the shape hierarchy above, the coordinates of a reference point for each shape may be held as members of the base class. The other classes may then inherit these common members from the base class, without the programmer having to recode them explicitly.

The shape hierarchy shows only *single* inheritance. That is to say, each derived class has only one immediate base class. It is also possible to have *multiple* inheritance, in which a class has more than one immediate base class.

Example

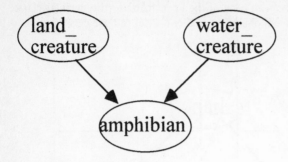

Here, *amphibian* inherits the members of both *land_creature* and *water_creature*.

However, multiple inheritance is a rarely-used technique and will not be mentioned further in this text.

1.2.4   Message-Passing

Encapsulation protects an object's data from the outside world, but it would be pointless to have objects operating entirely in isolation, of course. The whole purpose of writing a piece of software is to provide some service or to solve some problem. Unless there is some means of getting information to and from objects, they will not be able to contribute to the overall goal of the software. Grady Booch, one of the recognised 'gurus' of object orientation, defines OOP as :

> "... *a method of implementation in which programs are organised as cooperative collections of objects, each of which represents an instance of some class, and whose classes are members of a hierarchy united via inheritance relationships.*"

Communication with and between such objects is carried out via **message-passing**. OOP hides the internal details (the **implementation**) of an object from the surrounding program via encapsulation. However, it provides a *minimal interface* via which messages may be passed. An object's data should be **private** to the object. If other objects require (and are to be allowed) access to this data, they must use a **public** method supplied as part of the object's interface. This interface provides *controlled* access to members. It may provide no access at all to some members, read-only access to some and controlled modification of others. The particular needs of the application area(s) in which a class is to be used will determine the type of access to be granted when the class is designed.

Example

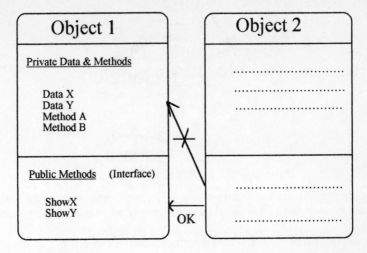

On receipt of a (valid) message, the corresponding method is executed. Here, Object 2 may send the message *ShowX* or *ShowY* to Object 1, since these methods are part of the latter object's public interface. However, Object 2 cannot call either of Object 1's private methods directly. Nor can it modify data members X and Y.

A class's interface (and, hence, the interface for any object of that class) is determined by the class designer on a 'need-to-know' basis. The outside world is allowed as much access to members as is legitimately required, but no more.

1.2.5   Polymorphism

Many authors quote the following as being the three fundamental concepts of object-orientation :

- encapsulation;
- inheritance;
- polymorphism.

[There is significant variation in the literature, though, with some authors listing **data abstraction** instead of inheritance, these authors regarding the latter simply as a mechanism for achieving polymorphism.]

Encapsulation and inheritance have already been introduced, but what is *polymorphism*? The word comes from two Greek words : *polus* (meaning 'many') and *morphe* (meaning 'shape'). Thus, polymorphism means 'taking on many shapes'. In order to simplify the explanation of what is meant by polymorphism in the context of object orientation, it seems appropriate to refer again to our simple shape hierarchy example...

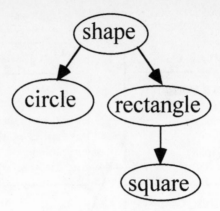

Suppose the *shape* class has a *draw* method. Classes *circle* and *rectangle* will both inherit this method, but will respond quite differently when receiving the same *draw* message.

Polymorphism applies only within inheritance hierarchies and allows the different 'sub-classes' to respond in different (but appropriate) ways to the same message(s). This is one of the major benefits attributed to object orientation.

1.3   The Motivation for a New Approach

From the mid-1960s up to very recently, structured programming has been the dominant approach to the production of software, the principles of structured programming having been introduced in an attempt to solve what has been called 'the software crisis'. This crisis was caused by a large amount of software being produced late, over budget, containing too many bugs, not doing what the customer really wanted and being difficult to maintain. The demand for reliable, quality software has outstripped the supply by a considerable margin for a number of years. This problem has been greatly exacerbated by the need to maintain old software systems ('legacy systems') which were often not designed with maintainability in mind, with the result that as much as 70% of total programming time has been spent on maintenance work in some sectors. Though structured programming was a considerable improvement on the software development methods (or lack of them) which preceded it, the demand for software still considerably exceeds the supply. In addition, it is felt by many software developers that structured programming does not necessarily produce the reliability and maintainability which is required of much software nowadays. Consequently, computer scientists have striven to find a better approach.

1.4   Why OOP?

Why is it that object-orientated programming is now seen by many software practitioners as being the natural successor to structured programming? What are its perceived benefits? The major ones which are claimed for it are shown below.

- *Code Reusability*

It has been recognised for a long time that there are standard data structures with associated standard algorithms which occur time and time again in programming problems. It is argued that the 'reinventing of the wheel' which occurs each time one of these structures or algorithms is coded for a new application is very wasteful and that it would be much more sensible to hold such code in standard libraries, which may then be included in any program requiring the use of them. OOP provides class libraries of such code, and so (in theory, at least) it provides the code reusability which, it is claimed, can greatly reduce initial development time and can also produce much more reliable software (since the code which is being reused comes from tried and tested libraries).

- *Easier Extendibility*

It may be that the class provided by a standard library does not provide the full structure or full functionality which is required for a particular application, but is a good approximation in most respects. The programmer is then at liberty to produce his/her own derived class which inherits all the members of the existing base class and to which he/she may add the missing members. It is also possible to overwrite existing members of the base class in the derived class, in order to modify existing functionality. Thus, the programmer (again in theory, at least) may reap the benefits of code reusability, but may 'tailor' the reused code to meet his/her specific requirements.

- *Easier Debugging*

Because of encapsulation, the source of a bug can usually be identified at the outset as being a particular object, which immediately narrows down the search area considerably and saves a significant amount of time.

- *Easier Management of Complexity*

It is claimed that this benefit results from the 'divide and conquer' approach inherent in modelling an application by identifying the fundamental objects contained within it.

- *A More Natural and Direct Mapping*

It is argued that the approach offered by object orientation involves a natural and direct mapping from objects in the problem domain to objects in the program. This is contrasted with the use of somewhat artificial programming structures in more traditional approaches to software development.

1.5   The Next Few Chapters

Before considering the C++ implementation of the concepts of object orientation, it
is necessary to become familiar with the more basic features of the language, those
features which are largely inherited from C. The next few chapters will cover these
basic features, with the implementation of O-O (object-orientated) features being
postponed until Chapter 7. At that point, it may be advisable to skim Sections 1.2
and 1.4, in order to refresh one's memory about the fundamental principles of object
orientation.

Chapter 2   First Steps in C++ Programming

Aims

- To familiarise the reader with the basic structure of a C++ program.
- To introduce the basic data types and the syntax for variable declarations.
- To familiarise the reader with standard input and output in C++.
- To give an understanding and appreciation of the concepts of scope and lifetime.
- To introduce the common operators.

2.1   The Basic Structure of a C++ Program

C++ is a high level language which allows easy access to the low level aspects of software and hardware. However, since it is a rather terse language, it is quite easy to write virtually unreadable programs in it! Consequently, it is even more important than it would be in more verbose languages to adhere to good programming practice, notably in the naming of variables and the adoption of sensible conventions for the layout of code. Leaving aside the O-O aspects for the time being, C++ may be regarded (and used) as simply a 'better C'. Adopting this approach for the time being, the basic components of an elementary C++ program (in the order in which they occur within a program) are :

- preprocessor directives;
- function prototypes;
- the function **main;**
- function definitions.

[Note that 'functions' serve the same purpose as both procedures and functions in a language such as Pascal. There is no such distinction made in C++.]
In practice, these four components would usually be split between several different files, as you will see shortly. However, for simplicity's sake, we shall deal only with single-file programs for the time being.

In addition to the four items listed above, any program should contain suitable comments, of course. Comments in C++ begin with a 'double slash' (*//*). No terminator for the comment is required, since it is assumed to run to the end of the line. For comments running over several lines, each line commences with *//*.

Example
```
//This is a C++ comment
//which runs over two lines.
```

Every program must have a function called main, since the system executes a C++ program by calling this function (from which other functions may then be called). In C++, a function may take a number of **arguments** (parameters), which are shown in brackets after the function name. Function main normally takes no arguments and so is commonly shown as the word main followed by empty brackets. Following this (and on separate lines) will be the central program declarations and statements, surrounded by chain brackets :

```
main()
{
     ..............;   //Each declaration or statement
     ..............;   //ends with a semi-colon (;).
     ..............;
}
```

Note that C++ (like C, Pascal and a number of other high level languages) is a *block-structured* language. Each block is surrounded by chain brackets and, as will be seen shortly, blocks may be 'nested' within other blocks.

It is worth mentioning the fact that some programmers prefer to emphasise the fact that main takes no arguments as follows :

```
main(void)
{
     ..................;
     ..................;
}
```

This is particularly common amongst C programmers, since a function followed by empty brackets indicates *any number* of arguments in C.
[The use of void will be explained more fully shortly.]

Some programmers also choose to show explicitly that function main returns an integer value :

```
int main(void)
{
     ..................;
     ..................;
}
```
[Details about return values will be given in Chapter 4.]

However, it is the author's personal preference (and is quite common practice) to employ the first option.

To simplify things further still, let's consider a full example program with no functions other than main...

```
//hello.cpp
//Displays a greeting to the user.

#include <iostream.h>
```

```
main ()
{
    cout << "Hello, user!\n";
    return 0 ;
}
```

Aside

The use of the first line two or three lines of a program file to provide the name of the file and a brief comment on its purpose is good practice and commonplace. However, the author would also draw attention to the alignment of chain brackets shown above, with each of those brackets occurring on a line on its own. It is common to see programs in which the brackets are misaligned as follows :

```
main (){
     ..................;
     ..................;
     ..................;
}
```

The author feels that this detracts from the readability of a program and makes it (quite unnecessarily) more difficult to spot missing brackets.

Even with a program as short and simple as the one above, a number of important points may be made...

- C++ (like C) is **case-sensitive**. By convention, almost everything in a C++ program appears in **lower case**.

- The names of Borland C++ source files (and those of some other C++ implementations) end in **.cpp** .
  [For Unix users, the source name will usually end in either **.cc** or **.c**.]

- The #include preprocessor directive specifies a 'header' file, part of the library which is supplied with any implementation of C++. This directive causes the code from the named header file to be made available to the current program. Header files have the suffix **.h**. [This is true in Unix systems also.]

- All input and output in C++ is carried out via **streams**. (Abstractly, a stream is simply a way of describing a flow of data from some source to some destination.) The necessary declarations for such I/O are contained in **iostream.h**. Thus, this header file is included in almost every C++ program.

- cout is C++'s standard output stream (and cin, though it does not occur in the example, is its standard input stream). In most situations, cout corresponds to the monitor and cin to the keyboard.

- << is the output or *insertion* operator (and >> the input or *extraction* operator).
  The former inserts a value onto the specified stream, while the latter extracts a value from the specified stream. Thus, these two are very frequently used with cout and cin.

- A single backslash followed by another character is called an *escape sequence* and is used to produce a non-printable character.
  \n is the 'newline' character (equivalent to carriage return + line-feed). Other useful escape sequences :

  \t   (tab)
  \a   (alarm/bell)

  If the backslash character itself is required, then a double backslash (\\) must be used.

- By convention, function main usually returns a value of 0. This simply indicates that all is well. (This return value is usually ignored by the system, but could be made use of in a batch processing environment, where the return value may determine which program is called next or what value is passed to it.)

2.2   Basic Data Types and Variable Declarations

C++ provides five basic data types :

- char
- int
- float
- double   (double precision floating point)
- void   (valueless)

A char variable usually holds a character, but may be used where an integer is expected, thereby undergoing an implicit type conversion (into its ASCII code). An int variable can hold only integers, while floats and doubles hold real numbers (i.e., numbers with fractional parts). A double will have more bits allocated to it than a float. The number of bits allocated for each will depend upon the architecture of the particular machine used.
The syntax for a variable declaration is :

<type>   <variable name>;

<u>Examples</u>
```
char letter;
float radius;
int length, breadth, height;      //Multiple declaration.
```

Each of the first four types may be preceded by one or more of the following 'modifiers' (though some combinations will not make much sense) :

```
                  signed
                  unsigned
                  short
                  long
```

<u>Examples</u>
```
unsigned float weight;
long int mark;
unsigned short int age;
```

short and long may be used on their own, in which case int is assumed.

<u>Example</u>
```
short result;        //Means short int result;
```

Variables may be initialised at declaration time by use of the equals symbol.

<u>Example</u>
```
int  total = 0;
```

The programmer may also declare his/her own types by using the word typedef.

<u>Example</u>
```
typedef unsigned int mark;  //Declares type mark to be
                            //an unsigned int.

mark maths, french;
//Variables of the newly-created type.
```

2.3   Type Conversions

Both implicit and explicit conversions from one type to another are allowed. For instance, as mentioned in the last section, there is an implicit conversion from char to int when a character is used where an integer is expected.

<u>Example</u>
```
int n = 'A';   //n set to 65, the ASCII code for 'A'.
```

The conversion can also be other way round.

<u>Example</u>
```
char c = 65;
```

Similar conversions occur when going from short to long integers, integers to doubles, etc. Such conversions are necessary, of course, when carrying out arithmetic with values of differing types. However, it is often safer and more readable to carry out explicit conversion, via **typecasts**...

Example
```
int i = 5;
float j;
double k;

j = float (i);    //Typecast value of i into a float.
k = double (i);   //Typecast value of i into a double.
```

Note that typecasting almost invariably involves a type **promotion** (i.e., a conversion into a type with a wider range of values). Typecasting to a type with a narrower range of values carries with it the inherent danger of *truncation* (i.e., loss of data), leading to meaningless values!

2.4   Constants

A constant is declared by commencing the declaration with the descriptor const. For historical reasons, upper case is used when naming constants.

Example
```
const float PI = 3.14159;
```

Character constants must be enclosed by inverted commas.

Examples
```
const char INITIAL = 'J';
const char NEWLINE = '\n';
//Single character made up of two symbols.
```

By default, the compiler fits a numeric literal constant into the smallest compatible data type which will hold it --- except for floating point constants, which are assumed to be of type double. It is possible to override the default by appending F (float), U (unsigned) and/or L (long) to a numeric literal.

Examples
```
34L          3819U
45.8F        68UL
```

Lower case may be used, but it is highly inadvisable to use a lower case L ('l'), as it is almost indistinguishable from the digit '1'.

Hexadecimal and octal constants may also be declared.

Examples
```
const int HEX = 0x80;
const int OCT =  012;    // Leading 0 indicates octal.
```

It is highly unlikely that you will wish to enter numbers in either hexadecimal or octal format, but it is important to realise that a number entered with a leading zero will be interpreted (by default) as an octal number! Failure to appreciate this fact can lead to some mysterious errors which are difficult to track down. This default action can be overridden and decimal interpretation enforced by use of the manipulator *dec* [See Appendix C and the note in Exercise 2 at the end of Chapter 11], but it is sometimes advisable simply to accept the number as a character string. This is especially convenient with values such as telephone numbers, which will never need to be subjected to arithmetic. Values which *do* need to be subjected to arithmetic will need to be manipulated into arithmetic form, of course.

2.5   Standard Input and Formatted Output

As was mentioned in Section 2.1, cin is the standard input stream and, in most situations, is associated with the keyboard. cin is normally used in combination with the input (or *insertion*) operator, >>. This operator 'inserts' values into the input stream as they are entered at the keyboard.

Example
        cin>>number;   //Here, *number* is a pre-declared variable.

The formatting of output (and input) may be modified by the use of **manipulators**, which are simply placed on the output (or input) stream in the same way that data values are placed on the stream. Those manipulators which need to be supplied with arguments (parameters) are declared in *iomanip.h*, while those which do not are declared in *iostream.h*.

The manipulator setiosflags is used to set a number of inbuilt *formatting flags*. These formatting flags are declared within an inbuilt class called **ios** and must be preceded by ios:: to indicate this. A common requirement when outputting real numbers (i.e., numbers with fractional parts) is to be able to use fixed point notation, rather than exponential form (though this may very well be the default format for your compiler) and the flag which does this is called fixed. Thus, setiosflags may be used to specify fixed point notation for values output on the standard output stream as follows :

        cout<<setiosflags(ios::fixed);

setprecision is the manipulator which specifies the number of decimal places in the value to be output (using rounding where required, rather than truncation). Since occurrences of the output operator may be 'chained', allowing several values to be placed on the output stream in succession, fixed point notation with two decimal places may be specified as follows :

        cout<<setiosflags(ios::fixed)<<setprecision(2);

[For further information on manipulators, see Section 6.2 and Appendix C.]

<u>Simple Example Program</u>

```
// circarea.cpp
// Calculates the area of a circle whose radius is supplied.

# include <iostream.h>
# include <iomanip.h>

main ()
{
   const float PI = 3.142;
   int radius;

   cout <<"Enter radius (in cm): ";
   cin>>radius;        //First example of standard input.
   cout<<"\n\nArea = "<<setiosflags(ios::fixed);
   cout<<setprecision(2)<<PI*radius*radius<<"sq cm\n";
   return 0;
}
```

Additional Points to Note

- It is possible to chain occurrences of the input operator in the same way as occurrences of the output operator have been chained above.

  Example
  ```
  cout<<"Enter 2 numbers : ";
  cin>>num1>>num2;
  //Values entered may be separated by
  //space(s) and/or <Return>.
  ```

- .It is the author's personal preference to make each physical program line into a single program statement, by placing a semi-colon at the end of the physical line. This means that cout must be specified for each consecutive physical line involving output above. Some programmers prefer to use just one program statement split across several physical lines, as follows :

  ```
  cout<<"\n\nArea = "
      <<setiosflags(ios::fixed)<<setprecision(2)
      <<PI*radius*radius<<"sq cm\n";
  ```

- Identifiers (the names of program entities such as variables) should be declared at the start of the block within which they will be used. More detail will be provided shortly.

2.6   Enumerated Types

These can help to make programs more readable, by giving meaningful names to integer values.

Syntax :

```
        enum <tag> {<List of names>};
```
[Note that the chain brackets are character literals here, and not part of extended BNF.]

Example
```
        enum colour {RED, BLUE, GREEN, YELLOW};
        colour col1, col2; //2 variables declared.
```

Alternatively,

```
        enum colour{RED, BLUE, GREEN, YELLOW} col1, col2;
```

By default, the contents of an enumerated type are given integer values numbered consecutively from zero upwards. Thus, RED-YELLOW above are given values 0-3. If other values are wanted, they must be stated explicitly.

Example
```
        enum colour {RED=5, BLUE=8, GREEN=1, YELLOW=6};
```

If consecutive values are required, only the first need be supplied.

Example
```
        enum season {SPRING = 1, SUMMER, AUTUMN, WINTER};
```

Since there is no inbuilt Boolean type in C++, one very useful application of the enumerated type facility is the creation of such a type...

```
        enum boolean{FALSE, TRUE};
```

As will be emphasised in the next chapter, FALSE is represented by **0** in C++. Thus, FALSE needs to be placed before TRUE in the above declaration (unless explicitly assigning 1 and 0 to TRUE and FALSE respectively.).

2.7   The Scope of a Variable

This is the portion of a program within which a variable is declared and may be referenced. If the variable is declared within a block, its scope extends from the point of declaration to the end of the block containing the declaration, making it a **local** declaration. If the declaration is not inside any block (i.e., it occurs before main), the scope extends from the point of declaration to the end of the file, making it a **global** declaration.

Example
```
        //example.cpp
        #include <iostream.h>

        int number;          //Has file scope.
```

```
main()
{
    ....................
    ....................
    {
        char letter;                //Has block scope.
        ...................
        ...................
    }
    ...................
}
```

Here, *number* can be accessed from anywhere within the program. *Letter*, on the other hand, is a local variable which has meaning and accessibility only within its immediately containing program block.

2.8   The Lifetime of a Variable

The concept of lifetime of a variable is closely associated with the variable's scope. By default, a variable declared within a block is created when the declaration is executed and destroyed when the end of the block is reached (when the variable goes 'out of scope'). If the block is subsequently re-executed, a new variable is created. Such variables are said to have a storage class of **automatic** --- a pretty meaningless name!

Variables declared globally (outside any block) remain in existence until the end of the program. Such variables are said to have a storage class of **static** (a little more meaningful). A variable declared within a block can be declared static explicitly.

Example

```
{
    ...................
    static int count;
    ...................
}
```

Here, *count* will remain in existence until the program reaches termination, retaining its value from one execution of the block to the next.

It is also possible to declare local variables to be automatic explicitly, by use of the keyword auto, but there is no point whatsoever in doing so (since this is the default storage class for such variables).

2.9   Common Operators

Before looking at the individual operators, it is necessary to point out one very important and fundamental characteristic of C++ : *every expression returns a value*. An 'expression' may comprise simply a single variable or single value, or it may involve several terms combined by means of operators. It may be that the value returned is ignored and effectively discarded, but the value is still returned initially.

2.9.1   The Assignment Operator

This is provided by the equals symbol (=).
[N.B. Though assignment and initialisation use the same symbol and have a similar effect, they are *different* operations.]

Example
```
total = 0;
```

 Since (a) every expression in C++ returns a value and (b) the assignment operator is right-associative (i.e., when there are multiple occurrences of it in the same statement, the assignments are executed starting from the rightmost one and moving left), assignments may be chained.

Example
```
num1 = num2 = 0;
```

Due to the right-associativity property, this is the same as :

```
num1 = (num2 = 0);
```

Thus, *num2* is first assigned the value 0 and then the value assigned (0) is returned as the value of the sub-expression *num2 = 0.* This value is then used in the other assignment :

```
num1 = 0;
```

2.9.2   Arithmetic Operators

The simple arithmetic operators (as opposed to the compound ones, which will be encountered shortly) are as follows :

```
+

*        (multiplication)
/        (integer or real division),
%        (remainder from integer division),
++       (increment --- add 1)
--       (decrement --- subtract 1)
```

Examples
```
result = num1 * num2 * num3;
quotient = 14/4;          //Integer division. 3 assigned.
remainder = 14%4;         //Value of 2 assigned.
```

When more than one operator is used in an expression, the order in which operations are carried out is dictated by the order shown below, which shows descending precedence (i.e., higher operations are carried out first).

```
++, --
*, /, %
+, -
```

<u>Example</u>
```
number = 5 + 4 * 3; //Value assigned is 17.
```

For operators at the same level of precedence, of course, the operations will be carried out in the order given (i.e., working from left to right).

There are both pre- and post-increment operators, as well as pre- and post-decrement operators.

<u>Examples</u>
```
count++;      //Add 1 to count.
++total ;     //Add 1 to total.
count--;      //Subtract 1 from count.
--total;      //Subtract 1 from total.
```
[This is where the origin of the name C++ lies --- 'one stage beyond C'.]

When the increment/decrement operator precedes the variable name, the value of the variable is changed *before* being returned as the value of the expression; when it follows the variable name, the (current) value is returned and *then* the value is changed.

<u>Example</u>
```
a = 5;
b = a++;      // Equivalent to :   b = 5; a = 6;
c = ++a;      // Equivalent to :   a = 7; c = 7;
```

2.9.3   The Bitwise Operators

For most people reading this book, it is highly unlikely that the need to operate on data at the bit level will ever arise (apart from the combining of formatting flags, as will be seen later), but here are the operators which will allow you to do this :

&	(AND)	~	(One's complement)
|	(OR)	>>	(Right-shift)
^	(XOR)	<<	(Left-shift)

2.9.4   Conditional Operator

This is made up of two symbols (though they do not appear consecutively when used) :
```
?:
```

It is C++'s only **ternary** operator --- i.e., it takes *three* operands.
Syntax :

```
(<conditional expression>) ? <exp.1> : <exp.2>;
```

This is equivalent to the following pseudocode :

```
        IF conditional expression is true THEN
                Return expression1
        ELSE
                Return expression2
        ENDIF
```

Example
```
        (a>b) ? max = a :   max = b; //Max set to larger value.
```

The result returned may be used to make this statement more succinct :

```
        max = (a>b)? a:b;
```

2.9.5   Compound Operators

The assignment operator may be combined with several of the other operators :

```
        +=              -=              *=              /=              %=
        <<=             >>=             &=              ^=              |=
```

Example
```
        total += value;
```

This is equivalent to :

```
        total = total + value;
```

2.9.6   Comma Operator

This operator allows us to combine two or more expressions into a single expression (the value returned by the overall expression being that of the last sub-expression).

Example
```
        i++,  j++;  // Return original value of j.
```

This operator is rarely, if ever, of any use in simple statements, but is occasionally of some use in *for* loops, as indicated by one of the examples in the next chapter.

Exercises

1. Accept the user's initials (using two char variables) and then display a greeting to the person, using his/her initials in the greeting.

2. Accept the lengths (in cm) of the two shortest sides of a right-angled triangle and then display the length of the hypotenuse to the nearest whole number, by adding 0.5 to the result and then using a typecast.
[In case your trigonometry is rather rusty, Pythagoras' Theorem states that, if h is the length of the hypotenuse and a and b are the lengths of the other two sides, then $h = \sqrt{(a^2 + b^2)}$.]
To find the square root, use function sqrt, which is declared in **math.h** (so you will need to use #include <math.h>). Example usage : *root = sqrt(number);*

3. Accept three integers and then display their arithmetic mean ('average') to one decimal place. (You will need a typecast.)

4. Initialise a character variable to hold the integer 65 (the ASCII code for 'A'). Use the increment, decrement and output operators on this variable so that the next three letters of the alphabet (i.e., 'B', 'C' and 'D') are output, first in alphabetical order and then in reverse order.

Chapter 3   Selections and Iterations

Aims

- To introduce the two types of selection statement in C++.
- To introduce the three types of iteration structure in C++.
- To familiarise the reader with the use of the relational operators and the logical operators in both selections and iterations.

3.1   The Relational Operators

These allow values to be compared. The full list is :

==	(Is equal to)
!=	(Is not equal to)
<	(Is less than)
>	(Is greater than)
<=	(Is less than or equal to)
>=	(Is greater than or equal to)

3.2   Selection Statements

There are two types of selection statement in C++ :

- the *if* statement;
- the *switch* statement.

3.2.1   The if Statement

As with a number of other high level programming languages, the if statement in C++ provides a one- or two-way selection facility. Basic syntax :

```
if (<expression>)
        <statement 1>;
[else
        <statement 2>;]
```

The expression following the keyword if will commonly involve one of the relational operators. If the condition being tested by the relational operator is false, then a value of **0** is returned by the expression; if it is false, then a non-zero value (usually 1) is returned.

[Note that, though most (if not all) implementations of C++ use 1 to represent TRUE, the specification of the C++ language does not dictate any particular value for TRUE, so it would be bad practice to rely upon TRUE being equal to 1. *Any* non-zero value is regarded as being equivalent to TRUE in C++.]

Examples

```
(i)            if (entry <0)
                   cout<<"Invalid entry!\n";

(ii)           if (number%2 == 1)
                   cout<<"Number is odd.\n";
               else
                   cout<<"Number is even.\n";
```

Note that C++ **demands** the use of a semi-colon after the statement which is subordinate to the `if` expression, even if there is an `else` clause following it. This does **not** terminate the whole `if` statement.

Note also that it is a **very** common error to confuse the equality and assignment operators. This is particularly dangerous, since the use of either of them is syntactically correct wherever the use of the other one is syntactically correct (though some compilers, including Borland's, do issue a warning if one of these operators is found where the other one might be expected). Failure to appreciate this fact can lead to bugs which are very difficult to track down.

Example

Suppose the following test is to be made in a program :

```
if (number==10)...........
```

If, instead, the programmer keys in

```
if (number=10)...........,
```

then there will be no syntax error generated and 'number' will be *assigned* the value 10. This value will then be returned and used by `if` as a truth value (i.e., 'TRUE' or 'FALSE'). Since any non-zero value indicates TRUE in C++ (as will be emphasised in the next section), the test will be regarded as returning 'TRUE', and so whatever statement follows the test will be executed. Thus, unless the original value of 'number' *was* 10, two serious errors will result :

- the value of 'number' will be overwritten by 10;
- the program will proceed to execute other statement(s) which should not be executed.

Often, several statements will be subordinate to the `if` and/or the `else`, in which case they must be 'blocked' together by means of chain brackets.

Example (Calculates income tax payable)

```
if (gross_pay > allowance)
{
    tax = (gross_pay - allowance) * TAX_RATE;
    //TAX_RATE is a constant here.
    cout<<"Tax payable = ";
    cout<<setiosflags(ios::fixed);
    cout<<setprecision(2)<<tax<<'\n';
}
else
    cout<<"No tax payable.\n";
```

It is also possible to have 'nested' ifs .

Example

```
if (rainfall < 0.5)
    cout<<"Low rainfall.\n";
else if (rainfall < 1.0)
    cout<<"Average rainfall.\n";
else if (rainfall < 2.0)
    cout<<"Heavy rainfall.\n";
else .........................
```

Note that the usual style of layout for nested ifs in C++ involves placing each subsequent if on the same line as the else which precedes it, rather than indenting the if on the next line as shown here :

```
if (rainfall < 0.5)
    cout<<"Low rainfall.\n";
else
    if (rainfall < 1.0)
        cout<<"Average rainfall.\n";
    else
        if ....................
```

However, there is no reason why you should not use this convention instead, if you wish.

Wherever possible (and it is possible only when dealing with a small number of *single* values, rather than a *range* of values as shown in the preceding example), a switch statement should be used in preference to nested ifs...

3.2.2 The switch Statement

This statement provides a multi-way selection facility.

Syntax :

```
switch (<control expression>)
{
    case <const 1> :    <statement sequence 1>
                        break;
    case <const 2> :    <statement sequence 2>
                        break;
    ...............................................
```

```
..................................................
    [default :                 <statement sequence>]
}
```

The case labels *const1*, *const2*, ... are the values which may be assumed by the control expression. The specific value which is assumed will dictate which statement sequence is executed.

N.B. It is very important to include the `break` statements above. If they are not included, then **all** statements from the selected case label to end of the `switch` statement will be executed!

The optional `default` clause specifies the action to be taken if the control expression assumes none of the listed values.

If the same statements are to be executed for more than one possible value of the control expression, then these values may be listed consecutively, followed by the statements to be executed, as shown below.

Example

```
switch (grade)
{
    case 'A' :
    case 'a':     cout <<"Grade A awarded.\n";
                  cout<< "Mark in range 70-100.\n";
                  break;
    case 'B':
    case 'b':     cout<<"Grade B awarded.\n";
                  cout<<"Mark in range 60-69.\n";
                  break;
    ..................................................
    ..................................................
    default:      cout<<"Invalid grade!\n";
}
```

3.3   Iterations

C++ caters for all the standard types of iteration (count-controlled, pre-conditioned and post-conditioned).

3.3.1   The `while` Statement

This provides a pre-conditioned iteration.

Syntax :

```
while (<condition>)
{
    <statement block>
}
```

Example

```
total = 0;
cout<<"Enter a positive value (or 0 to quit) : ";
cin>>value;
while (value>0)
```

```
        {
             total+=value;
             cout<<"\nEnter next value (or 0 to quit) : ";
             cin>>value;
        }
```

3.3.2   The do Statement

This provides a post-conditioned iteration.
Syntax :

```
        do
        {
             <statement block>
        }while (<condition>);
```

<u>Example</u>

```
        do
        {
             cout<<"\nEnter a number greater than 0 : ";
             cin>>number;
             if (number <=0)
                   cout<<"\n\nInvalid entry! Try again...\n";
        }while (number<=0);
```

3.3.3   The for Statement

Though this statement is used solely for count-controlled ('deterministic') iterations
in other languages, it may be used for both count-controlled and condition-
controlled ('non-deterministic') iterations in C++. However, it is most commonly
used for count-controlled iterations.
Syntax :

```
        for (<initialisation>; <condition>; <step>)
        {
             <statement block>
        }
```

The initialisation statement is often used to set a counter to an initial value, though it
is occasionally used for other things (such as setting a pointer to the head of a linked
list prior to traversal of the list).
The condition statement specifies the condition for the loop to be executed (or re-
executed).
N.B. If the condition is false the first time it is tested, the loop *will not be executed
at all*.
The step statement is used to step a control variable through a series of values and
frequently makes use of the increment and decrement operators (++ and --).

<u>Example</u>

```
        total = 0;
        for (int count=0; count<10; count++)
        {
             cin >> value;
```

```
          total += value;
     }
```

Note that the initialisation statement here is a variable declaration. The variable may, instead, be declared beforehand.

Example
```
     int count;
     for (count=1; count<=100; count++)
          cout<<count<<'\n';
```

By use of the comma operator, a for loop may step through more than one variable.

Example
```
     int i,j;
     for (i=0, j=10; i<5; i++, j++)
          cout<< "i = "<<i<<"     j = "<<j<<'\n';
```

i and j could have been declared in the *for* statement :

```
     for (int i=0, j=10; i<5; i++, j++)
```

In this case, however, the first comma is acting as a *separator* of variable declarations, not as an operator. (In practice, of course, it is highly unlikely that this distinction will be of any practical value.)

3.4   The Use of `break` and `continue`

The statements `break` and `continue` may be used to depart from the normal sequence of operations within a loop. They might be considered by some people as versions of the notorious `goto` statement, leading to the conclusion that their use is bad practice and should be avoided. However, there is no 'jump' to a specified label, line number or memory location. With both statements, the alteration to the flow of execution is relative to the loop body. In the case of `break`, execution leaves the loop and continues from the first statement following the loop. With `continue`, on the other hand, only the current iteration of the loop is abandoned and the next one (if there is another one) commenced.

Example
Counts the number of positive values entered and keeps a running total of them.

```
     int number=0, count=0;
     do
     {
          cout<<"Enter a positive integer (0 to quit) :   ";
          cin>>number;
          if (number==0) break;    //Leave loop.

          if (number<0) continue;
          //Ignore any negative number and begin next
          //iteration of loop (prompting for next number).
```

```
        total+=number';        //Add positive integer to total
        count++;                //and increment counter.
    }while (1);
    //While 'TRUE' --- i.e., 'forever' (until a break).
```

3.5   The Logical Operators

There are three logical operators :

&&	(AND)
||	(OR)
!	(NOT)

These may be used to combine or negate conditions and may feature in both if statements and iterations.

<u>Example</u>

```
    do
    {
        cout<<"Do you wish to try again? (y/n) : ";
        cin>>reply;
    }while ((reply!='y') && (reply!='n'));
```

Exercises

1. Accept three integers and output the largest one.

2. Accept a single digit ('0'...'9') into a `char` variable and then use a `switch` statement to output the text name of the digit ('zero'...'nine'), outputting an error message if anything other than a digit is entered.

3. Accept a series of positive integers (terminated by zero) and count the number of odd integers entered, outputting this value. [You will find it useful to employ the remainder operator, %.]

4. Accept an integer in the range 2-7. For as long as the user enters a value outside this range, re-prompt and accept a new value. Once a value in the required range has been entered, output its factorial value.
[For a positive integer n, factorial n (denoted *n!*) = n x (n-1) x (n-2) x ... x 1.]

5. Accept a positive integer and determine whether or not it is a prime number. Any value smaller than 2 should be rejected, with the user being prompted (as many times as is necessary) to enter a value greater than 1. Try to make use of a Boolean enumerated type.

Chapter 4   Functions and Header Files

Aims

- To give the reader an appreciation of the value of separating function declarations from their definitions.
- To familiarise the reader with the syntax for the declaration, definition and use of functions.
- To give the reader an understanding of the concept of linkage and its implementation in a C++ program.
- To familiarise the reader with the procedure required for creating his/her own header files.

4.1   Functions

4.1.1   The C++ Approach and Rationale

C++ demands that the declaration of a function be separated from its definition (unless the function is a very small one, in which case the two may be combined into an *inline* function, as described shortly). A function is *declared* via a **function prototype**, a forward declaration which specifies the name of the function, its return type and the types of its arguments (parameters). The *definition* (or *implementation*) of a function is the function body, comprising executable statements (and possibly local data declarations). One major reason for this separation is that function definitions/implementations will often be held in separate files (header files), allowing the implementations to be modified at a later date without the programs which use these functions requiring any modification at all (provided that neither the function name nor argument list changes). Any subsequent change in the implementation of a particular function will be completely transparent to the users of that function. The other major reason for this separation is that it allows the compiler to check the arguments passed to a function against the types specified in the prototype. Because of this, C++ is said to have **typesafe linkage**.

4.1.2   Function Syntax

The syntax for a function prototype is :

```
<Return type>   <Func name>([<Arg. list>]);
```

(Note that the argument list is optional, and so may be empty, but the surrounding brackets will still be required.)

Example
```
float comp_amount(float principal, float rate, int time);
//Calculates the final value of an investment, given
//an initial sum of money (the principal) which earns
//a specified rate of compound interest over a
//specified number of years.
```

When called, this function must be supplied with values for *principal*, *rate* and *time*, and will return a result through its return type (the first float).
The names of the arguments are optional in the prototype and may be omitted as follows :
```
float comp_amount(float, float, int);
```

N.B. Though allowable, this is not advocated as good practice by the author. If it *is* done, then there is a greater onus on the programmer to provide comments on the purpose of the arguments.

Once declared via its prototype, a function can be used within a program, provided that its definition is available to the program. This definition will repeat the information specified in the prototype and will then supply the executable code for the function. For the time being, we shall continue to keep things relatively straightforward by placing all our program code (apart from items held within iostream.h) in one file. In this case, then, a function whose prototype appears at the start of a program should have a matching function definition which appears after main. If a function is not required to return a value, then its return type is specified as being void. If the function has a non-void return type, then a value must be returned through the return statement.

Example
```
//invest.cpp
//Calculates the final value of an investment
//which earns compound interest.

#include <iostream.h>
#include <iomanip.h>

float compound(float principal, float rate, int time);

main()
{
    int principal, time;
    float rate;

    cout<<"Enter principal: ";
    cin>> principal;
    cout<<"\nEnter rate of interest (as a percentage): ";
    cin>>rate;
    cout <<\n"Enter time (in years): ";
    cin>>time;
    cout<<"\n\nFinal value : ";
    cout<<setiosflags(ios::fixed)<<setprecision(2);
    cout<<comp_amount(principal, rate, time);
```

```
        return 0;
}

float  comp_amount (int p, float r, int t)
{
        for (int count = 0; count < t; count++)
            p *= (1 + r/100);   //Same as :   p = p*(1+r/100);
        return p;
}
```

4.1.3   Inline Functions

Some overhead is associated with each function call and return when prototyping is used. If the function accomplishes a substantial task, this overhead is small in comparison with the time spent doing useful work. If, however, the function body is very small, then this overhead is substantial and, in some processing-intensive applications (such as graphical routines or sorting operations on large volumes of data), this could present a problem. The solution is to use an **inline function**. In this case, the definition of the function is supplied with the declaration, preceded by the word `inline`.

Example
Adapting the example from Section 2.9.4 involving the use of the conditional operator (?:), we can make use of an inline function which returns the larger of two integers which are passed to it...

```
//bigger.cpp
//Accepts two integers and makes use of an
//inline function to return the larger value.

#include <iostream.h>

inline int larger(int num1, int num2)
{
        return (num1 > num2) ? num1 : num2;
}

main()
{
        int first, second;

        cout<<"Enter two integers (separated by space) :  ";
        cin>>first>>second;
        cout<<"\nLarger integer = "<<larger(first, second);
        return 0;
}
```

Note that the declaration and definition of the inline function have been merged. When an inline function is used in a program, the compiler will replace every call to the function with the actual body of the function (as opposed to the *address* of the function, as would be the case for normal function calls).

4.2 Linkage

Most programs in C++ are made up of more than one source file. In order to operate as one program, the individual files must be compiled and then *linked* together. This latter operation is carried out by a piece of software called the *linker*, which must determine which identifiers are accessible to which files within the program. An identifier with *internal* linkage is accessible only within the source file in which it is declared. An identifier with *external* linkage is accessible from *all* source files within the program. It is not often necessary to specify linkage explicitly, since default values are assumed in the absence of explicit linkage specifications and these default values are usually the ones which are wanted.

Default Linkage

- Local identifiers have **internal** linkage.

- Global variables (those declared with file scope) have **external** linkage.

- Identifiers declared with const have **internal** linkage.

- Inline functions have **internal** linkage.

- Non-inline functions have **external** linkage.

These defaults can be overridden by using the words static and extern to force internal or external linkage respectively.

Examples

```
static int anyfunc (int, int);
extern const MAXIMUM=25;
```

N.B. The word static has more than one meaning in C++. This meaning has **nothing** to do with the use of static to specify lifetime of a variable, as described in Section 2.7.

4.3 Non-System Header Files

Just as header files are used to hold the prototypes for system-supplied functions, so header files may be used by an individual programmer to hold prototypes for his/her functions. As for system header files, these header files will have the suffix **.h**. The function definitions will be held in separate **.cpp** files (or .cc/.c files on Unix systems). Apart from the advantages derived from separating function declarations from their corresponding definitions (already stated in 4.1), the purpose of separating functions from the programs which use them is to allow the same functions to be used by many different programs (simply by using the #include directive to 'pull in' the functions). This *reusability* is considered a major benefit.

Functions which are not really reusable (i.e., are specific to a particular program) do not have to be placed in separate files, but, if there are more than a small number of them, programmers may choose to separate them in this way, in order to split a program into separate (and more manageable) compilation modules.

Example (Very artificial!)
Suppose we have a simple stock control system holding the current levels of just three items of stock, with those items numbered 1,2 and 3.

```
//stock.h
//Declarations for simple stock control system.
//N.B. If you are thinking of keying in and running
//this code, then see the next section first!

extern int  level1, level2, level3;
//It is rarely necessary to hold individual variables
//in a header file, but this allows a demonstration of
//the use of extern.

inline void init_levels()
//Sets all stock levels to 0.
//Inline function must be in header.
{
     level1=level2=level3=0;
}

char get_option();
//Accepts menu option selected by user.

void set_levels();
//Sets stock levels to values supplied by user.
//No value to be returned, so void specified
//as return type.

int get_level(int item);
//Returns current level of specified stock item.

enum boolean{FALSE, TRUE};

boolean change_level(int item, int level);
//Changes current level of specified item
//to specified value.
//Returns TRUE if change is possible and FALSE
//if an invalid number is specified.
.................................................
.................................................

-----------------------------------------------------------

//stock.cpp
//Definitions for simple stock control system.

#include <iostream.h>
#include "stock.h"
//Note the use of speech marks, instead of angle
//brackets, for a non-system header file.
```

```
int level1, level2, level3;
//These are  the variable definitions corresponding to
//the declarations in the header file.
//Further explanation is given after the code.

char get_option()
{
    char option = '0';
    //The use of char, rather than int, avoids a
    //runtime  error if the user enters a non-digit
    //value and is good programming practice.

    cout<< "\n\n1.Set levels.\n";
    cout<< "2.Get individual level.\n";
    cout<< "3. Change individual level.\n";
    cout<< "4. Quit.\n";
    do
    {
        cout<<"\n\nEnter choice (1-4) :  ";
        cin>> option;
    } while ((option<'1') || (option>'4'));
    return option;
}

void set_levels()
{
    cout<<"Enter starting level for item 1 :  ";
    cin>> level1;
    cout<<"Enter starting level for item 2 :  ";
    cin>> level2;
    cout<<"Enter starting level for item 3 :  ";
    cin>> level3;
}

int get_level(int item)
{
    switch (item)
    {
        case 1  :    return level1; break;
        case 2  :    return level2; break;
        case 3  :    return level3; break;
        default :    return |1;
                     //Indicates invalid entry.
    }
}

boolean change_level (int item, int level)
{
    switch (item)
    {
        case 1  :    level1 = level; break;
        case 2  :    level2 = level; break;
        case 3  :    level3 = level; break;
        default :    return FALSE;
    }
    return TRUE;
}
.......................................................
.......................................................
```

```
//usestock.cpp
//Stock control program

#include <iostream.h>
#include "stock.h"

main()
{
    char option;
    int item, level;
    init_levels();
    do
    {
        option = get_option();
        switch (option)
        {
            case '1':  set_levels();
                       break;
            case '2':  cout<<"Enter item no.(1- 3): ";
                       cin>>item;
                       level = get_level(item);
                       if (level!=-1)
                           cout<<"Level= "
                               <<level<<'\n';
                       else
                           cout<<"Invalid item!\n";
                       break;
            case '3':  cout<<"Enter item no (1-3) : ";
                       cin >> item;
                       cout<<"Enter new level : ";
                       cin>>level;
                       if (!change_level (item, level))
                           cout<<"\a*Invalid item!*\n";
        }
    } while (option!='4');
    return 0;
}
```

In general, then, each main file will make use of a number of pairs of files (often only one pair for programs of modest size), each pair comprising a header file (containing declarations) and an implementation file (a file of function definitions for the prototypes in the header file).
N.B. The header file must be included in both the main file and its own implementation file!

Points Requiring Further Explanation

- The use of extern before *level1*, *level2* and *level3* makes the line a **declaration**, rather than a **definition**, of the three variables. The difference is that a definition *allocates memory* for variables, while a declaration does not. Both *usestock.cpp* and *stock.cpp* require access to these variables, which they obtain by including the header file. However, the definition must occur only once — in the definition/implementation file.

- The use of angle brackets around a header file indicates that the file is a system-supplied one and is held in a particular system directory, where the system will look for it. Speech marks indicate that the file is a programmer-supplied one and is in the directory whose path is supplied inside speech marks (which will be the current directory if the pathname is absent, of course).

4.4   The Multiple Inclusion Problem

Since the main file and at least one other .cpp file require access to the same header file, there is the potential problem of having the same header file included more than once in a source file compilation. In some circumstances, this can lead to *multiple definitions*, which will usually result in compilation errors. The problem may be avoided by using the preprocessor directives #ifndef ('if not defined'), #define and #endif around the declarations.

Example

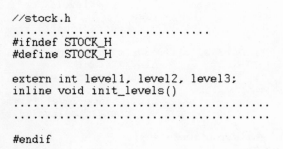

```
//stock.h
.............................
#ifndef STOCK_H
#define STOCK_H

extern int level1, level2, level3;
inline void init_levels()
.......................................
.......................................

#endif
```

The basic idea is to define a macro constant for each header file. This is precisely the method which is employed in the system library's header files. The first time the preprocessor meets the macro name (here, *STOCK_H*), it is not defined, and so it passes it to the compiler for subsequent compilation. The next time the preprocessor encounters the name, it recognises it and ignores the block of code following the macro name. Although the omission of the #ifndef/#define/#endif combination will not often cause problems, there are occasions when it most certainly will and it is good programming practice to get into the habit of using such macros in *all* your header files. You are perfectly at liberty to use whatever names you wish for these macros, of course, but adopting the above convention of using the same name as that for the header file and using an underscore in place of a full stop (which would be illegal) will save an effort of imagination.

4.5   Function Overloading

It is often convenient to use the same function name with different argument types and/or different numbers of arguments. Such reuse of a function name is called *function overloading*.

Example
```
inline long square(long n)
{
    return n*n;
}

inline double square(double x)
{
    return x*x;
}
```

Note that a function cannot be overloaded simply by varying its return type. Thus, the following would not be allowed by the compiler :

```
int func(int, float);
double func(int, float); // Compilation error!
```


4.6   Default Arguments

C++ allows default arguments to be specified for functions. If a function requires the same value(s) for a significant proportion of the occasions on which it will be called, then this facility can save the programmer and/or user the tedium of having to supply the same value(s) each time that the function is called. The arguments to be supplied with default values are initialised with those values *in the function prototype* (which will usually be in a header file).

Example
```
void set_level(int stock_code, int stock_level = 0);
```

The following calls may then be made :

```
set_level(item, 100);
set_level(item);  //Default value of 0 assumed for level.
```

It is possible to have more than one default argument. However, *only trailing arguments may have default values*. (Otherwise, the compiler would have no way of knowing which arguments were to be supplied with default values — unless the types of the arguments could always be guaranteed to be different, which is not practical.)

Examples
```
float amount (int p, float r=7.5, int t=5); //Legal.
float amount (int p, float r=7.5, int t);   //Illegal!
```

Exercises

Use header files (with appropriate use of #ifndef, #define and #endif) for each of the programs below.

1. Rewrite Exercise 1 from Chapter 3 so that it makes use of a function called *max*. [It is unlikely that the function will be reusable for precisely three values. However, for the purposes of this exercise, assume that it will be.]

2,. Write a function which will display the multiplication table for any integer in the range 2-12 which the user enters. Allow the user to enter as many values in this range as he/she wishes, the process being terminated by any value outside the range.

3. Rewrite Exercise 4 from Chapter 3 so that a function is used for calculating the factorial value.

4. Rewrite Exercise 5 from Chapter 3 so that it makes use of a function called *is_prime*, which returns a Boolean value.

5. Write a function called *gcd* which will calculate and return the greatest common divisor of any two positive integers which it receives (i.e., the largest positive integer by which each is exactly divisible). Allow the user to enter as many pairs of positive integers as he/she wishes, until he/she answers 'n' when asked if another pair is to be entered.

Chapter 5   Arrays, Pointers and References

Aims

- To familiarise the reader with the declaration and processing of arrays with simple base types (int, char, etc.).
- To introduce the use of pointers to the simple types and to make the reader aware of the close connection between pointers and array names.
- To introduce string-handling and the standard library functions most commonly used for this.
- To demonstrate the way in which reference types may be used (in preference to pointers) to achieve argument-passing by reference.

5.1   Structured Types

So far, the only types encountered have been the inbuilt ones (int, char, float, double and void). These are *unstructured* types, which means that an identifier of any of these types can have only one, individual value at any given time. Quite often, however, it is desirable to be able to group together several values and to refer to them by the same name. (E.g., a list of examination marks or a person's name, address and telephone number.) In common with most other high level programming languages, C++ allows the creation of such *structured* types. The most common and most straightforward of C++'s structured types is the **array**. As in other languages, this is used to group together elements which are all of exactly the same type (either an inbuilt type or a user-created type).

5.2   Array Declaration and Usage

The general form of an array declaration is :

> ⟨*Base type*⟩ ⟨*Array name*⟩ [⟨*Array size*⟩];

<u>Examples</u>

```
int mark[10];       //A list of 10 integers.
char letter[25];    //A sequence of 25 characters.
```

In order to refer to an individual element of an array, we use the array name, followed by an integer in square brackets.

Examples

```
cout<<mark[5];
mark[7] = 63;
```

The integer is called an *index* or *subscript* (something of a misnomer, since it is not 'below the writing') and specifies the element's position within the array or 'list' of values.

N.B. Array elements in C++ are numbered from **0**, not from 1. Thus, the array declaration *int mark[10]* reserves space for 10 integers, which may then be referred to individually by the names *mark[0]*, *mark[1]*, ..., *mark[9]*. It would be foolish and potentially very dangerous to attempt to manipulate an element called *mark[10]* here!

> *Aside*
> When choosing names for arrays, it is necessary to make a choice between a singular noun and its plural equivalent. (E.g., *mark* v *marks*.) At declaration time, the use of the plural seems much more natural, since we know that we are referring to a group of values. However, when we carry out operations on individual elements of the array (which is all that we can do after the initial declaration of the array, apart from passing the whole array to a function), it is rather more readable to use the singular. Thus, for example, *mark[3] = 49* is rather better than *marks[3] = 49*. Therefore, it is the author's opinion that the singular should always be used.

Assignment of a whole array to another whole array (even one with the same base type and number of elements) is **not allowed** in C++. For example, the following is not allowed :

```
array1 = array2;    //Illegal
```

5.3   Array Initialisation

An array may be initialised at declaration time. This is achieved by use of the equals symbol followed by the list of initial values (called an *initialisation list*) contained within chain brackets.

Example

```
int number[3] = {15, 27, 19};
```

For a numeric array, if the number of elements supplied is fewer than the number of elements in the array, then the remaining elements are initialised to zero. Thus,

```
int num[4] = {7, 18};
```

is equivalent to :

```
int num[4] = {7, 18, 0, 0};
```

It is not absolutely necessary to state the size of an initialised array explicitly. If the number of elements for the initialised array is not specified, then the number of initial values supplied determines the number of elements in the array.

Example
```
        int num[] = {12, 5, 7, 9};   //An array of 4 elements.
```
This is referred to as an 'open' array.

Elements of a static numeric array (one declared outside any block or explicitly declared with the keyword *static*) are automatically initialised to zero if no initialisation is specified by the user. Non-static, uninitialised arrays contain unpredictable values! It is, therefore, highly advisable to initialise such arrays before they are used.

5.4   Array Processing

Frequently, the same operation needs to be carried out on all elements of an array at the same point in a program. In these circumstances, the processing will almost invariably involve the use of a for loop.

Example
```
        float weight [20];

        for (int count = 0; count < 20; count++)
        {
            cout<<"Enter weight "<<(count + 1)<< " : ";
            cin>>weight[count];
        }
```

Character arrays can also be declared and then used to store individual characters.

Example
```
        char letter[] = {'a', 'b', 'c', 'd'};
```

However, this is a set of individual characters and cannot be interpreted as a *string* (a word or block of text). See the next section for coverage of strings.

Multi-dimensional arrays are also allowed. Though more dimensions than two are allowed, it is rarely useful to consider more than two dimensions. Two-dimensional arrays are very useful for representing *tables* of values, with one dimension representing rows and the other representing columns. The processing of such arrays is conveniently carried out by *nested* for loops.

Example
```
        int mark[10][4];    //Marks of 10 students in 4 exams.
```

```
for (int row = 0; row <10; row++)
{
    cout<<"\nStudent "<<(row + 1)<< "\n\n";

    for (int col = 0; col < 4; col++)
    {
        cout<<"Enter mark for exam "<<(col+1)<<" : ";
        cin>>mark[row][col];
    }
}
```

It is not necessary to specify the size of the first dimension explicitly if the array is initialised when it is declared, but all remaining dimensions must be stated explicitly.

Example
```
int dim3_array[][2][3] = {{ {1,2,3}, {37,9,14} },
                          { {8,97,4}, {13,5,63} },
                          { {42,18,6}, {17,1,99} }  };
```

In this example, the first dimension of the array is implicitly taken to be 3 by the compiler, resulting in a 3 x 2 x 3 array. (This may be interpreted as an array of three rows and two columns in which each element is itself a one-dimensional array holding three integers.)

5.5   Strings

A string is a sequence of characters which may be regarded and used as a single entity. Often, a string will be a word. In C++, a string is stored as an array of characters, with the final character followed by the null character, '\0'. This character is essential for termination of the string. Thus, the number of array elements must be one more than the number of characters in the string.

Character arrays may be initialised to hold strings by specifying a sequence of characters held within speech marks.

Example
```
char word[8]= "Example"; //7 letters + null character.
```

This is equivalent to :

```
char word[8] = {'E','x','a','m','p','l','e','\0'};
```

As usual, we can leave it up to the computer to determine the number of elements for an initialised array.

Example
```
char text[] = "Computing";
```

5.6   Pointers

Pointers are very widely used in C++. A pointer is a type of variable which is capable of holding the address of a data element of a specific type. Thus, for example, a pointer might hold the address of an int or that of a float. In the diagram below, *int_ptr* holds the address of an int, while *float_ptr* holds the address of a float.

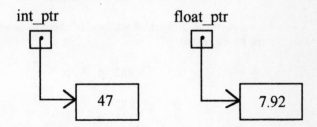

When first encountering pointers, it is very easy to become confused betwen the pointers themselves and the data items to which they are pointing. Remember that the two are **separate** and that the value held in a pointer is an **address**, not data.

There is a close connection between pointers and arrays in C++, but, before this connection is discussed, we shall consider the syntax and general usage of pointers in C++.

Syntax for a pointer declaration :

```
< type> *   < identifier> ;
```

<u>Examples</u>
```
int*  int_ptr;       //Holds address of a single integer.
float*  float_ptr;   //Holds address of a single float.
```

Aside
A lot of C programmers place the pointer asterisk immediately before the identifier, and this custom has spread amongst some C++ programmers (since many of them were originally C programmers).

```
E.g.,   int  *int_ptr;       //Common C-style.
```

However, it is the author's firm opinion that this is considerably less logical and less readable, since the pointer symbol (the asterisk) should be associated with the base type and not with the identifier. Thus, for instance, the first of the two examples above declares an identifier *int_ptr* of type int* ('pointer-to-int'), not an (invalid) identifier *int_ptr* of type int.

However, this does mean that some care must be exercised with multiple pointer declarations. For instance, if we wish to declare three pointers-to-int, the following line would **not** be the way to do it :

```
int*  p, q, r;          //Wrong!
```

This means :

```
int  *p;  int q;  int r;
//One pointer and two ints.
```

To achieve the desired effect, one of the following two options must be employed :

(i)   int* p, * q, * r;

(ii)   int* p;
         int* q;
         int* r;

In order to de-reference a pointer (i.e., to get at the data whose address is held in the pointer), the pointer name must be *preceded* by an asterisk. Thus, *int_ptr* is read as 'the value whose address is held in int_ptr' or 'the contents of location int_ptr'. In order to obtain the address of any identifier within a program, we must use the 'address-of' operator, **&** (the ampersand), which is followed by the identifier whose address is required. Thus, *&total* will return the address of the variable *total*.

Example
```
int number = 5;
int*  num_ptr = &number;   //Holds address of number.

cout<<"Initial value of number : "<<*num_ptr<<'\n';
                            //Value of 5 is output.
*num_ptr = 10;      //Same effect as :  number = 10;
cout<<"New value of number : "<<*num_ptr<<'\n';
                            //Value of 10 is output.
```

5.7   Pointers and Arguments

For all the inbuilt types apart from arrays, 'ordinary' arguments to functions in C++ are passed **by value only**. This means that any value supplied in a function call is passed on to the function's corresponding formal argument (the one named in the function definition), which is a local variable whose scope is the function definition itself. This local variable holds a *copy* of the original variable. Any changes which are made to this variable during execution of the function will be lost once function execution has finished. Thus, variables passed to a function as 'ordinary' arguments cannot be updated by the function. If only one value were in need of being updated, then there would be no great problem, since the new value could be returned via the function's return type and used to update the variable (even though this is a little indirect). However, when two or more values are to be updated, this solution is not feasible.

Example

Suppose the following function definition is intended to reverse the values of its arguments :

```
void swap(int num1, int num2)
{
    int dummy = num1;
    num1 = num2;
    num2 = dummy;
} //Incorrect definition!
```

The following call to this function might then be made, but would have no effect on its arguments :

```
swap(first, second);        //Won't work!
```

After execution of the above line, *first* and *second* will still have their original values, since the arguments are passed **by value** to *num1* and *num2*, which are **local** to the function definition.

One solution to this problem is to use *pointers* to pass the addresses of the arguments. Once the addresses of the variables in the function call have been passed, of course, the function may alter the contents of these locations, thereby achieving **passing by reference** of the arguments. That is, the function is given access to the original variables, not just (temporary) copies of the values held in those variables.

Pointer Solution to Problem

The new function definition becomes :

```
void swap(int* num1_ptr, int* num2_ptr)
{
    int dummy = *num1_ptr;
    //Accesses contents of address.

    *num1_ptr = *num2_ptr;
    *num2_ptr = dummy;
}
```

When this function is called, the address-of operator is used to pass the addresses of the two values which are to be exchanged :

```
swap(&first, &second);
```

Though this is a perfectly legitimate method for passing arguments by reference in C++, it does carry with it the danger of omitting the ampersand operator before the identifiers. A better technique in C++ is to make use of *reference types*, which will be introduced at the end of this chapter.

5.8   Arrays and Pointers

There is a close connection between arrays and pointers in C++, since an array name
in C++ holds the address of the first element (element 0) of the array. Since the
remaining elements of the array will be stored in consecutive locations following the
first element, the array name is effectively a *pointer* to the array. For example, if
int_array is the name of an array, then this name is equivalent to *&int_array[0]*.
Thus, unlike other variables, arrays can **only** be passed to functions by reference
(i.e., by address).

When coding a function definition which involves an array as one of its
arguments, the programmer may use either array notation or explicit pointer
notation to specify the array. If the latter technique is used, then elements of the
array may be accessed via the pointer by using an integer index in square brackets in
exactly the same way as that in which array elements are normally accessed. In fact,
the use of an open array and that of an explicit pointer to the base type of the array
when specifying an argument to a function may be treated as equivalent (though the
compiler will recognise a type difference), and it is usually merely a matter of
personal preference which one is used.

Example
Suppose a set of examination marks is held in an array and that the marks may need
to be increased by a given percentage (subject to a maximum mark of 100). The
following function definition will achieve this :

```
int adjust_up(int* array_ptr, int size, int percent)
//Note use of pointer to first integer in array.
//As an alternative, the argument could have been
//supplied as an open array :      int array[]
{
    int temp;

    for (int count=0; count<size; count++)
    {
        temp =
        int(float(array_ptr[count])*(1+percent)+0.5);
        //Rounds result to nearest integer.

        if (temp > 100)
            array_ptr[count] = 100;
        //Explicit pointer argument used with index in
        //exactly same way as array name would be.
        else
            array_ptr[count] = temp;
    }
}
```

To increase by 10% the results held in an array *mark* of size 30, the following call
would then be made :

```
adjust_up(mark, 30, 10);
```

5.9   The NULL Pointer

As in other languages which support pointers, there exists a **null pointer** in C++. This does not point to anything and is used to indicate the absence of a valid pointer. As will be seen in a later chapter, such a pointer is particularly useful for indicating the end of a linked list. The special constant NULL is used in C++ to indicate the null pointer. Though many programmers use 0 instead, since C++ will convert between NULL and the integer constant 0 as required, it is advisable to use NULL for program readability when referring to pointers.

5.10   Strings Revisited

Since an array name is a pointer to the first element of the array, its type is *<Base type>**. For example, an array of integers is of type int*. In particular, a character array name has type char* ('pointer-to-char'). Thus, the following is a valid declaration :

```
char*  string_ptr = text;
//Assuming that 'text' is a string.
```

In addition, when a string literal is used, it yields a pointer to the first character of the string. This means that the following is also a valid declaration :

```
char*  string_ptr = "Example";
//Takes up 8 characters, including null character.
```

Being arrays, strings are passed to operators and functions as pointers. When their values are output, however, the pointers are automatically de-referenced and their text contents sent to the specified stream. Thus, given *string_ptr* as above, the statement

```
cout<<string_ptr;
```

will cause the following output to be produced :

```
Example
```

5.11   Functions for String Processing

When handling strings, there are certain operations which are frequently required. The inbuilt header file *string.h* contains the function prototypes for these commonly-required operations. The most useful of these functions are strcpy, strlen, strcmp and strcat. Other functions which may be of occasional use are strupr and strlwr.

`strcpy`

Prototype :   `char* strcpy(char* dest, const char* source);`

This copies string *source* (i.e., the string pointed to by *source*) into string *dest* (i.e., the string pointed to by *dest*).
(The use of `const` in the prototype ensures that the function will not change string *source*, which is good programming practice.)
The function returns a pointer to the copy which has been created.

Example

```
char word[15];
strcpy(word, "kitchen");
```

Here, 'kitchen' is copied into the first eight character positions of array *word* (including the null character), with the remaining seven positions unused and with unknown contents.

`strlen`

Prototype :   `int strlen(char* string);`

This function returns the number of characters in its string argument (excluding the null character).

Example

```
char* word = "frog";
//N.B. If initialisation is not used here,
//array notation MUST be used, in order to
//allocate space for array.

cout<<strlen(word); //'4' is output.
```

`strcmp`

Prototype :   `int strcmp(const char* str1, const char* str2);`

This function compares two strings and returns 0 if they are equal, a negative number if the first string precedes the second and a positive number if the second string precedes the first. An easy way to remember all this is to think of the function as carrying out the 'subtraction' *str1-str2*, with the 'smaller' string being the one which precedes the other alphabetically. Thus, for instance, if *str2* is 'bigger' than *str1* (i.e., comes after it alphabetically), `strcmp` will return a negative result.

Example

```
char word1[15];
char word2[15];

cout<<"Enter first word : ";
cin>>word1;
cout<<"Enter second word : ";
```

```
        cin>>word2;
        cout<<"\n\n";
        if (strcmp(word1, word2) < 0)
            cout<<word1<<" precedes "<<word2;
        else if (strcmp(word1, word2) > 0)
            cout<<word2<<" precedes "<<word1;
        else
            cout<<"These words are identical.";
```

strcat

Prototype :   *char* strcat(char* dest, const char* source);*

This function appends string *source* to string *dest* (leaving string *source* unchanged) and returns a pointer to the concatenated result (i.e., to modified *dest*).

Example

```
        char word1[25];
        char word2[15];

        cout<<"Enter 2 words, separated by space(s) : ";
        cin>>word1>>word2;
        if (strlen(word1) + strlen(word2) < 25)
            cout<<"Concatenated result : "
                <<strcat(word1,word2);
        else
            cout<<"Insufficient space available for result! ";
        //Dynamic memory allocation would need to be employed
        //here to overcome this problem and will be covered in
        //a later chapter.
```

strupr

Prototype :   *char* strupr(char* string_in);*

This function converts *string_in* into its upper case equivalent, returning a pointer to the converted string.

Example

```
        char word[20];
        .......................................
        .......................................
        cin>>word;
        strupr(word);
        cout<<word<<"\n\n";
```

If 'example' is entered by the user when the above code is executed, then 'EXAMPLE' will be output.

strlwr

Prototype :   *char* strlwr(char* string_in);*

This function converts *string_in* into its lower case equivalent, returning a pointer to the converted string.

Example
```
        char word[20];
        .........................................
        .........................................
        cin>>word;
        cout<<strlwr(word)<<"\n\n";
        //Previous example could also have used this shortened
        //form, but illustrated that contents of 'word' had
        //actually been changed.
```

If 'eXAMplE' is entered by the user when the above code is executed, then 'example' will be output.

5.12   Memory Allocation for Strings

Unless memory is subsequently allocated dynamically [See Chapter 7 for details of this], a character string **must** have sufficient space allocated for it at declaration time. This may be done *either* by explicitly stating the maximum size of the string (as in example (i) below) *or* by initialising the string to a particular value (as shown in examples (ii) and (iii)).

Examples

```
(i)    char string[10];      //Maximum of 9 characters + '\0'.
(ii)   char* word = "cat"; //Maximum of 3 characters + '\0'.
(iii)  char[] word = "dog"; //As for (ii) above.
```

It is **highly dangerous** to allocate insufficient space, since you may then overwrite other data or part of the program! In particular, a lack of familiarity with string pointers often leads novice C++ programmers to allocate *no memory* for a string.

Example
```
        char*  word; //No space allocated.
        .................................
        strcpy(word, "anything");
```

This will almost certainly result in unpredictable behaviour from the program (often involving a program crash or the display of strange character sequences on the screen when attempting ouput of the string concerned). The precise result will depend on what previously occupied the address held in *word*.

5.13   Reference Types

As seen in section 5.7, C++ allows the use of pointers to create 'aliases' for other variables, notably when passing arguments 'by reference' to functions (as opposed to passing them 'by value'). However, this is really the C method for passing arguments by reference. C++ allows a more convenient way of doing this, by providing *reference types*. These are used to create *references* to existing variables. Such 'references' are new names (aliases) for these variables. Like pointers, they contain the addresses of these variables. Unlike pointers, though, they are *implicitly de-referenced* when used, making them look like ordinary variables. The general syntax for a reference declaration is :

```
<Base type>& <Identifier>;
```

Example
```
float length = 5.63;
float& length_ref = length;
//Establishes correspondence.
```

The reference identifier *length_ref* is now an alias for *length*, so that both refer to the same variable, the same memory location. Thus, the following statements have exactly the same output :

```
cout<<length;
cout<<length_ref;
```

The following assignment changes the value of both *length* and *length_ref* to 7.95 :

```
length_ref = 7.95;
```

N.B. A reference **must** be initialised (i.e., 'tied' to a particular variable) when declared, except when used as an argument to a function. [See next section for an example of the latter.] Once initialised, it cannot be reassigned to point to another variable.

It is not possible to create a reference to a reference or a pointer to a reference, though it *is* possible to create a reference to a pointer.

5.14   References as Arguments

References are most commonly used for passing arguments to functions by reference.

Example
```
void swap(int& num1, int& num2)
{
    int dummy = num1;
    num1 = num2;
    num2 = dummy;
}
```
This avoids the explicit de-referencing of a pointer shown in the same example in Section 5.7.

Reference types can also be used as function return types, but this facility is only usually of any great use when passing back references to objects of programmer-defined classes, as will be demonstrated in a later chapter.

Exercises

1. Accept three integers, using variables *first*, *second* and *third* to hold them. Employing a function which makes use of pointers, rearrange the contents of *first*, *second* and *third* so that they are in ascending order and then output the values in order.

2. Rewrite the previous program so that, instead of using pointers, the function uses reference types.

3. Use arrays to accept the surnames and examination marks in English, Mathematics and French of four school pupils. When all names and marks have been entered, display the results in tabular form, including the average mark (to 1 decimal place) for each subject.
N.B. A two-dimensional array should be used for names, since an individual name will itself be an array of characters.

4. Write definitions of the two string-handling functions described below and then write a program which will demonstrate their use by prompting the user for appropriate values and displaying the results.

(i)   `int strpos(const char* s, const char c);`
Returns the position of the first occurrence of character *c* in string *s*. If *c* is not contained in *s*, 0 is returned.
If a non-zero value is returned, you should display the substring starting at the specified position.

(ii)   `char* strcat(char* str1, const char* str2);`
(Operates as described in 5.11.)

Chapter 6   Adding Sophistication to Basic I/O

Aims

- To demonstrate how text containing 'whitespace' may be accepted in full.
- To extend the use of manipulators for improving the format of screen output.

6.1   Handling 'Whitespace' in Text Input

'Whitespace' comprises spaces, tabs, newlines and form-feeds. When input is received through cin, the end of an individual item is signalled by any whitespace character. A consequence of this is that it is not possible to enter a character sequence containing spaces (such as a sentence or someone's full name) directly through cin, since cin will consider the data item to be terminated by the first space character.

<u>Example</u>

```
main()
{
    char name[31]; //Up to 30 characters + '\0'.

    cout<<"Please enter your full name : ";
    cin>>name;
    cout<<"\n\nName entered : "<<name<<'\n';
    return 0;
}
```

If the user keys in 'Andrew Paul Mallinson' when this code is run, then the dialogue will look like this :

```
Please enter your full name :  Andrew Paul Mallinson

Name entered :  Andrew
```

However, as will be explained in more detail at a later stage, cin is a *class object* which has a number of *member functions*. One of these functions is getline, which takes three arguments :

```
char* text        (pointer to the character string to be accepted);
int max_length    (maximum no. of characters which will be accepted);
char terminator   (terminating character).
```

This member function may be used to accept a line of text. The second argument specifies one character more than the maximum length of the string (allowing space for the null character, '\0'), while the third argument specifies the character which will be used to signal termination of the character sequence. cin will accept characters until *either* the terminating character is encountered *or* the maximum number of characters (*max_length-1*) has been accepted (whichever comes first). The terminating character is *not* stored as part of the character sequence. This terminating character will normally be the newline character, in which case the final argument may be expressed as :

```
char terminator = '\n'
```

However, the terminating character has a default value of '\n' anyway, so this argument is frequently omitted. The syntax for calling this member function, then, is usually :

```
cin.getline(<string>, <length>);
```

Example
```
main()
{
    char name[31];

    cout<<"Please enter your full name : ";
    cin.getline(name, 31);
    cout<<"\n\nName entered : "<<name<<'\n';
    return 0;
}
```

This time, if 'Andrew Paul Mallinson' is entered again when the code is run, the output will look like this :

```
Please enter your full name :  Andrew Paul Mallinson

Name entered :  Andrew  Paul Mallinson
```

However, there is a further problem to be overcome before getline can be used effectively...

The input operator (>>) does not remove the newline character from the input stream. This causes no problem if the next input is also accepted via the input operator, since this operator ignores whitespace characters, by default (though it is possible to change this feature via a manipulator). When input is accepted via getline, however, whitespace is **not** ignored. This means that the newline character which has been left on the input stream will be accepted by getline, signalling immediate termination of string entry! What we need is some way of getting rid of this unwanted newline character before we attempt to accept further input with getline. Fortunately, there is another member function of cin which will allow us to do this : ignore. This function takes two arguments :

```
int length        (maximum no. of characters to be discarded);
int terminator     (terminating character).
```

Function `ignore` extracts and discards characters until *either* it meets the terminating character *or* the number of characters specified by *length* has been discarded. There is a special constant EOF (probably = -1) which is used to indicate the end of file input. [See Chapter 12 for details of file I/O.] Thus, for file input, the final argument may be expressed as :

```
int terminator = EOF
```

This is the default value, and so is the value which will be assumed for this argument if none is supplied.

[The reason that -1 is normally used (and so type `int` is required, rather than `char`) is that -1 cannot possibly be the code for a valid character.]

For keyboard input, however, the terminating character will normally be the newline character, so that the final argument may be expressed as :

```
int terminator = '\n'
```

Thus, for keyboard input, the call will normally be :

```
cin.ignore(<length>, '\n');
```

If there is any input via >> before the use of `getline`, `getline` should be immediately preceded by `ignore`.

Example
```
main()
{
    int year;
    char name[31];

    cout<<"Enter the year : ";
    cin>>year;
    cin.ignore(80, '\n');
    //Above call gets rid of surplus character(s).
    cout<<"\nEnter your full name : ";
    cin.getline(name, 31);
    cout<<"\n\nName entered : "<<name<<'\n';
    return 0;
}
```

Try running the above code (including <iostream.h>, of course) both with and without the line which calls function `ignore`, observing the difference in output.

6.2   The Formatting of Output Via Manipulators

The example program in Section 2.5 featured one type of formatting which is frequently required : the output of a real number (i.e., a number with a fractional part) to a specified number of decimal places. This section shows further ways in which the format of output may be modified via the use of manipulators, particularly for real numbers, but also for integers and character strings.

[For lists of the available formatting flags and associated manipulators, refer to Appendix C.]

6.2.1   Common Manipulators

Manipulators dec, oct and hex may be used to ensure decimal, octal or hexadecimal conversion respectively of numeric output.

Example

```
cout<<oct<<157;
//'235' is output. (157 = 2x64 + 3x8 + 5x1)
```

Manipulator setw ('set width') sets the field width for the next item to be output. Unlike any of the other manipulators, it applies only to the next item output and must be reset for each subsequent value output (even if the field width is not to change).

Example

```
cout<<setw(2)<<day<<'/'<<setw(2)<<month<<'/'<<setw(2)<<year;
```

If setw is not specified before the next item output, then the field width is automatically reset to 0. This is rather misleading, though, since a field width of 0 is interpreted by the system as the minimum width necessary to accommodate an item. Thus, there is no truncation of output.

Manipulator setfill is used to specify the character which will be used to 'pad' out or fill out a field to the size specified by setw (if the number of characters in the item is fewer than that specified by setw).
Note that, since the argument is of type char, it must be enclosed by inverted commas, even if it is a digit.

Example

```
cout<<setfill('0')<<setw(2)<<day<<'/';
cout<<setw(2)<<month<<'/'<<setw(2)<<year;
```

If *day*, *month* and *year* hold the values 5, 2 and 98 when the lines above are executed, then the output will be as follows :

```
05/02/98
```

The combination of setw and setfill is very useful for such things as the output of dates and times in specific formats and the insertion of leading asterisks for protection of printed cheques.

As seen in Section 2.5, the manipulator setprecision is used to specify the number of decimal places for real numbers. It should be used in combination with manipulator setiosflags, the latter being used to ensure fixed point notation.

Example
```
cout<<setiosflags(ios::fixed)<<setprecision(2)<<29.726;
```

Execution of the above line will result in the following output :

```
27.73
```

The more general use of setiosflags will be covered in the next section.

6.2.2   Common Formatting Flags

There are several inbuilt formatting flags which may be used to alter the format of output. Each of these flags is stored as a single bit within an enumerated type, so that each has an associated name. As noted in Section 2.5, any reference to one of these flags must be preceded by ios::, to indicate the name of the inbuilt class which holds the enumerated type. The manipulator setiosflags may be used to set these formatting flags, either singly or in combination (the latter by 'OR-ing' the bit flags). The most commonly required formatting flags are the following :

```
left, right, showpoint and fixed.
```

The first two of these are used to produce left and right justification respectively and may be used in combination with setw to align columns in tables of output. They may be used with both numeric and character/string data, as may setw. By default, all screen output in C++ commences at the next available position (and so is 'left justified'). Often, however, numeric values in a table need to be output with their rightmost digits aligned (i.e., 'right justified'). This may be accomplished by setting flag right via setiosflags.

Example
```
cout<<setiosflags(ios::right)<< ...
```

If real numbers are being output, then flag *fixed* may be set at the same time by 'OR-ing' it with the above flag :

```
cout<<setiosflags(ios::fixed|ios::right)<< ...
```

[It may be that your implementation of C++ defaults to fixed point output, as do the latest Borland implementations, but it will do no harm to play safe.]

Where tables of figures are involved, it is normal to use setw to set field width to a value which will accommodate the longest value which will be displayed. This width will, of course, need to be specified for each value to be output.

Example
```
cout<<setw(6)<<num<<'\n'<<setw(6)<<num<<'\n'<< ...
```

If real numbers are being output and a particular value has no fractional part (i.e., it is a whole number), then the usual default action is to show a whole number with no decimal point. In many applications, however, it is highly desirable that the decimal point be retained, with one or more zeroes displayed after it. In particular, applications relating to monetary figures frequently require numeric output to be shown to two decimal places (so that *.00* is shown at the end of any whole number). In such cases, flag showpoint ('show decimal point') needs to be set. Like the other flags, it can be set separately or it can be 'OR-ed' with other flags.

Example
```
cout<<setiosflags(ios::fixed|ios::right|ios::showpoint)<< ...
```

Once flag right has been set, it will affect all output which follows, until overridden by the setting of flag left. In particular, it will affect the output of strings. However, tabular output is normally required with columns of string data left justified and columns of numeric data right justified. This means that, for tables involving a mixture of column types, we shall need to specify the justification for individual columns.

Example
```
const char name[3] = {"Smith", "Reynolds", "Williamson"};
const int age[3] = {5, 36, 100};
const float savings[3] = {0, 512.85, 14278.92};

for (int count=0; count<3; count++)
{
    cout<<setiosflags(ios::left)<<setw(15)<<name[count];
    cout<<setiosflags(ios::right)<<setw(4)<<age[count];
    cout<<setiosflags(ios::fixed|ios::showpoint)<<setw(10);
    cout<<setprecision(2)<<savings[count]<<'\n';
}
```

Execution of this code produces the following output :

```
Smith                5        0.00
Reynolds            36      512.85
Williamson         100    14278.92
```

Exercises

1. Rewrite Exercise 3 from the previous chapter, this time ensuring that columns are correctly aligned.

2. Modify the above program to accept and display *full* names.

3. Accept the stock codes and current levels of ten items of stock, with stock codes being entered as strings. Then allow the user to retrieve the stock level of any item whose stock code he/she enters. The user should be allowed to enter the code in upper, lower or mixed case. Allow as many repetitions as the user wishes, stopping when the user enters 'n' in response to being asked whether he/she wishes to retrieve another stock level. [Single-key input is preferable for accepting the user's response to a prompt for another retrieval, but is implementation-dependent. See Appendix B for further information.]

4. Accept an integer in each of the number bases 8, 10 and 16 and then output the value of each of these integers in each of the other two number bases.

5. Accept five real numbers from the user and then display these numbers in a column, using a field width of 10 and showing 2 decimal places (even if the fractional part is 0). Make each value occupy the same number of screen positions by specifying a 'fill' character of '*' (asterisk).

Chapter 7   Classes in C++

Aims

- To familiarise the reader with structs, as a prelude to the introduction of explicit classes.
- To introduce the reader to the implementation of the class construct in C++.
- To familiarise the reader with the use of class member functions, particularly constructors and destructors.
- To introduce the use of static class members.

7.1   Structures

The word 'structure' in the context of C/C++ is somewhat misleading, since its meaning is considerably narrower than that normally attributed to the word 'structure' in computer science. A structure in C++, indicated by the keyword **struct**, is the equivalent of a **record** in a number of other high level languages. That is to say, it is a *composite* type, made up of two or more members. Unlike the members of an array, the members of a struct may be of differing types.

The syntax of the type declaration for a structure is as follows :

```
struct <tag name>
{
    <Member list>
};
```

N.B. It is very easy to omit the terminating semi-colon. Doing so is likely to lead to a non-helpful error message!

Once a structure declaration has been encountered by the compiler, it will be regarded as a genuine type, so that variables of this type may be declared.

<u>Example</u>
```
struct item
{
    unsigned long int code;   //First of 3 members
    unsigned int quantity;
    float price;
};

item stock1, stock2;        //Two variables of type item.
```

Structures may be 'nested' --- i.e., they may be members of other structures.

Example

```
struct order
{
    unsigned int invoice_num;
    item goods;        // Nested structure.
};
```

A structure can be initialised by using a list of values inside chain brackets, in the same way in which an array is initialised.

Example

```
item part= {5794832, 150, 42.75};
```

The individual members of a structure are referenced via the **dot operator** (.).
Syntax :

```
<struct name>.<member name>
```

Example

```
stock1.quantity = 150;
```

It is quite common in C++ to access a structure via a pointer. In order to access a member of the structure via the pointer, the **arrow operator (->)**, which is made up of the two keyboard characters '-' and '>', is used.

Example

```
item* stock_ptr = &stock1;
cout<<stock_ptr->quantity;
//Outputs value of stock1.quantity
```

Alternatively, it is possible to dereference the pointer first, in order to get at the whole structure, and then to use the dot operator to get at the required member.

Example

```
cout<<(*stock_ptr).quantity;
```

However, it should be readily appreciated that the latter option is considerably less elegant!

Since structure members can be pointers, structures are often used to form **linked lists**. However, consideration of this technique will be postponed until the next chapter.

In C++, structs are genuine *class types*. This means that they may have *functions*, as well as data items, as members.

Example

```
struct point
{
    int x, y;        //Coordinates of point.

//Function prototypes :
    void set_values (int x_val, int y_val);
    void get_values(int& x_val, int& y_val);
};
```

The data members are known as **instance variables** (or simply **data members**) and the functions as **member functions** (or **methods**).

The author would rarely use a struct for holding more than data. A much more common way of declaring classes is to use the keyword *class*, as described in the next section.

7.2 Explicit Class Declarations

The syntax for a standalone class declaration is as follows :

```
class <class name>
{
private:
    <private members>
public:
    <public members>
};
```

(The precise meaning of the keywords *private* and *public* will be explained in the next section.)

As for structs, *beware omission of the final semi-colon!*

Class Declaration Example

```
class point
{
private:
    int x,y;
public:
    void set_values(int x_val, int y_val);
    void get_values(int& x_val, int& y_val);
};
```

7.3 Access Control

The keywords `private` and `public` specify access control for the members of a class. This means that they specify which parts of a program can gain access to the members. (There is a third category of access control, but this will only be of use when inheritance has been covered and will not be described here.)

7.3.1 Private Access

A member declared with such access control is accessible only to member functions of its class. This allows **information hiding** to take place. For information hiding to be effective, the following rule should be adhered to in C++ programs :

- *all instance variables (data members) should be private.*

Nothing within the language prevents instance variables from being declared with *public* access, but it would be quite pointless (and foolish) to do so, since this would remove the protection afforded by encapsulation.

7.3.2   Public Access

A member declared with such access control is accessible to *any* part of a program which has included the class. Usually, most/all of a class's functions will be public, providing an *interface* to the class. As stated in Chapter 1, such an interface provides controlled access to instance variables (possibly only to some instance variables). The access provided will be minimal and will be determined by the class designer on a 'need-to-know' basis for the application programs which will make use of the class.

Occasionally, one or more of the public functions may need to make use of ancillary functions, which the outside world need know nothing about. Thus, it is quite legitimate (and appropriate) for such ancillary functions to be declared private.

7.3.3   Default Access Levels

If the access levels are not specified, then certain default values are assumed. For a struct, members are assumed to be `public`; for a class, they are assumed to be `private`. The author considers it good practice always to declare access levels explicitly, rather than leaving the defaults to apply, since it is then quite clear what access levels were intended.

7.4   Member Function Definitions

The syntax for a member function definition is an extension of that for a standalone function definition :

```
<Return type> <Class name>::<Function name> ([<Argument list>])
{
     <Function body>
}
```

The only difference is the insertion of the class name and the double colon (called the **scope resolution operator**) between the return type and the function name. The member function body will have direct access to all the private members of the class.

Example

```
void point :: set_values(int x_val, int y_val)
{
     x = x_val;
     y = y_val;
}
```

7.5   Using a Class

As an example, suppose we wish to declare an abstract data type (a class) called *rational_num*, which will hold a vulgar fraction (2/5, -8/9, 27/18, -5/4, etc.) which is not necessarily in its lowest terms. Thus, for example, 9/12 will be held as 9/12, and not in its reduced form of 3/4. Functions will be required for setting the value of the a *rational_num* object, for returning its current (unadjusted) value and for returning the current value in its lowest terms. Firstly, though, it is necessary to show the syntax for calling a member function :

```
<object name>.<function name> ([<arguments>]);
```

Example
```
my_circle.draw(radius);
```

Now for the code for the rational number example...

```
//rat_nums.h
//Declaration of rational number class.

#ifndef RAT_NUMS_H
#define RAT_NUMS_H

#include <iostream.h>
#include <stdlib.h>
//The above header file is needed for access to the function exit.
//Execution of this function causes immediate exit from program.

class rational_num
{
private:
    int numerator;        //'Top' number in fraction.
    int denominator;      //'Bottom' number.
public:
    void set_value(int num, int denom);
    void get_value(int& num, int& denom);
    void get_lowest_terms(int& num, int& denom);
};
#endif
```

```
//rat_nums.cpp
//Implementation of rational number class.

#include "rat_nums.h"

enum boolean{FALSE, TRUE};

void rational_num::set_value(int num, int denom)
{
    if (denom == 0)
    {
        cout<<"\n\n\n\a";
        cout<<"*** Denominator of zero not allowed! ***\n\n";
        exit(1);    //Traditionally, any non-zero
```

```
                       //value here indicates an error.

    if (denom<0)        //Only numerator may be signed.
    {                       //Thus, e.g., 5/(-7) is disallowed.
        numerator = -num;
        denominator = -denom;
    }
    else
    {
        numerator = num;
        denominator = denom;
    }
}

void rational_num::get_value(int& num, int& denom)
{
    num = numerator;
    denom = denominator;
}

void rational_num::get_lowest_terms(int& num, int& denom)
{
    //If your maths is not very good, you would probably
    //be well advised to skip the details of this function!

    int sign_adjuster = 1;
    if (numerator < 0)
    {
        sign_adjuster = -1;
        num = -numerator;      //Must be positive for
                               //arithmetic which follows.
    }
    else
        num = numerator;
    denom = denominator;
    if (num%denom == 0)        //Num exactly divisible by denom.
    {
        num = (num/denom) * sign_adjuster;
        denom = 1;
        return;
    }
    if (denom%num == 0)        //Denom exactly divisible by num.
    {
        denom/=num;
        num = 1*sign_adjuster;
        return;
    }

    int greatest_divisor;
    //Will hold greatest possible common divisor.
    if (num < denom)
        greatest_divisor = num/2;
    else
        greatest_divisor = denom/2;
    boolean divisor_found = FALSE;
    while ((greatest_divisor>1) && (!divisor_found))
    {
        if ((num%greatest_divisor == 0)
        && (denom%greatest_divisor == 0))
            divisor_found = TRUE;
```

```
            else
                greatest_divisor--;
        }
    num = (num/greatest_divisor) * sign_adjuster;
    denom/=greatest_divisor;
}
```

```
//rnumdemo.cpp
//Demonstrates use of rational number class.

#include <iostream.h>

#include <ctype.h>
//Above needed for function tolower.

#include "rat_nums.h"

main()
{
    rational_num rat_num;
    char reply = 'y';
    int num, denom;

    do
    {
        cout<<"\n\n\nEnter numerator :   ";
        cin>>num;
        cout<<"Enter denominator :   ";
        cin>>denom;
        rat_num.set_value(num, denom);
        rat_num.get_lowest_terms(num,denom);
        cout<<"\n\nFraction in lowest terms :   ";
        cout<<num<<'/'<<denom;
        cout<<"\n\nDo you wish to do this again? (y/n) :   ";
        cin>>reply;
    }while (tolower(reply) == 'y');
    return 0;
}
```

A sample piece of output is shown below.

```
Enter numerator :   10
Enter denominator :   -45

Fraction in lowest terms :   -2/9

Do you wish to do this again? (y/n) :
```

7.6   Inline Member Functions

Like standalone functions, member functions may be *inline*. Unlike standalone functions, though, inline member functions are not preceded by the word 'inline'.

Example

The earlier function *get_value* is an obvious candidate for being an inline function.

```
class rational_num
{
private:
    int numerator;
    int denominator;
public:
    ..............................
    void get_value(int& num, int& denom)
    {//Inline function.
        num=numerator;
        denom=denominator;
    }
    ..............................
};
```

Member functions may, of course, call other member functions.

Example

```
void rational_num::adjust_value()
{
    int num, denom;

    get_lowest_terms(num, denom);
    set_value(num,denom);
}
```

7.7   Constructors

7.7.1   General Purpose, Syntax and Rationale

Constructors are special member functions which provide automatic initialisation of objects at the time of declaration, whilst preserving data hiding. That is to say, no direct access to instance variables is granted. The only manipulation of instance variables which occurs is that which was built into the constructor definition by the class designer. A program making use of objects of this class cannot modify the action of the constructor in any way other than providing values for its arguments (if the constructor has any arguments). Constructors can not only set values for the members of an object, but can also perform other kinds of operation (such as allocating memory dynamically, opening files, etc.).

A constructor is a special member function which has *same name* as its class (which makes its definition look a little peculiar, due to duplication of the class name) and has *no return type*, since it is effectively returning an object of the class, having created that object.

Example

```
class rational_num
{
```

```
            private:
                int numerator;
                int denominator;
            public:
                rational_num(int num, int denom);   //Constructor.
                int set_value(int num, int denom);
                .................................
                .................................
            };

        ---------------------------------------------------------------

        //Within implementation file...

        rational_num::rational_num (int num,int denom)
        {
            set_value(num, denom);
            //Makes use of another member function.
        }
```

A constructor is called when an object of the class is declared. One way of doing this is to make a direct call to the constructor.

Example

```
        rational_num rat_num = rational_num(2,5);
```

However, there is a shorter way (and this is the method which is normally used) :

```
        rational_num rat_num(2,5);
```

Why have constructors at all? Why are they considered important (as, indeed, they are)? Well, having constructors coupled with object declarations makes those objects **more robust**. They guarantee that objects will be initialised properly before being used. If the class designer were to rely on programmers remembering to carry out all necessary initialisation at the start of a program, then there would undoubtedly be some programmers who would forget to do this. Using constructors removes this possibility. For example, our *rational_num* constructor above means that it is no longer possible to retrieve the value of a *rational_num* object before it has been set. If this were to happen, then a meaningless and unpredictable value would be returned.

7.7.2   Constructor Overloading

Like other functions, constructors may be overloaded. In fact, it is quite common for them to be overloaded.

Example

Suppose we have a **date** class which stores the date as three integers (for day, month and year). One date constructor might accept the date as three such values, while the other accepts it as two integers, the first integer specifying the day of the year as a value in the range 1 to 365/366 and the second integer specifying the year. Shown

below is the code for the *date* class and a program which makes use of the class.
This is a somewhat longer example than has been presented so far in this book (even
though some of the details have deliberately been suppressed to cut down on the
volume of code), but the main items on which to focus are the two constructors.

```
//dates.h

#ifndef DATES_H
#define DATES_H

enum boolean {FALSE, TRUE};

class date
{
private:
    int day, month, year;
    int max_day;        //365 or 366
    int max_feb_day;    //28 or 29

    //The following methods are used only by other methods of
    //the class, and so have been declared public :

    int days_in_month(int month_in);
                            //Returns no. of days in month_in.

    void set_max_days(int year_in); //Sets max_day to 365/366
                                    //and max_feb_day to 28/29.

    boolean leap_year(int year_in); //Indicates whether year_in
                                    //is a leap year or not.

    void check_date(int day_in, int month_in, int year_in);
                            //Checks validity of date.

    void quit_with_error();     //Executed for invalid date.

public:
    date(int day_in, int year_in);
                                //Range of day_in is 1-365/366.
    date(int day_in, int month_in, int year_in);
    void set_date(int day_in, int month_in, int year_in);
    void add_day();                     //Moves date on by one day.
    void get_date(int& day_out, int& month_out, int& year_out);
};

#endif
```

```
//dates.cpp
//Implementation file for date class.

#include <iostream.h>
#include <stdlib.h>
//Above header file included for 'exit' function.

#include "dates.h"

int date::days_in_month(int month_in)
```

```
    {
        int month_length[12] =
          {31, max_feb_day, 31, 30, 31, 30, 31, 31, 30, 31, 30, 31};
        //Declarations in C++ may occur anywhere within a block,
        //allowing them to be more closely associated with the code
        //which uses them.

        return month_length[month_in-1];
        //Array elements numbered 0-11, not 1-12.
    }

void date::set_max_days(int year_in)
    {
        max_day = 365;
        max_feb_day = 28;
        if (leap_year(year_in))
        {
            max_day++;
            max_feb_day++;
        }
    }

boolean date::leap_year(int year_in)
    {
        ......................
        ......................
    }//Details omitted.

void date::check_date(int day_in, int month_in, int year_in)
    {
        if ((day_in<1) || (day_in>31)
                      || (month_in<1) || (month_in>12))
        {
            quit_with_error();
        }

        //Otherwise, set max_day to 365/366 and max_feb_day to
        //28/29 (as appropriate) :
        set_max_days(year_in);

        switch (month_in)
        //Check that day_in doesn't exceed last day
        //for a short month_in.
        {
            case 4:  case 6:            //April, June,
            case 9:  case 11:           //September, November
                      if (day_in==31)
                          quit_with_error();
                      break;
            case 2:   if (day_in>max_feb_day)
                          quit_with_error();
        }
    }

void date::quit_with_error()
    {
        cout<<"\n\n\n\a*** Invalid date! ***\n\n";
        exit(1);
        //Non-zero return value indicates an error.
    }
```

```
date::date(int day_in, int year_in)
{
    set_max_days(year_in);
    if (day_in>max_day)
        quit_with_error();
    day = day_in;
    year = year_in;

    int month_length[12] =
      {31, max_feb_day, 31, 30, 31, 30, 31, 31, 30, 31, 30, 31};

    month = 1;

    while (day>month_length[month-1])
    //(Array elements numbered from 0.)
    {
        //If the value held in day > length (in days) of
        //current array month, subtract length of current
        //month from day and move on to next month :

        day-=month_length[month-1];
        month++;
    }
}

date::date(int day_in, int month_in, int year_in)
{
    set_date(day_in, month_in, year_in);
    //Convenient simply to make use of another
    //member function here.
}

void date::set_date(int day_in, int month_in, int year_in)
{
    check_date(day_in, month_in, year_in);

    //If OK, assign values to instance variables :
    day = day_in;
    month = month_in;
    year = year_in;
}

void date::add_day()
{
    int month_days = days_in_month(month);

    day++;
    if (day > month_days)
    {
        //Set date to first day of next month.
        day = 1;
        month++;
        if (month > 12) //New Year!
        {
            month = 1;
            year++;
        }
    }
}
```

```
    void date::get_date(int& day_out, int& month_out,
                                         int& year_out)
    {
        day_out = day;
        month_out = month;
        year_out = year;
    }
```

```
//dateuser.cpp
//Tests date class.

#include <iostream.h>
#include "dates.h"

main()
{
    date date1(29, 2, 1996);
    date date2(60, 1996);    //Same as 29/2/96.
    int day1, day2;
    int month1, month2;
    int year1, year2;

    date1.get_date(day1, month1, year1);
    date2.get_date(day2, month2, year2);
    cout<<"Original value for date1 :   ";
    cout<<day1<<'/'<<month1<<'/'<<year1;
    cout<<"\nOriginal value for date2 :   ";
    cout<<day2<<'/'<<month2<<'/'<<year2;
    date1.add_day();
    date2.add_day();
    date1.get_date(day1, month1, year1);
    date2.get_date(day2, month2, year2);
    cout<<"\n\nNew value for date1 :   ";
    cout<<day1<<'/'<<month1<<'/'<<year1;
    cout<<"\nNew value for date2 :   ";
    cout<<day2<<'/'<<month2<<'/'<<year2;
    return 0;
}
```

The output from this program is shown below.

```
Original value for date1 :   29/2/1996
Original value for date2 :   29/2/1996

New value for date1 :   1/3/1996
New value for date2 :   1/3/1996
```

7.7.3   Default Constructors

A default constructor is a constructor which either takes no arguments or has arguments which all have default values.

<u>Examples</u>

```
        (i)      rational_num::rational_num()
```

```
              {
                  numerator = 1;
                  denominator = 1;
              }

(ii)      date::date(int day_in=1, int month_=1,
                                    year_in=1999)
              {
                  day=day_in;
                  month=month_in;
                  year=year_in;
              }
```

Such constructors are useful for implicit initialisation of objects (i.e., objects which are initialised without values being supplied by the programmer or user).

Example

```
          date new_date;
          //Using constructor in example (ii) above,
          //date is set to 1/1/99.
```

Default values may be overridden, of course.

Example

```
          rational_num rat_num(5);
          //Overrides first default in example(i),
          //making value 5/1.
```

7.7.4   Copy Constructors

A copy constructor is a constructor whose first argument is a reference to the same type as the class itself. If there are more arguments, then they must all be default arguments for the constructor to be a copy constructor.

Example

```
          rational_num::rational_num(rational_num& rat_num)
          {
              numerator = rat_num.numerator;
              denominator = rat_num.denominator;
          }
```

The copy constructor is called up when one object is being used to initialise another object of the same class.

Example

```
          rational_num  rat_num1(7,9);         //Fraction 7/9.

          rational_num  rat_num2 = rat_num1;
          //Call copy constructor.
```

If no copy constructor exists, then the system will generate a default constructor, which performs a memberwise copy. In many cases, this will be precisely what is required, but, as will be seen in the next chapter, this is not so where dynamic memory allocation is involved.

N.B. Whenever an object is passed as an argument, it should be passed as a *reference* argument (even if its contents are not to be changed). If this is not done, the argument will be treated as a new local variable, causing the class constructor to be called redundantly. This is also true for most objects which are returned through the function's return type (the notable exceptions being cases in which a *locally* created object is being returned, since a compilation error will result from attempting to return a reference to a local variable).

7.8   Destructors

These are the counterparts to constructors. They are used to perform cleanup activities for objects which are no longer required. Typically (though not necessarily), a destructor will be used to deallocate memory which has been allocated dynamically by a constructor. [This will be seen in the next chapter.] A destructor has same name as the class to which it belongs, but is preceded by the tilde character (~).

An object's destructor is never called explicitly — it is called **automatically** by the system when program execution leaves the scope of the object (the program block within which the object was declared). Like constructors, destructors have no return values.

<u>Example</u> (Rather artificial!)

```
//dates.h

class date
{
private:
    ..............................
    ..............................
public:
    ...............................
    ...............................
    ~date();
};


---------------------------------------------------------

//dates.cpp
..................................
..................................
date::~date()
//Simply displays a message giving the date held in the
//object as the object goes out of scope.
{
    cout<<"\n\nDate object with value "
    cout<<day<<'/'<<month<<'/'<<year;
    cout<<" going out of scope!\n\n";
}
```

Apart from being called implicitly and having no return types, destructors have two other notable characteristics :

- a class can have only *one* destructor;
- destructors can't have arguments.

7.9   Arrays of Objects

Recall that arrays of the simple types can be initialised by using a list of values inside chain brackets.

<u>Example</u>
```
int mark[4] = {57, 35, 86, 63};
```

In a similar way, an array of objects may be initialised by using a list which calls a constructor for each object.

<u>Example</u> (Extension of *date* class)
Suppose that a businessman needs to keep notes about important dates...

```
class date
{
private:
    int day, month, year;
    ....................................
    ....................................
    //Members above are same as before.
    char memo[60];          //Additional member.
public:
    ....................................
    ....................................
};

------------------------------------------------------------

//Within application program...

....................................

date event[] =
        {   date(5,12,1997), date(18,12,1997),
            date(4,1,1998), date(23,1,1998), ...};
....................................
```

7.10   Objects Within Objects

It is perfectly possible to have objects which are members of other objects. When creating and destroying the container objects, it is necessary to give consideration to the creation and destruction of the member objects. The creation of member objects is carried out by **member initialisation lists**. Such lists may be used to initialise both simple members and member objects, but they are only really of use with member objects, since simple members may be initialised by straightforward assignment statements (as seen in previous examples). A member initialisation list is placed between the argument list of a constructor and the body of the constructor. It is separated from the argument list by a colon and comprises a list of items, separated by commas. Each item in the list comprises an object name followed by an initialisation value in brackets.

<u>Example</u>   (Extension of example from 7.2)

Suppose we have a class *point*, whose private members x and *y* specify the coordinates of the *point* object. The *point* object may then be used to specify the diagonally opposite corners of a *rectangle* object, as shown below.

```
class point
{
private:
    int x, y;
public:
    point (int x_val, int y_val)
    {
        x=x_val; y=y_val;
    }
    void set_values(int x_val, int y_val);
    void get_values(int& x_val, int& y_val);
};

class rectangle
{
private:
    point upper_left;
    point lower_right;
public:
    rectangle(int xupleft, int yupleft, int xlowright,
                                        int ylowright);
};

-----------------------------------------------------------

//Within implementation file...

rectangle::rectangle (int xupleft, int yupleft,
int xlowright, int ylowright)
: upper_left(xupleft, yupleft), lower_right(xlowright,
 ylowright)
{
    //Nothing else to do after
    //member constructor executed.
}
```

Note that the arguments required by the member objects are passed to their constructors in the member initialisation list after having been received by the constructor for the container object. Assignments in the member initialisation list are executed after the arguments have been passed, but before the body of the main constructor is executed. Thus, member constructors are executed before the main constructor. With destructors, this order is reversed --- the main object is destroyed first and then the member objects (in the reverse order to that in which they are declared within the container object).

Note also that, if the constructor for a member object is a default constructor (and so does not need to be supplied with values for any arguments), there is no need to initialise the object via a member initialisation list. If arguments *do* need to be supplied, however, a member initialisation list *must* be used!

7.11   The `this` Pointer

The methods of a class occur just **once** in memory, no matter how many objects of the class are created. Instance variables, on the other hand, must be created afresh for each new object and maintain their own individual values, unaffected by the values held by any other object. When a method of the class is called up, then, it needs to be supplied with the address of the object upon which it is to act. A pointer holding this address is passed automatically by the compiler to the member function as the function's *first argument* (though this process is completely transparent to the programmer). The pointer which is passed is called `this` and every member function has this item as an invisible first argument. It is rarely necessary to use `this` explicitly. Below is an example showing a redundant (but harmless) use of `this` to access the members of a *rational_num* object.

Example

```
void rational_num::get_value(int& num, int& denom)
{
        num = this->numerator;
        denom = this->denominator;
}
```

7.12   Static Class Members

Member variables appearing in a class declaration are normally *instance variables*. This means that a separate copy (an *instance*) of each is created for each class object which is created during the running of a program. Normally, of course, this is what is wanted. We would not usually expect the values of one object's instance variables to be affected by those of another object's. Sometimes, however, it is convenient or desirable to have variables which are associated with *the class itself*, rather than with any particular class object. Such variables are called **class variables**. Whereas every instance (object) of a class has its own private copy of any instance variables, each accesses the same class variables. These variables occur only **once** and are declared via the keyword **static** (providing further unfortunate overloading of this descriptor!). It is also possible to have member functions which are declared *static*. Such functions can operate *only* on static data members (class variables). They cannot access the instance variables of a class object.

Example

```
class my_class
{
private:
    int data1;
    static int data2;
public:
    my_class(int d1, int d2)
    {
        data1 = d1;
        data2 = d2;
    }
    static void set_data2(int d2)
    {
        data2 = d2;
    }
};
```

Here, *data2* is a class variable. It will occur only *once*, no matter how many objects of the class *my_class* are created. The member *data1* is an ordinary instance variable, a fresh copy of which will be created for each new object of the class. Function *set_data2* has access to the class variable *data2*, but cannot access the instance variable *data1*. Ordinary member functions, however, can access both instance variables and class variables. In the example, the constructor does just that.

An unusual feature of static variables is that, like non-inline member functions, they are declared in a class declaration (as is *data2* in the example above), but are defined in the corresponding implementation file.

[Remember that the difference between a variable declaration and its definition is that the definition is what causes memory to be allocated for the variable. Normally, a variable declaration will also be its definition, but recall the example of external linkage in Section 4.3, where the two were separated.]

The definitions of static variables are similar to ordinary variable declarations/definitions, but include the class name and scope resolution operator, in the same way that the definitions of member functions do.

Example

```
int my_class::data2;
```

The definition may include initialisation of the variable.

Example

```
int my_class::data2 = 0;
//(Explicit initialisation is actually redundant here,
//since static numeric values are automatically
//initialised to 0.)
```

Like static member variables, static member functions are associated with their *class*, rather than with any particular class object. They may be invoked via the name of the class (and the scope resolution operator) or any object of that class.

Example

```
my_class my_obj;
```

```
. . . . . . . . . . . . . . . . . . . . . . . . . . . . . . . .
my_class::set_data2(5);    //Call function through class.
. . . . . . . . . . . . . . . . . . . . . . . . . . . . . . . .
my_obj.set_data2(1);       //Call function through object.
```

Since we can use the name of the class to invoke a static function, we can call the function *even if no class objects have been created*. This may not seem particularly useful, but suppose we are creating objects by means of dynamic memory allocation [See Chapter 8 for details of how to do this] and that we wish to keep a running total of the number of objects in existence. We can hold the running total (initialised to 0) in a class variable and have the constructor increment this total whenever it is called to create a new object. Similarly, we can have the destructor decrement this running total.

Exercises

1. Use an array of structures to hold the names and current levels of six items of stock. (Each structure will hold the name and stock level of a single item.) The names and levels are to be requested from the user and then the user is to be allowed to retrieve the stock level of any item whose name he/she supplies. The user should be allowed an indefinite number of requests, with an 'Item not found!' error message being displayed whenever he/she enters an invalid item.
N.B. You are not to use the structs as class objects, but simply as containers for data.

2. Define a *robot* class, an instance of which the user is to be allowed to move around conceptually (i.e., no graphics will be involved). The location of the robot is to be specified by a pair of (x,y) co-ordinates and the robot can face any of the four directions defined by :
enum direction {NORTH, SOUTH, EAST, WEST};
(x increases as the robot moves east and y increases as the robot moves north.)

The public interface for the robot is to be defined by the functions shown below.

robot(int x, int y, direction d);
// Constructor to create robot at given location facing given direction.
void move(int distance);
// Moves robot a given distance in the direction it is currently facing.
void left_face();
// Turns robot anticlockwise 90 degrees.
void right_face();
// Turns robot clockwise 90 degrees.
int x_pos();
// Returns robot's current x coordinate.
int y_pos();
// Returns robot's current y coordinate.
direction orientation();
// Returns direction robot is currently facing.
(You will find *switch* statements very useful.)

Write a program to use this class, with the user being allowed to enter single-letter commands *l* (left-turn), *r* (right-turn), *d* (distance) and *q* (quit) until q is entered. Whenever *d* is entered, the user must be prompted to enter a distance.
After each user command, the program is to display the robot's current location and orientation.

3. (Rather artificial, but provides practice in the use of member initialisation lists and an appreciation of the operation of constructors and destructors.)
Extend the *point* class featured in Section 7.10 so that the constructor displays a greeting and the object's coordinates as it is created and displays a farewell message and the point's coordinates as it goes out of scope. In addition, define a class triangle with the following structure :

```
class triangle
{
private:
    point vertex1, vertex2, vertex3;
public:
    triangle(int x1,int y1,int x2,int y2,int x3,int y3);
    ~triangle();
};
```

The constructor and destructor for this class should also display greeting and
farewell messages as the object is created and destroyed.

Write a simple program which has nothing in main other than the declaration of a
triangle object (and the return 0 statement, of course). Observe the order in which
the constructors and destructors are executed as the program is run.

Chapter 8   Dynamic Memory Management

Aims

- To demonstrate the need for dynamic management, identifying those circumstances under which it is required.
- To familiarise the reader with the implementation of dynamic memory management in C++.
- To demonstrate the application of dynamic memory management techniques to the implementation of linked lists.
- To make the reader aware of the close connection between (a) constructors and destructors and (b) operators *new* and *delete* when objects are created and destroyed dynamically.

8.1   Introduction

Up to this point, only two options for the lifetime of a data item have been mentioned : *static* and *automatic*. A data item declared with the keyword **static** has memory allocated for it at compilation time and remains in existence for the entire duration of its program. Global variables (those declared outside any program block) are the main examples of such data items. A data item with storage class *automatic*, on the other hand, is local to a particular program block. Memory for such an item is allocated from the system stack at runtime as the item's declaration is encountered and deallocated when the item goes out of scope — i.e., when program execution leaves the block within which the item was declared.

For many programming applications, these two categories of lifetime are quite sufficient. However, there are other application areas for which these two categories alone do not provide sufficient flexibility and attempting to use them alone to solve such problems would be impractical. These applications are ones in which the memory requirements are difficult or impossible to predict and which require the ability to allocate and deallocate memory freely at runtime, according to changing circumstances (usually dictated by preferences expressed by the user via the program interface). This memory which is allocated and deallocated at runtime is called *dynamic memory* and the handling of such memory is known as *dynamic memory management*.

8.2   new **and** delete

Dynamic memory management is achieved in C++ by use of the operators new and delete. These operators give programmers the ability to allocate memory for data items at any time during the running of a program and to deallocate it when it is no longer required. Such dynamic memory is allocated from a system-managed data structure called the *heap*. As might be expected from their names, new is used for the allocation of dynamic memory, while delete is used for its deallocation. Where classes are involved, these operators work hand in hand with constructors and destructors (as will be seen shortly).

Operator new is used to create data objects of any type, whether they be of the inbuilt types or of user-defined classes. It is applied to the *type* of the data object to be created and returns a **pointer** to the object it creates (i.e., the *address* of that object in memory).

Example
```
        int*  num_ptr;
        num_ptr = new int;
        //Allocate memory dynamically and store address
        //in num_ptr.
```

Exactly the same result may be achieved with the following single statement :

```
        int*  num_ptr = new int;
```

We can also use new to allocate space for arrays dynamically. The syntax for this is a simple extension of that used in the example above :

```
        <Ptr type> <Ptr name> = new <Type>[<Size>];
```

Example
```
        float*  real_ptr = new float[100];
```

This example sets *real_ptr* to point to the first element of a newly-created array of 100 reals (which will be accessed via the names *real_ptr[0]*, *real_ptr[1]*, ..., *real_ptr[99]*).

When memory which has been allocated dynamically is no longer required, it should be deallocated (i.e., placed back on the heap, making it available for use elsewhere). This deallocation is achieved by use of the delete operator, which is applied to the pointer holding the address of the allocated memory.

Example
```
        delete num_ptr;
```

To deallocate memory for all the elements in a dynamically-allocated array, it is necessary to use empty square brackets immediately after the word delete.

Example
```
        delete[] real_ptr;
```

When new allocates memory for an array, it stores the size of the array, so delete knows how many elements to free and does not need to be told explicitly. Omitting the square brackets would result in only the first element of the array having its memory deallocated!

8.3   Dynamic Memory Usage with Classes

Powerful though new and delete are in the examples of the preceding section, they are even more powerful when used to allocate and deallocate memory dynamically for objects which have constructors and destructors. When new is used with such objects, the object's constructor (or *one* of its constructors, if there are more than one) will be called automatically, as will its destructor if delete is used.

Example
Suppose we have a class called *personnel* whose constructor sets a person's payroll number, name, job title and department. We can use new to create a *personnel* object and supply arguments for the constructor as follows :

```
personnel*  person_ptr =
    new personnel(782539, "SMITH", "BRIAN", "Clerk", "Accounts");
```

8.4   Dynamic Data Structures

The most common application of dynamic memory management is the creation and processing of dynamic data structures, notably linked lists. For the benefit of the reader who is unfamiliar with this powerful and widely used data structure, a linked list comprises a series of *nodes*, all of which have the same structure : a *data part* (which, for a given linked list, could be as simple as a single integer or could involve a series of data items of various types) and a *pointer part*. The pointer holds the address of the next node in the list and space for each node is allocated dynamically. Since each node holds the address of the next node in the list, the whole list may be traversed (and data retrieved/modified or nodes inserted/deleted) by following the 'chain' of pointers. It is also necessary to hold a separate pointer to the first node in the list (the 'head' of the list) and to store an empty/null pointer in the last node (to indicate that there are no further nodes).

Diagrammatically :

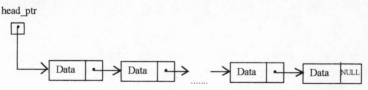

[This is a singly (or one-way) linked list. It is also possible to have doubly (or two-way) linked lists, but consideration of these is not relevant to this text and will not be mentioned further.]

Coming up shortly is a full working example of a linked list application. Since the list in the example is an unordered one, each new node will simply be inserted at the head of the list (rather than the program having to traverse the list to find the correct insertion position). The updating of pointers which is necessary when inserting a new node at the head of the list is shown diagrammatically below. This insertion is carried out in the example by the member function *insert_node*.

Situation before insertion :

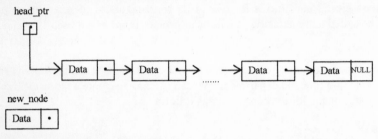

Situation after insertion :

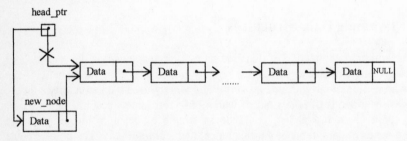

Note that the new node now points to the old head of the list, while *head_ptr* has been updated to hold the address of the new node (now the head of the list).

The updating of pointers required when deleting a node is shown below. In the worked example, this deletion is carried out by the member function *delete_node*.

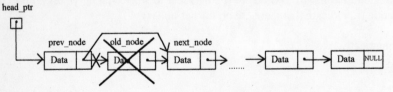

Here, the node to be removed has address *old_node*. In order to effect its removal, the previous node has to be given the address of the node following the removal node and then memory deallocated for the removed node.

Now for the worked example, which concerns the holding of stock orders in a linked list...

Linked List Example

```
//stoklist.h
//Header file for linked list class of stock orders.

#ifndef STOKLIST_H
#define STOKLIST_H

struct order  //Declares the structure of a node in the list.
{
    unsigned long invoice_num;      //First of 3 data fields.
    unsigned long stock_code;
    unsigned int qty;

    order* next_order;              //Pointer to next node in list.
};

enum boolean{FALSE, TRUE};

class stoklist
{
private:
    order* head_ptr; //Holds address of head of list.
    //Provides starting point for all list processing.
public:
    stoklist() {head_ptr = NULL;}
    //Constructor creates empty list.

    boolean find_node(unsigned long inv_num,
                order*&  current_order, order*&  prev_order);
    //Searches for specified invoice number.
    //Returns TRUE if found, FALSE if not.
    //If found, pointers to the node holding the order
    //and to the previous node are returned.
    //This function is called by both get_order and remove_order,
    //but get_order uses only the first pointer.
    //N.B. Reference arguments are required, in order to prevent
    //the creation of local pointers!

    void insert_node(order*& new_order)
    //Inserts a new node at head of list.
    {
        new_order->next_order = head_ptr;
        //Places node at head, with its next_order field
        //pointing to the old head.

        head_ptr = new_order;  //Updates head_ptr.
    }

    void delete_node(order*& current_order, order*& prev_order);
    //Removes node whose address is held in current_order.

    void display_list();    //Displays full list of orders.
    ~stoklist();            //Deallocates memory used for nodes.
};

void  insert_order(stoklist&);
//Accepts order and calls insert_node to place it in list.

void get_order(stoklist&);
```

```
//Retrieves order for specified invoice number.
//Displays error message if not found.

void remove_order(stoklist&);
//Accepts invoice number and removes relevant node.
//Displays error message if not found.

#endif
```

> **Aside**
> Some texts show additional pointers such as *current, next* and/or
> *previous* as additional instance variables of linked list classes.
> This is *unambiguously wrong*! The **only** value which needs to be
> known (and the only value which *should* be known) in order to
> process a (one-way) linked list is the location of the *head* of the
> list. The concepts of 'current', 'next' and 'previous' have meaning
> only during the local processing within a member function. At the
> end of such processing, these local values are worthless, since any
> subsequent processing action will require only the address of the
> head of the list.

```
//stoklist.cpp
//Implementation of linked list class of stock orders.

#include <iostream.h>
#include <iomanip.h>
#include "stoklist.h"

boolean stoklist::find_node(unsigned long inv_num,
        order*& current_order, order*& prev_order)
{
     prev_order = head_ptr;
     current_order = head_ptr;

     while (current_order != NULL)  //Not at end of list.
     {
          //Check invoice number at current node.
          if (current_order->invoice_num == inv_num)
               return TRUE;    //Invoice number found.
          else
          {
               //Move pointers along a node.
               prev_order = current_order;
               current_order = current_order->next_order;
          }
     }
     return FALSE;    //Invoice number not in list.
}

void stoklist::delete_node(order*& current_order,
                                order*& prev_order);
{
     if (current_order == head_ptr) //Node is at head of list.
          head_ptr = head_ptr->next_order;
          //Give head_ptr address of second node in list.
     else
          prev_order->next_order = current_order->next_order;
```

```
                    //Make node before removal node point to node
                    //after removal node.
              delete current_order;      //Deallocate memory for removal node.
        }


        void stoklist::display_list()
        {
              order* current_order;

              cout<<setiosflags(ios::left)<<setw(15)<<"Invoice No.";
              cout<<setw(15)<<"Stock Code"<<"Quantity\n";
              cout<<setw(15)<<"------- --";
              cout<<setw(15)<<"----- ----"<<"--------\n\n";
              current_order = head_ptr;

              //Visit each node in turn until end of list.
              while (current_order != NULL)
              {
                    cout<<setiosflags(ios::left)<<setw(15);
                    cout<<current_order->invoice_num;
                    cout<<setw(15)<<current_order->stock_code;
                    cout<<setiosflags(ios::right)<<setw(6);
                    cout<<current_order->qty<<'\n';
                    current_order = current_order->next_order;
              }
        }


        stoklist::~stoklist()
        {
              order* current_order = head_ptr;
              order* prev_order;

              while (current_order != NULL)
              {
                    prev_order = current_order;
                    current_order = current_order->next_order;
                    delete prev_order;  //Deallocate memory.
              }
        }
        //Above function will be called automatically when list
        //goes out of scope.
        //In the example program, this will be as the program terminates.

        void insert_order(stoklist& list)
        {
              order* new_order = new order;  //Create new node.

              //Accept values into new node, via
              //pointer to node...

              cout<<"\n\nEnter invoice number :  ";
              cin>>new_order->invoice_num;
              cout<<"\nEnter stock code      :  ";
              cin>>new_order->stock_code;
              cout<<"\nEnter order quantity  :  ";
              cin>>new_order->qty;

              list.insert_node(new_order);
              //Member function inserts node at head of list.
        }
```

```cpp
void get_order(stoklist& list)
{
    unsigned long inv_num;
    order* current_order;
    order* prev_order;

    cout<<"\n\nEnter invoice number :   ";
    cin>>inv_num;
    cout<<"\n\n";
    if (list.find_node(inv_num, current_order, prev_order))
    {
        cout<<"Stock code : "<<current_order->stock_code;
        cout<<"\nQuantity ordered : "<<current_order->qty<<'\n';
    }
    else
        cout<<"\a        *** Invoice number not found! ***\n";
}

void remove_order(stoklist& list)
{
    unsigned long inv_num;
    order* current_order;
    order* prev_order;

    cout<<"\n\nEnter invoice number :   ";
    cin>>inv_num;
    cout<<"\n\n";
    if (!list.find_node(inv_num, current_order, prev_order))
        cout<<"\a        *** Invoice number not found! ***\n";
    else
        list.delete_node(current_order, prev_order);
}


//-----------------------------------------------------------------


//listmenu.cpp
//Menu-driven program which makes use of a linked list
//of stock orders.

#include <iostream.h>
#include "stoklist.h"

void display_menu();

main()
{
    stoklist list;
    char choice, any_key;

    do
    {
        display_menu();
        cout<<"Enter your choice :   ";
        cin>>choice;
        switch (choice)
        {
            case '1' :  insert_order(list);
                        break;
            case '2' :  get_order(list);
                        break;
```

```
            case '3' :   remove_order(list);
                         break;
            case '4' :   list.display_list();
                         break;
            case '5' :   //'Quit' option.
                         break;
            default  :   cout<<"\n\n";
                         cout<<"\a          *** Invalid option! ***";
        }

        if (choice != '5')
        {
            cout<<"\n\n";
            cout<<"Press any key  and <Return> to continue...";
            cin>>any_key;
            //Much neater to use a function such as getch (as in
            //Borland and Unix) to accept a single keypress, if
            //your implementation has such such a function.
        }
    }while (choice != '5');

    return 0;         //Destructor called automatically.
}

void display_menu()
{
    cout<<"\n\n\n       Stock Orders Program";
    cout<<"         ----- ------ -------\n\n";
    cout<<"1. Insert a new order in the list.\n\n";
    cout<<"2. Retrieve an order. \n\n";
    cout<<"3. Remove an order from the list.\n\n";
    cout<<"4. Display full list of orders.\n\n";
    cout<<"5. Quit.\n\n\n";
}
```

Aside

Note that it is good practice to avoid member functions which involve a dialogue with the user, since this dialogue is not part of the fundamental processing of an object of any class. Instead, standalone (i.e., non-member) functions should be used to elicit responses from the user. These standalone functions will then make use of the lower-level member functions, which carry out the real work (and whose structure is of no interest to the user). As a consequence, functions *insert_order*, *get_order* and *remove_order* have been made standalone functions above. The first two of these call the member function *find_node*, while *remove_order* calls *delete_node*.

8.5   Dynamic Arrays of Objects

When using *new* to allocate space dynamically for an array of objects, it is **not possible** to initialise the elements of the array by using an initialiser list. This is because *there is no way of passing arguments to the constructor of each object*. However, if the objects have a *default* constructor (i.e., a constructor which either

takes no arguments or has only default arguments), then the objects will be
initialised implicitly by having the default constructor called for each object in the
array.

<u>Example</u>

```
//Within header file :

class account          //(Bank account)
{
private:
    float balance;
public:
    account() {balance = 0.0;}      //Takes no arguments.
    ...........................     //Other members.
    ...........................
};

----------------------------------------------------------

//Within user program :

account* acct_ptr = new account[5];
//Default constructor called for each of the 5 accounts.
```

In fact, if an array of objects is declared dynamically, then it must have *either* a
default constructor *or* no constructor at all (in which case, the system will
automatically generate one).

8.6   Dynamic Instance Variables

When memory is allocated dynamically for instance variables, care must be taken to
ensure that this memory is freed when the containing object goes out of scope and
its destructor is called. Since all that will be held in the object is a *pointer* to this
memory, only the memory occupied *by the pointer itself* will be disposed of
automatically and **not** the memory to which it is pointing. A common case is that of
strings which have had space allocated for them dynamically.

<u>Example</u>
Suppose we have a linked list of words entered by the user...

```
struct node
{
    char*  word;
    node*  next_node;
};

class word_list
{
private:
    node* head_ptr;
public:
    word_list() {head_ptr = NULL;}
    void insert_node(node*&);
```

```
........................ //Other member functions.
........................ //(Of no interest to us.)
~word_list();
};
```

Suppose also that there is a function called *accept_word* which will accept a word from the user and will insert it into the list by calling the private member function *insert_node*. *accept_word* is a non-member function which has the following prototype :

```
void accept_word(char*, word_list&);
//First argument is the word to be accepted.
//Second argument is the list into which the word
//is to be inserted.
```

Before *accept_word* calls *insert_node*, though, it will need to allocate space dynamically for the string which has been entered. The full function definition is as follows :

```
void accept_word(char word_in[30], word_list list)
{//A comfortable maximum size used for word.
    node*  new_node = new node;

    cout<<"Enter word : ";
    cin>>word_in;

    new_node->word = new char[strlen(word_in) + 1];
    //Allocate space dynamically for new word
    //(inc. the null character) and assign address
    //to instance variable word.

    strcpy(new_node->word, word_in);
    //Copy string into space allocated by new.

    list.insert_node(new_node);
}
```

The destructor for the list will have to deallocate space for these strings explicitly :

```
word_list::~word_list()
//Traverses the list, deallocating space for each node.
{
    node*  old_head;

    while (head_ptr != NULL)
    {
        delete[] head_ptr->word;
        //Remember to use square brackets!

        old_head = head_ptr;

        delete head_ptr;
        //Remove other contents of node.

        head_ptr = old_head->next_node;
    }
}
```

Exercises

1. Write a program which will create and process a linked list of examination results. Use a *structure* to hold a single node and define an *unordered* linked list class which will encapsulate the data and methods associated with a linked list made up of such nodes. (Since the list is unordered, each new node may simply be added at the *head* of the list.)
For simplicity, each node should contain just three fields :

        (i)   a surname (using an **array** of 15 characters);
        (ii)   an examination mark;
        (iii)   a pointer to the next node in the list.

Starting with an empty list, your program is to be menu-driven and is to provide the options listed below.

        1.   Insert a new result.
        2.   Remove a result.
        3.   Retrieve the mark for a given person.
        4.   Display all results in the list.
        5.   Quit.

(Don't forget to deallocate space for nodes in your destructor.)

2. Modify the above program so that dynamic memory management is employed for surnames. (Remember to modify the list destructor.)

3. Modify the program further so that it is alphabetically-ordered on surname.
(This may, in turn, be extended to include first names, maintaining alphabetical ordering on surname + first name.)

Chapter 9   Inheritance

Aims

- To remind the reader of what is meant by inheritance in the context of object orientation and to reinforce his/her understanding of the concept.
- To introduce the reader to the implementation of inheritance in C++.
- To provide some basic guidelines for the design of a class hierarchy for a given application.

9.1   Inheritance in the Context of Object Orientation

Recall that inheritance is one of the three fundamental concepts of object orientation (the other two being encapsulation and polymorphism). In many object-orientated programs, there will be a *hierarchy* of classes, with each of the lower classes (the *derived* classes) *inheriting* data and methods from one of the higher classes (a *base* class). Moving down through the hierarchy, each new derived class becomes a *specialisation* of its base class, modifying or extending its data and/or methods in some way.

<u>Shape Hierarchy Example</u>

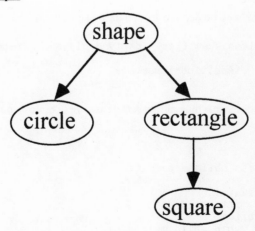

When forming a class hierarchy, make sure that each derived class has an 'IS-A' relationship with its immediate base class. (E.g., a square IS-A rectangle, a rectangle

IS-A shape, etc.). In particular, take care not to incorporate 'HAS-A' relationships. For example, it would be wrong to have a class *line* or a class *point* derived from *square*.

The essential purpose of inheritance in object orientation is to avoid 'reinventing the wheel'. It has long been recognised that the same types of data structure and associated algorithms are required across a large number of programs and application areas. In order to avoid the explicit recoding which would otherwise be necessary, object orientation allows the common features of these structures and algorithms to be coded just once, placed in a base class and then inherited by other (derived) classes. This, it is argued, promotes reusability of code and provides the programmer with code which is tried and tested.

> *Aside*
> The author's personal opinion is one of considerable scepticism about the feasibility of much code reusability across the full spectrum of application areas (other than *very* general-purpose classes such as streams), since this requires programmers to have an intimate working knowledge of what are often *very* large libraries of code. The author regards reusability of code as being much more practicable within a specific application area amongst programmers who are working with a manageable set of frequently-required objects. However, it is appreciated that many people may disagree with this viewpoint!

9.2   Inheritance in C++

9.2.1   Syntax

In C++, a class may be derived from a base class via the following syntax :

```
<class specifier> <derived class> : <base class>
{
    <Additional members>
};
```

`<class specifier>` may be either `class` or `struct`, but is almost invariably `class`.

Example
```
class child : parent
{
private:
    int child_data;
public:
    void child_method();
};
```

Here, class child will inherit all the members of parent and has two additional members (one instance variable and one method).

9.2.2   Access Rights of Derived Classes

By default, the private members of a base class are not directly accessible to anything outside the class itself — not even to the member functions of a derived class! Frequently, of course, the member functions of a derived class will need to manipulate instance variables inherited from the base class. The keyword protected provides the required access. A member which is declared protected will be accessible both to member functions of its own class *and to member functions of any derived classes.*

Example
```
class parent
{
protected:
    int parent_data;
public:
    void parent_method();
};
```

Class *child* will now have direct access to the inherited member *parent_data* (as will any other class derived from *parent*), but *parent_data* will still not be directly accessible to anything outside the inheritance hierarchy.

However, the declaration in the base class of private, public or protected access is only one of two factors governing access rights within a derived class. The other factor is specified within the derived class itself and involves *declaring the derived class to be either public or private.*

Example
```
class child : public parent
{
private:
    int child_data;
public:
    void child_method();
};
```

The table below shows the access rights for all possible combinations of the two factors.

Base Class Member	Derived Class + Public Base Class	Derived Class + Private Base Class
private	inaccessible	inaccessible
public	public	private
protected	protected	private

There is no need whatsoever to memorise this table, since there are a couple of simple rules which cover most circumstances. Firstly, if you are designing a class and you feel that there is even a remote possibility of a derived class needing direct access to the instance variables of the base class, then you should declare those members to be protected. (Even if you *don't* think it remotely likely that such access will be required, it is unlikely to do any harm if you declare those members to be protected anyway.) Secondly, you will almost invariably declare a derived class to have public access to a base class. You would only use a private base class if you needed to provide a different set of functions for users of the derived class, and so wished to block access to the base class functions.

Access is private by default, which is not usually what is wanted. Even if it *is* what is wanted, it is good practice to state the access explicitly.

9.2.3   Base Class Constructors In Initialisation Lists

Because an instance (an object) of a derived class contains instance variables from both base class and derived class, constructors for both the base class and the derived class must be called in order to initialise the instance. This is similar to the way in which constructors needed to be called for both a 'container' class and a member object in Section 7.10. Once again, an *initialisation list* is used, this time containing a call to the base class constructor.

Example

```
//shapes.h
//Declarations for shape hierarchy.

class shape
//Base class.
{
protected:
    float x, y;  //Coordinates of reference point.
public:
    shape(float x_val, float y_val)
    {
        x = x_val;
        y = y_val;
    }
};

class circle : public shape
{
protected:
    float radius;
public:
    circle(float x_val, float y_val, float rad);
    ............................................
    ............................................
};
    ............................................
    ............................................

-----------------------------------------------------------
```

```
//shapes.cpp
//Implementation of shape hierarchy.

#include "shapes.h"

circle::circle(float x_val, float y_val, float rad)
: shape(x_val,y_val)
//No types appear in initialisation list, since already
//specified in arguments to derived class constructor.

{
    radius = rad;
}
...................................................
...................................................
```

A base class constructor which is a default constructor (i.e., either has no arguments or has only arguments with default values) need not appear in the initialisation list and will be called automatically. If a base class constructor does not appear in the list and there is no default constructor, then a constructor with no arguments is created and called.

Base class constructors are called *before* the constructor for a derived class is executed, while destructors for base classes are called *after* the destructor for the derived class has been executed.

9.2.4   Bringing it all Together

When a derived class is declared, the declaration for both it and its base class must be included in the source file. The simplest way of achieving this is to declare the base class and derived class in the same header file, and this is the way in which it is usually done.

The concepts introduced in 9.2.1-9.2.3 will now be illustrated by means of a worked example.

Example
Consider a bank which offers just three kinds of account :

- *savings account* (providing interest and withdrawal facilities);
- *current account* (a standard account for the cashing of cheques);
- *deposit account* (allowing only interest to be withdrawn).

Obviously, all three classes will have features (members) in common. In such circumstances, we should identify those common members, place them in a base class and allow the three original classes to **inherit** those members, thereby avoiding explicit code duplication. We shall call this generic class *account*. It will be an *abstract* base class, since it will not contain enough specific details to allow it to be used for the creation of objects itself. It will simply define the *common properties* of real account types. In addition, classes *savings_account* and *deposit_account* will both have interest facilities, with *deposit_account* requiring an extra member which will specify the funds currently available for withdrawal. Thus, we can allow *deposit_account* to inherit from *savings_account*. Our full class hierarchy, then, looks like this :

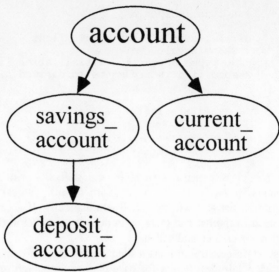

Now for the code itself...

```
//account.h
//Header file for account classes

#ifndef ACCOUNT_H
#define ACCOUNT_H

class account
{
protected:
    //Accessible only to class account
    //and its derived classes.
    unsigned long int acct_num;
    double balance;
public:
    account(unsigned long acct_no, double balance_in=0.0)
    {
        acct_num = acct_no;
        balance = balance_in;
    }
    void deposit(double amount) {balance+=amount;}
    double get_balance() {return balance;}
};

class savings_account: public account
{
protected:
    float rate;              //Rate of interest.
public:
    savings_account(unsigned long acct_no, float rate_in,
                                double balance_in = 0.0);
    double compound();   //Compute and deposit interest.
    double withdraw(double amount);
```

```
    };

    class current_account : public account
    {
    protected:
        float limit;    //Minimum limit for free transactions.
        float charge;   //Per cheque charge for a low balance.
    public:
        current_account(unsigned long acct_no,
        double balance_in=0.0, float limit_in=0.0,
                                        float charge_in=0.50);
        double cash_cheque(double amount);
    };

    class deposit_account : public savings_account
    {
    protected:
        double disposable;              //Accumulated interest.
    public:
        deposit_account(unsigned long acct_no,
                float rate_in, double balance_in=0.0);
        double compound();                  //Redefinition.
        double withdraw(double amount);   //Redefinition
        double get_disposable() {return disposable;}
    };

    #endif

    ------------------------------------------------------------

    //account.cpp
    //Implementation of account classes

    #include "account.h"

    savings_account::savings_account(unsigned long acct_no,
    float rate_in, double balance_in) : account(balance_in)
    //Constructor for base class called.
    {
        rate = rate_in/100;
    }

    double savings_account::compound()
    {
        double interest = rate * balance;
        balance += interest;
        return interest;
    }

    double savings_account::withdraw(double amount)
    {
        if (amount <= balance)
        {
            balance -= amount;
            return amount;
        }
        else
            return 0;
    }
}
```

```
current_account::current_account(unsigned long acct_no,
double balance_in, float limit_in, float charge_in)
: account (balance_in)
//Constructor for base class called.
{
    limit = limit_in;
    charge = charge_in;
}

double current_account::cash_cheque(double amount)
{
    if ((balance < limit) && (amount+charge <= balance))
    {
        balance -= (amount+charge);
        return (amount+charge);
    }
    else if ((balance >= limit) && (amount <= balance))
    {
        balance -= amount;
        return amount;
    }
    else
        return 0.0;              //Insufficient funds!
}

deposit_account::deposit_account(unsigned long acct_no,
float rate_in, double balance_in)
: savings_account(balance_in, rate_in)
//Again, constructor for base class called.
{
    disposable = 0.0;
}

//Redefine inherited function.
double deposit_account::compound()
{
    double interest = savings_account::compound();
    //Call base class function to do first part.
    //Not really worth it here, but illustrates
    //required syntax for reusing base class code.

    disposable += interest;
    return interest;
}

//Redefine inherited function.
double deposit_account::withdraw(double amount)
{
    if (amount <= disposable)
    {
        disposable -= amount;
        balance -= amount;
        return amount;
    }
    else
        return 0;
}
```

9.2.5 Redefining Inherited Functions

In the last example, functions *compound* and *withdraw* were redefined in the derived class *deposit_account*. The redefined function *compound* had to carry out the same actions as original function, but also add interest to *funds_available*. To achieve the former, it had to call the original definition first. In order to tell the compiler that it was the original version which was to be executed, the function call had to be preceded by the class name and scope resolution operator :

```
double interest = savings_account::compound();
```

The qualified name *savings_account::compound* **must** be used, in order to avoid undesired (and uncontrolled) recursion!
[If you haven't been introduced to recursion yet, don't be concerned if you don't understand the last statement. If you *have* met recursion, you should be well aware of the unfortunate consequences if it is uncontrolled.]

9.2.6 The Assignment Compatibility Rule

A derived class is treated as a **subtype** of its base class. As a consequence, a derived class object is assignment-compatible with a base class object — but **only** when assigning a derived class object to a base class object. For instance, if *circle* is a derived class of *shape*, then a *circle* object may be assigned to a *shape* object without typecasting.

Example
```
        shape shape_obj;
        circle circle_obj;
        .....................
        .....................
        shape_obj = circle_obj;
```

However, the reverse assignment would be illegal. The basic reason is that a *circle* object contains all the members defined in (and required by) a *shape* object, but the reverse is not true. More will be said about this rule in the next chapter.

9.3 Designing a Class Hierarchy

9.3.1 Existing Methods

The field of object-orientated analysis and design is still a very new and fluid one. Several notable methods have sprung up over the past ten years and some of the better known ones are listed below.

- OMT   (Object Modelling Technique)
- Booch
- Coad-Yourdon

- • Schlaer-Mellor
- • Objectory
- • CRC   (Class-Responsibility-Collaboration)
- • Fusion   (OMT + CRC + Booch + Z/VDM)

Though none has achieved dominance over all the others, recent collaboration between Booch, Rumbaugh (the leading force behind OMT) and Jacobson (Objectory) has resulted in the Unified Modelling Language (UML), which attempts to combine the best features of the three aforementioned methods. It seems likely that this will be a widely used method in the near future. Almost all the methods listed above involve a substantial amount of graphical notation, with associated sets of conventions. Instead of using any of the full methods, the author will adopt something of a minimalistic approach, employing a few fundamental heuristics in the initial identification of classes and very basic diagrams for graphical representation of class hierarchies. In identifying classes, he feels that the simplistic, yet powerful, approach of CRC can have much to offer when working in software project teams. CRC is an exploratory technique, rather than a full method, and deals primarily with the *design* stage of development. It involves recording the initial classes on index cards (approximately postcard-sized), working from the initial requirements document. Each class which is identified has a card assigned to it, this card listing the responsibilities (methods) of the class and those classes with which it collaborates.

Class name :	
Superclasses :	
Subclasses :	
Responsibilities	Collaborators

The members of the project team then enact system scenarios, role-playing individual classes by passing messages to other classes. As the role-playing progresses, the classes are refined, with new classes being introduced or old classes merged as appropriate.

9.3.2   General Principles

Regardless of the method used, it is necessary to produce an initial list of classes from the requirements document. The basic principle which is usually followed is to examine the nouns which occur in the document and decide which of these are 'candidate classes'. The next step will usually involve identifying the members of these classes. As this process is carried out, it will often become apparent that there are common properties across some of the classes, which will lead to the introduction of base classes to hold these common properties, allowing them to be inherited by other classes. This, then, is something of a 'bottom-up' approach. During this same process, it may also become apparent that the classes already identified need to be divided into further categories (sub-classes). This, of course, is 'top-down' design. Thus, the process may be partly 'bottom-up' and partly 'top-down'. The approach adopted is not nearly as rigid or well-defined as that of structured software development. Another fundamental difference is that the O-O approach generally involves iteration of the analysis, design and even implementation stages. The process is an incremental and evolutionary one, with each iteration adding further refinements to the design. In passing, it is worth noting that the distinction between analysis and design is not nearly as clear as it is in the structured approach.

When looking for similarities between classes, it is similarities in the methods which will be used to communicate with those classes (their interfaces) which are important, rather than similarities in their instance variables. Classes are characterised principally by the operations which may be performed upon them, rather than their detailed data structures (though similarities in data structure will also be identified, where appropriate).

Each of the next two sections illustrates the principles covered in this section by means of an example. The first involves a rather general windows interface problem, which needs very little by way of problem statement, while the second is rather more detailed and offers more scope for initial textual analysis.

9.3.3   Windows Interface Example

Suppose that we wish to define a windows interface. Required objects will be pull-down menus, icons, etc. Initially, we may decide that the two main classes are *Window* and *Icon*. As indicated in the previous section, there are two ways in which we may now proceed with our analysis and design : upwards and downwards. Moving upwards first of all, we need to ask ourselves whether there are any characteristics which are shared by *Window* and *Icon* which may then be isolated and placed in a 'super-class' (a base class), from which both *Window* and *Icon* may inherit members. A few minutes of thought is likely to produce something like the list of members shown below.

Data	Methods
Position	Open
Status (Active/Inactive)	Close
	Move

Thus, we can define a base class called *ScreenObject* which will hold these common properties, with *Window* and *Icon* inheriting these properties as derived classes. Methods *Open* and *Close* will probably be empty in *ScreenObject*, since they are likely to be different for each of *Window* and *Icon*, so that no specifics may be inherited. However, the general interface will have been established in *ScreenObject* and, as will be seen in the next chapter, **polymorphism** will allow us to specify the appropriate implementation in each derived class.

Now we can give consideration to those classes which lie below *Window* and *Icon* (i.e., the derived classes of *Window* and *Icon*). Our deliberations will probably lead to something like the design which is shown graphically below.

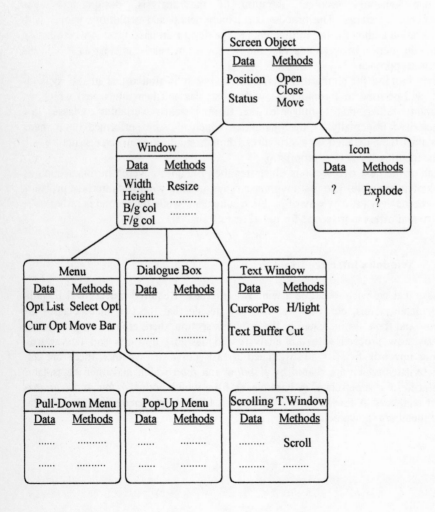

9.3.4   M.I.S. Example

Problem Statement

A Management Information System (MIS) is required for managing the running of courses within a university computing department. As well as holding details of available courses, the system must maintain details of all individuals involved in such courses. In addition to students and lecturers, this will mean technicians (since each computer laboratory will be the responsibility of a particular technician) and administrative staff (one or more of whom will be responsible for the administration associated with each particular course).

Courses are divided into (first) degrees and HND/Cs, the latter of which may be studied on a full-time or part-time basis. (Postgraduate courses are to be outside the system.) Each course is modular in structure, with the system holding details of the modules. Each module may involve students from more than one course and it must be possible to produce a list of students associated with any module.

In order to produce semester timetables for courses, details of each room (size, equipment, availability, etc.) must be held. The system must be capable of producing the timetable for any individual student or lecturer, for any year group of students on any course and for any room. Associated with each third year undergraduate student and each second year full-time HND student, there will be a work placement, details of which must be held by the system. Finally, at the end of each semester, details of examinations will be required from the system, involving rooms to be used.

Carrying out a textual analysis of the problem statement and isolating nouns, we arrive at the list of 'candidate classes' shown below.

Course	System
Department	Module
Individual	List
Student	Timetable
Lecturer	Room
Technician	Size
Laboratory	Equipment
Responsibility	Availability
Admin. staff	Year group
Administration	Work placement
Degree	Semester
HND/C	Examination

Taking each of these in turn and eliminating those which are members of other classes (e.g., size, equipment and availability), are implicit in the overall system (e.g., department and system) or are implied by a relationship between classes (e.g., responsibility), we should arrive at a list of classes similar to that shown below.

Course   Module
Degree   Room
HND/C   Placement
Department Person ('Individual')   Timetable
Student
Lecturer
Technician
Admin. Person

Now we need to decide upon detailed class responsibilities and the relationships between classes (including identification of class hierarchies). This may be done in several ways :

(i)   by following the formal steps of a recognised method;
(ii)   by following the somewhat less formal CRC procedure;
(iii)   simply by following a process of reflection and 'trial and error' (experimenting on paper with various design options).

In general, the approach used will depend upon (a) whether one has a choice in the matter, (b) personal preference (if one does have a choice) and (c) the scale of the problem. Whichever option is chosen for the present problem, though, will probably lead to a design something like that shown graphically on the following pages.

```
┌─────────────────────────────────┐
│             Course              │
├──────────────────┬──────────────┤
│ Responsibilities │ Collaborators│
│ Show structure   │ Timetable    │
│ Print timetable  │ Admin Person │
│ Show admin. person│ Lecturer    │
│ Show lecturers   │ Module       │
│ Show exam T/T    │              │
└──────────────────┴──────────────┘
```

```
┌───────────────────────────┐   ┌───────────────────────────────┐
│          Degree           │   │            HND/C              │
├──────────────────┬────────┤   ├──────────────────┬────────────┤
│ Responsibilities │Collaborators│ Responsibilities │Collaborators│
│ ..............   │        │   │ ..............   │            │
│ ..............   │        │   │ ..............   │            │
└──────────────────┴────────┘   └──────────────────┴────────────┘
```

```
┌───────────────────────────┐   ┌───────────────────────────────┐
│       F/Time HND/C        │   │         P/Time HND/C          │
├──────────────────┬────────┤   ├──────────────────┬────────────┤
│ Responsibilities │Collaborators│ Responsibilities │Collaborators│
│ ..............   │        │   │ ..............   │            │
│ ..............   │        │   │ ..............   │            │
└──────────────────┴────────┘   └──────────────────┴────────────┘
```

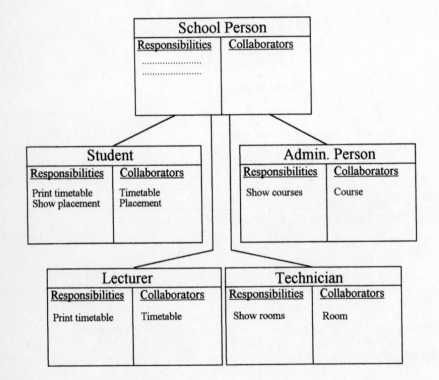

Module	
Responsibilities	Collaborators
Show students Show exam details	Student Course

Room	
Responsibilities	Collaborators
Show technician Show timetable	Technician Timetable

Placement	
Responsibilities	Collaborators
Show details	Student

Timetable	
Responsibilities	Collaborators
Show timetable	Course Student Lecturer Room

◄ [Member (instance variable) of Lecturer, Student and Course.]

Individual Timetable	
Responsibilities	Collaborators

Group Timetable	
Responsibilities	Collaborators

Note that further sub-classes (derived classes) have appeared during this process.

Exercises

1. Key in the simple (and very artificial) program listed below. Then run the
program and observe the operation of the constructors and destructors within the
inheritance hierarchy.

```
//inherit.h
//Simple class hierarchy.

#ifndef INHERIT_H
#define INHERIT_H

class base
{
private:
    char x;
public:
    base(char x_in);
    ~base();
};

class derived : public base
{
private:
    char y;
public:
    derived(char x_in, char y_in) ;
    ~derived();
};

#endif
```

```
//inherit.cpp
//Function definitions for simple class hierarchy.

#include <iostream.h>
#include "inherit.h"

base::base(char x_in)
{
    x = x_in;
    cout<<"\nBase class object "<<x;
    cout<<" constructed.\n\n";
}

base::~base()
{
    cout<<"\nBase class object "<<x;
    cout<<" destroyed.\n\n";
}

derived::derived(char x_in, char y_in) : base(x_in)
{
    y = y_in;
    cout<<"\nDerived class object "<<y;
    cout<<" constructed.\n\n";
}
```

```
derived::~derived()
{
        cout<<"\nDerived class object "<<y;
        cout<<" destroyed.\n\n";
}
```

```
//mainprog.cpp

#include "inherit.h"

main()
{
    base b1('A');
    base b2('B');

    derived d1('X', 'x');
    derived d2('Y', 'y');

    return 0;
}
```

2. Define a base class called **employee** and derive classes **manager** and **staff** from this class. Instance variables and member functions for these three classes should be as shown below. Note that empty brackets are used here to indicate *general* functions, not necessarily functions with no arguments. It is up to *you* to allocate arguments where appropriate.

employee	manager	staff
protected	private	private
name	salary	hours_per_wk
start_date		hourly_rate
emp_number		
dept	public	
	manager()	public
public	~manager()	staff()
employee()	get_salary()	~staff()
~employee()	change_salary()	change_hours()
get_name()		change_rate()
get_start_date()		get_wage()
get_emp_no()	[N.B. The 'get' functions simply *return*	
get_dept()	*values* of instance variables.]	
change_name()		

Write a program which will create three managers and five members of staff, splitting both between three departments and using initialiser lists to provide data for the arrays holding managers and staff. Your program should then display in tabular form the names, employee numbers and salaries/wages of all employees (having calculated wages).

A default value of £35 000 should be used in the constructor for a manager and a default value of 40 hours for a member of staff. Though these should be overridden for most employees, create one manager with the default salary and two members of staff with the default hours.

Upon termination of the program, destructors should display each person's name and status (i.e., manager or staff member).

Chapter 10   Polymorphism

Aims

- To give the reader an appreciation of why the techniques encountered so far are inadequate for the implementation of true polymorphism.

- To introduce virtual functions as the means by which polymorphism is achieved in C++ and to demonstrate how polymorphism is applied.

10.1   Polymorphism in the Context of Object Orientation

In Chapter 1, the definition of the word 'polymorphism' was given as 'taking on many shapes'.   In the context of object orientation, an essential feature of polymorphism is that messages can be sent to an object without its precise class being known and yet the messages will be interpreted in a way which is appropriate to the object's class.   Polymorphism cannot be applied across classes wholesale, however.   It is applicable only to objects within the same class hierarchy. Before meeting the mechanism which is used for implementing polymorphism in C++ , it is instructive to consider whether any of the techniques encountered so far might be used for this...

10.2   The Assignment Compatibility Rule Revisited

Recall that the assignment compatibility rule (Section 9.2.6) allows us to assign a derived class object to a base class object. However, this will often prove to be not particularly useful, since a derived class object will usually have extra instance variables which will be lost in the assignment.

Example
```
//emps.h
//Employee class hierarchy.

#ifndef EMPS_H
#define EMPS_H

#include <string.h>

class employee
{
```

```
protected:
   char name[30];
   long int payroll_number;
public:
   employee(char* name_in="", long int pay_num=0)
   {
     strcpy(name, name_in);
     payroll_number = pay_num;
   }

   float pay() {return 0.0;}

   char* get_name() {return name;}
   ...............................        //Other
   ...............................        //functions.
};

class manager:public employee
{
protected:
     //Could be private, but allows
     //future class derivation.
     long int salary;
public:
     manager(char* name_in, long int pay_num,
     long int sal) : employee(name_in, pay_num)
     {
         salary = sal;
     }

     float pay() {return salary;}
     //Implicit type conversion.
     //Function overloaded.
     ...............................      //Other
     ...............................      //functions.
};

class staff:public employee
{
protected:
     //Again, could be private, but allows
     //future class derivation.
     float hourly_rate;
     float weekly_hours;
public:
     staff(char* name_in, long int pay_num, float rate,
     float hours) : employee(name_in, pay_num)
     {
         hourly_rate = rate;
         weekly_hours = hours;
     }

     float pay() {return (hourly_rate * weekly_hours);}
     //Function overloaded.
     ...............................      //Other
     ...............................      //functions.
};

#endif
```

```
//polyemps.cpp
//Attempts to implement polymorphism,
//using the assignment compatibility rule.

#include "emps.h"

main()
{
    employee emp1, emp2;            //Defaults used.
    manager boss("William Jones", 278594L, 38000L);
    staff subord("John Phillips", 304569L, 8.75, 37);
    ...................................................
    ...................................................
    emp1 = boss;            //Salary lost.
    emp2 = subord;          //Rate and hours lost.
    ...................................................
    ...................................................
}
```

However, the assignment compatibility rule also applies to pointers and references. That is to say, we can assign the address of a derived class object to a base class pointer and we can initialise a base class reference to a derived class object (implicitly, the address of the derived class object).   Since pointers and references both refer to objects via their addresses, which have the same size regardless of the class to which an object belongs, there will be no loss of members. This approach would appear to offer rather more promise than the direct assignment of a derived class object to a base class object. Using the class hierarchy from the previous example, then, let's see what happens when we employ pointers, rather than the objects themselves...

```
//emp_ptrs.cpp
//Attempts to implement polymorphism
//via the use of pointers to objects.

#include <iostream.h>
#include <iomanip.h>
#include "emps.h"

main()
{
    employee* emp1;
    employee* emp2;
    manager boss("William Jones", 278594L, 38000L);
    staff subord("John Phillips", 304569L, 8.75, 37);
    //In passing, note the use of the character 'L'
    //to specify long integer literals.

    emp1 = &boss;
    emp2 = &subord;
    cout<<"Salary for "<<emp1->get_name();
    cout<<" :  £"<<emp1->pay();

    cout<<setiosflags(ios::fixed|ios::showpoint);
    //Flag showpoint causes decimal places to be shown,
    //even if zero.

    cout<<setprecision(2);
    cout<<"\n\nWage for "<<emp2->get_name()<<" :  £";
}
```

```
        cout<<emp2->pay()<<"\n\n";
        return 0;
}
```

Unfortunately, this produces the output shown below.

```
Salary for William Jones : £0
Wage for John Phillips : £0.00
```

The fundamental problem is that the operation of overloaded functions is determined *statically* (i.e., at compilation time). Since emp1 and emp2 are declared as pointers to employee objects, it is the *pay* function for a base class object which is called for each of these pointers. What we need is some mechanism which allows the version of the function to be determined *dynamically* (i.e., at runtime). Before we look at the mechanism which is used for this in C++, however, it is necessary to say a little about **function binding**.

10.3   Function Binding

When a function call is linked up to the code constituting the function body, the process is called *function binding*. There are two types of function binding available in C++ : *static* and *dynamic*. The former (sometimes called 'early binding') is what takes place with normal function calls and is carried out at compilation time. The compiler takes the name of the function, the arguments (if there are any) and, if it is a member function, the class name of the object. From this information, it determines (before the program is run) which function to call. Functions which are overloaded are subject to *static* binding. With *dynamic binding* (also known as *late binding*), the function to be called is determined *at runtime*. This is achieved in C++ by the use of **virtual functions**, which make use of tables of *pointers* to the member functions (though this use of pointers is managed entirely by the system and is transparent to the programmer).

10.4   Virtual Functions

A member function is declared virtual simply by placing the keyword virtual before its prototype.

Example

```
class employee
{
protected:
    char name [30];
    long int payroll_number;
public:
    ...................................
    virtual float pay() {return 0.0;}
    ...................................
};
```

This means that the version of the *pay* function which is to be called will be determined *at runtime*, according to the object's precise type within the class hierarchy.   Once a function has been declared virtual in a base class, it will be virtual for all subsequent derived classes, so it is not actually necessary to specify the keyword `virtual` in the derived classes. However, the author believes that it is good practice to do so, in order to enhance the readability and understandability of source code.

Example

```
class manager : public employee
{
protected:
    long int salary;
public:
    ..................................
    virtual float pay() {return salary;}
    //(Implicit typecast carried out.)
    ..................................
};

class staff : public employee
{
protected:
    float hourly_rate;
    float weekly_hours;
public:
    ..................................
    virtual float pay()
    {
        return (hourly_rate * weekly_hours);
    }
    ..................................
};
```

If the example from the preceding section is modified as shown above (at least by inclusion of the keyword `virtual` before the base class function prototype) and then re-run, the output will be as shown below.

```
Salary for William Jones :   £38000
Wage for John Phillips :   £342.25
```

10.5   Constructors and Destructors

Should constructors and destructors be declared virtual?

Well, a virtual constructor would be useless, since a constructor is always called to create an object of a *specific* class. As a consequence, *constructors are not inherited*, and so **cannot** be virtual. Destructors, on the other hand, can (and possibly should) be virtual.   When the destructor for a base class is declared virtual, the destructors in the derived classes override the base class destructor (even though they have different names).   When an object referred to by a pointer or reference is destroyed, the precise class of the object determines which definition of the virtual destructor is called initially. However, if the object is of a derived class, the base class destructor will be executed after the derived class destructor, as seen in the output from the example program below.

Example

```
//emps.h
//Employee class hierarchy.

#ifndef EMPS_H
#define EMPS_H

#include <iostream.h>
#include <string.h>

class employee
{
protected:
    ................................
    ................................
public:
    ................................
    ................................
    char* get_name() {return name;}
    virtual ~employee()
    {
        cout<<"\nGeneral employee removed.\n\n";
    }
};

class manager:public employee
{
protected:
    ................................
public:
    ................................
    ................................
    virtual ~manager()
    {//Keyword virtual not essential here.
        cout<<"\nManager "<<get_name()<<" removed.\n\n";
    }
};

class staff:public employee
{
protected:
    ................................
    ................................
public:
    ................................
    ................................
    virtual ~staff()
    {//Again, keyword virtual not essential.
        cout<<"\nStaff member "<<get_name();
        cout<<" removed.\n\n";
    }
};

#endif
```

```
//emp_demo.cpp
//Simply creates a manager object and a staff object
//and then allows them to go out of scope (as the
//program ends).

#include "emps.h"

main()
{
    employee* emp1;
    employee* emp2;
    manager boss("William Jones",278594L,38000L);
    staff subordinate("John Phillips",304569L,9.25,37);

    emp1 = &boss;
    emp2 = &subordinate;

    return 0;
}
```

Output from this program :

```
Staff member John Phillips removed
General employee removed.
Manager William Jones removed.
General employee removed.
```

Unfortunately the base class destructor is also called for each object (since each derived class object contains an instance of a base class object). In order to suppress the base class message, we can simply make the base class definition empty :

```
virtual ~employee() {}
```

10.6   Pure Virtual Functions and Abstract Base Classes

In most situations, the base class of an inheritance hierarchy should be very general and should contain very little code, leaving the specifics to the derived classes. In some cases, it makes sense for the base class to be so general that it isn't used directly in the creation of objects, but simply provides the general interface for all objects within the hierarchy (and common instance variables, if appropriate). A class which is used only for deriving other classes, and not for creating class objects, is called an **abstract base class**. For such classes, it is possible to declare virtual functions *without definitions* (even empty ones). Such functions are called **pure virtual functions**.
 Syntax for a pure virtual function declaration :

```
virtual <Return type> <Function name> ([<Arg. list>]) = 0;
```

Example
```
        virtual float pay() = 0;
```

The assignment to 0 should be regarded as 'setting the body to nothing'.

The distinguishing feature of an abstract base class is that it contains at least one pure virtual function.

Example

```
class employee
{
protected:
    .........................
    .........................
public:
    .........................
    .........................
    virtual float pay()=0;
};
//Objects of class employee can no longer be declared
//(which would probably not make much sense anyway).
```

In a class derived from an abstract base class, each pure virtual function must be either defined or redeclared as a pure virtual function. In the latter case, of course, the derived class will also be an abstract base class (meaning that it cannot be used directly in the creation of objects).

Looking back at the employee example in the previous section, it might now seem more logical to make the base class destructor (~*employee*) a *pure* virtual function. However, this leads to the linker objecting to a missing definition for the base class destructor.

In the next section, we shall look at the use of polymorphism in a practical application.

10.7   Heterogeneous Linked Lists

Because of virtual functions, the nodes in a linked list need not all be of precisely the same class (though they will be from the same class hierarchy). A linked list made up of nodes from different classes is called a *heterogeneous* list. As an example, we can create a linked list of employees, using the same employee class hierarchy featured in previous examples. In addition to the employee classes, we shall need to define both a linked list class and a structure for individual nodes in the list.

The linked list class will contain an instance variable of type pointer-to-node, which will hold the address of the node at the head of the list. As seen in Chapter 8, a node will normally hold both the data and a pointer to the next node in the list. In order to implement polymorphism, however, we cannot store the data directly in the node. Instead, we shall have to store an instance variable of type pointer-to-employee (i.e., *employee**) in the node. At runtime, this pointer may receive the address of either a manager object or a staff object, prior to the node being inserted in the list. Now for the code...

```
//emp_list.h
//Holds class declaration for a linked list of employees
//and structure declaration for a node of this list.
```

```
#ifndef EMP_LIST_H
#define EMP_LIST_H

#include "emps.h"

struct emp_node
{
    employee* emp_ptr;
    emp_node* next_node;
};

class emp_list
{
private:
    emp_node* head_ptr;  //Holds address of head of list.
public:
    emp_list() {head_ptr = NULL;}  //Creates empty list.

    void insert_emp(employee* new_emp);
    //Inserts new node at head of list.
    //New node will hold a pointer to
    //an employee's details.

    void display_names();  //Displays full list of names.

    ~emp_list();     //Deallocates memory used for nodes.
};

#endif

---------------------------------------------------------

//emp_list.cpp
//Holds definitions of member functions for
//linked list of employees.

#include <iostream.h>
#include "emp_list.h"

void emp_list::insert_emp(employee* new_emp)
{
    emp_node* new_node = new emp_node;

    new_node->emp_ptr = new_emp;
    //Insert pointer to employee's details in node.

    new_node->next_node = head_ptr;
    //Place node at head of list.

    head_ptr = new_node;       //Update head_ptr.
}

void emp_list::display_names()
{
    emp_node* current_node = head_ptr;
    cout<<"\n\n";
    while (current_node != NULL)
    {
        cout<<current_node->emp_ptr->get_name()<<'\n';
        //Dereference pointer to node and then,
```

```
            //from node, dereference pointer to employee's
            //details and call member function for
            //displaying employee's name.

            current_node = current_node->next_node;
            //Move to next node.
        }
        cout<<"\n\n";
    }

    emp_list::~emp_list()
    {
        emp_node* old_head;
        while (head_ptr != NULL)
        {
            old_head = head_ptr;
            head_ptr = head_ptr->next_node;

            delete old_head;
            //Destructor for manager/staff
            //called automatically.
        }
    }
```

```
//elstdemo.cpp
//Demonstrates use of heterogeneous linked list
//of employees.

#include <iostream.h>
#include <iomanip.h>
#include "emp_list.h"

main()
{
    emp_list list;
    manager boss1("William Jones", 278594L, 38000L);
    manager boss2("Karen Jane Watson", 245012L, 36500L);
    staff subord1("John Phillips", 304569L, 9.25, 37);
    staff subord2("Brian Hardcastle", 345062L, 8.75, 40);

    list.insert_emp(&boss1);
    list.insert_emp(&boss2);
    list.insert_emp(&subord1);
    list.insert_emp(&subord2);
    list.display_names();
    return 0;
}
//List destructor executed
//automatically, causing employee
//destructor to be called for each node.
```

The output produced by this program is shown below.

```
Brian Hardcastle
John Phillips
Karen Jane Watson
William Jones
```

Staff member Brian Hardcastle removed.

Staff member John Phillips removed.

Manager Karen Jane Watson removed.

Manager William Jones removed.

Exercises

1. Using classes *account*, *savings_account*, and *current_account* from the example in 9.2.4, but omitting all functions apart from the constructors, add virtual destructors which will display the contents of the protected members of an object as it goes out of scope. (The balance will be displayed by the base class destructor for both savings accounts and current accounts.) Create one *savings_account* object and one *current_account* object and then allow the program to terminate, so that the destructors will be called.

2. Using the example shown in 9.2.3 as the basis for a class hierarchy relating to geometric shapes, add a class *rectangle* with protected members *length* and *breadth* and a virtual function which will return the area of an object. (For a circle this will be Πr^2, requiring a constant PI to be defined with a value of 3.142; for a rectangle, of course, the area will be length x breadth.)   Add a class variable (a *static member* --- refer to 7.12) which will keep a count of the number of shapes in existence. The base class constructor should increment this count, while the base class destructor should decrement the shape count, displaying the number of objects left. The specific class destructor should display the area of the object as it is destroyed. Declare an array of pointers-to-shape (i.e., of type *shape**) which can hold up to 6 shape pointers. Allow the user to enter details of up to 6 shapes (circles and rectangles), using dynamic memory allocation to create space for these shapes and storing their addresses in the array. Then simply call up a function which will loop through the elements of the array, deallocating memory for the shapes whose addresses are held. (This will cause the destructors to be called.)

3. Define a base class *stock* and derived classes *part* and *car* for a car manufacturer. Instance variables and number functions for these three classes should be as shown below. Note that empty brackets are used here simply to indicate *general* functions, not necessarily functions with no arguments. It is up to you to allocate arguments where appropriate.

> **stock**
>
> <u>protected</u>
> current_level
> price   // For a part, cost to firm; for a car, sale price to dealers.
> <u>public</u>
> stock()
> get_level()   //Returns current level.
> change_level()   //Can increase or decrease.
> charge_price()
> ~stock()   //Displays level of part/model.

Function *change_level* will have to be virtual, since a warning will need to be generated if the reorder level is reached when parts are taken out of stock, but cars do not have reorder levels. The destructor should also be virtual.

part	**car**
<u>private</u>	<u>private</u>
reorder_level	model
part_num //1 letter and 2 digits.	engine_size
	max_speed
<u>public</u>	
part()	<u>public</u>
get_partnum() //Returns part no.	car()
set_reorder() //Resets reorder level.	get_model() //Returns model.
~part () // Displays part number	~car () // Displays model name.

Create a heterogeneous linked list class for holding stock and write a menu-driven program which will create and maintain such a list of parts and cars, allowing the user to select from the options below.

1. Add a part.
2. Add a model.
3. Change level if a part.
4. Change no. of cars of a model.
5. Query current part level.
6. Display full stock list.
7. Quit.

In order to distinguish between a part node and a car node, maintain an extra single-character field in each node with a value of 'p' or 'c'.
You will find that you need to use typecasts from *stock** to *part** and *car**.
N.B. This is quite a lengthy and testing problem!

Chapter 11   Friend Functions and Operator Functions

Aims

- To establish some of the circumstances under which the access facilities so far encountered are inadequate.

- To introduce the use of friend functions and friend classes as the means of overcoming the above inadequacies.

- To demonstrate how the inbuilt operators may be defined to work as naturally with class objects as they do with the inbuilt types.

11.1   Access Problems

There are certain circumstances under which the facilities so far encountered for accessing members of objects are inadequate or awkward. The two main categories of problem area are probably the following :

- situations in which a function needs to access the instance variables of more than one object and so should not really be associated with one particular object (even though it could process the instance variables of another object of the same class by using the object's name);

- situations in which a function's required argument list would conflict with that for a member function, due to the automatic generation by the system of the *this* pointer.

Member functions are merely inappropriate for the first category, but they are **unusable** for the second.   As an example of the second category, the C library function *qsort*, which implements the Quicksort algorithm in a generic way (i.e., it can sort elements of any given type) cannot operate as a member function, since the system's generation of the `this` pointer as the first item in any member function's argument list conflicts with the prototype for *qsort*. (Another example, which will be encountered later in this chapter, is the use of the output operator, <<, to place class objects on an output stream.)

The solution to these problems is to use *friend functions*...

11.2   Friend Functions

These are functions which can bypass the normal access restrictions of a class and
use its private members. Though they are declared friends within the body of the
class declaration, they are **not** member functions (and so do not cause the this
pointer to be generated). We can declare a single function to be a friend of a class
or we can declare a whole class to be a friend of another class.

11.2.1   Individual Friend Functions

For an individual function to be a friend of a class, the function's prototype must
appear within the body of the class declaration, preceded by the word friend.

Example
Suppose we need a function which will allow us to compare the salaries of any two
managers.

```
class manager : public employee
{
protected:
    long int salary;
public:
    ...................................................
    ...................................................
    friend int sal_diff(manager& mgr1, manager& mgr2);
};


//Within the implementation file...

int sal_diff (manager& mgr1, manager& mgr2)
{
    return (mgr1.salary-mgr2.salary);
}
```

As stated earlier, such a function is **not** a member function. It has direct access to
the private members of the class, but **it is not within the scope of the class** (despite
the physical location of the friend declaration). This means that class members must
be preceded by object names when used within a friend function. Because the
function is not a member of the class, its definition is not preceded by the class
name or scope resolution operator. When used, the function will be passed the
names of class objects.

Example
```
  main ()
  {
    manager mgr_a("Janet Thompson", 199074L, 36750L),
            mgr_b("Peter John Barrett", 185247L, 35500L);
    long int diff = sal_diff(mgr_a, mgrb);

    if (diff <0)
```

```
        cout<<"\nManager " <<mgr_b.get_name()<<"earns more.\n";
    else if (diff >0)
        cout<<"\nManager "<<mgr_a.get_name()<<" earns more.\n";
    else
        cout <<"\nSalaries are the same!\n";
    return 0;
}
```

Further points to note :

- • a class determines which its friend functions are — the functions themselves **cannot** ['We choose our own friends'];
- • friend functions are always **public**, even if they are declared within the private section of a class.

Though the example above featured a standalone function as a friend of a class, there is nothing to prevent a member function of one class being a friend of another class.

Example
Suppose that our employee hierarchy does not have a public method for returning the pay for a member of staff, but that a manager object requires this information.

```
class staff : public employee
{
protected:
    float hourly_rate;
    float weekly_hours;
public:
    ........................................
    ........................................
    friend float manager::get_pay(staff& worker);
};

class manager : public employee
{
protected:
    long int salary;
public:
    ......................................
    ......................................
    float get_pay(staff& worker)
    {
        return (worker.hourly_rate*worker.weekly_hours);
    }
};
```

Any manager object can now gain access to the pay for any staff object.

Example
```
staff emp ("Fred Jones", 315794L, 9.85, 37.5);
manager mgr("Gordon Brown", 125972L, 42000L);
float wages;
..............................
..............................
```

```
wages = mgr.get_pay(emp);
```

11.2.2   Friend Classes

Instead of making a single member function a friend of another class, we can make the whole of one class a friend of another class. This means that **all** the functions of the first class are friends of the second, and so they all have access to the private members of the second class. This is achieved via the following syntax :

```
friend class <class name>;
```

Examples

```
i)   class staff : public employee
     {
     protected:
         .....................
         .....................
     public:
         .....................
         .....................
         friend class manager;
     };

     class manager : public employee
     {
     protected:
         .....................
     public:
         .....................
         .....................
         float get_rate (staff& worker);
         float get_hours (staff& worker);
     };
```

Here, functions *get_rate* and *get_hours* will both have access to the private members of a staff object.

```
ii)  Suppose we have a linked list formed from explicit class objects, rather
     than struct objects, and that we declare the instance variables to be
     private.
```

```
     class node
     {
     private:
         int data;
         node* next_node;
     public:
         node()
         {
             data = 0;
             next_node = NULL;
         }
         friend class linked_list;
         //Needs to access instance variables of node.
     };
```

```
class linked_list
{
private:
    node* head_ptr;
public:
    linked_list() {head_ptr = NULL;}
    ..............................
    ..............................
};
```

Here, all the members functions of *linked_list* will require access to the instance variables of *node* objects.

11.3   Operator Functions and Operator Overloading

11.3.1   General Use of Operator Functions

Operator functions are special types of function which are used to redefine/overload the existing operators to work on our own classes as straightforwardly as they do on the inbuilt types (int, char, etc.). For example, we could create a *string* class and redefine the addition operator ('+') to concatenate objects of this class.

Many operators are already overloaded in this way. For instance, the addition operator can be applied to operands of type int, long, float and double. Programmers are at liberty to specify additional overloading to suit the needs of their classes. The compiler will know which definition of the operator to apply by examining the types of the operands.

The syntax for an operator function prototype is the same as that for an ordinary function prototype, but the name of the function comprises the reserved word operator followed by the symbol for the operator which is being overloaded :

```
<Return type> operator <Op. symbol> ([<Argument list>]);
```

Example

```
string operator+(string str1, string str2);
//(Assumes the existence of class string.)
```

The arguments of the function correspond to the operator's operands.

The syntax for an operator function definition follows a similar pattern :

```
< Return type> operator<Op. symbol> ([<Argument list>])
{
    <Function body>
}
```

N.B. In a programmer-supplied operator definition, at least one of the operands must be a class object. If this were not so, the programmer would be able to provide function definitions which conflicted with the inbuilt ones. He/she could, for instance, change the meaning of addition for integers!

Example of Operator Overloading

Suppose we have a class *time*, objects of which hold times of the day in hours, minutes and seconds (on the 24-hour clock). Suppose also that we wish to overload the += operator for this class, so that we can then add a number of seconds to the time held in a time object.

```
//timclass.h
//Class holding time in hours, minutes and seconds
//on the 24-hour clock.

#ifndef TIMCLASS_H
#define TIMCLASS_H

class time
{
private:
    int hours, minutes, seconds;
public:
    time (unsigned int hrs = 0, unsigned int mins = 0,
                                 unsigned int secs = 0)
    {
        set_time(hrs, mins, secs);
        //Another member function.
    }

    void get_time(int& hrs, int& mins, int& secs);

    void set_time (unsigned int hrs, unsigned int mins,
                                     unsigned int secs);
};

time& operator+=(time& t, unsigned int add_secs);
//Prototype for operator function.

#endif

-----------------------------------------------------------

//timclass.cpp
//Implementation file for class time.

#include "timclass.h"

void time::get_time(int& hrs, int& mins, int& secs)
{
    hrs = hours;
    mins = minutes;
    secs = seconds;
}

void time::set_time (unsigned int hrs, unsigned int mins,
                                       unsigned int secs)
{
//Values not allowed to fall outside
```

```
        //legitimate ranges.
        //% operator yields remainder from integer division.

            hours = hrs%24;
            minutes = mins%60;
            seconds = secs%60;
    }

    time& operator+=(time& t, unsigned int add_secs)
    {
            int hrs = add_secs/3600;         //Integer division.
            int add_mins = (add_secs - add_hrs*3600)/60;
            //Value in range 0-59.

            add_secs%=60;    //Value in range 0-59.
            add_hrs%=24;    //Value in range 0-23.

            int min_carry = (seconds + add_secs)/60;
            //Holds 1 if sum > 59; otherwise, holds 0.

            int new_seconds = (seconds + add_secs)%60;
            int hour_carry = (minutes + add_mins + min_carry)/60;
            //hour_carry set to 0 or 1.

            int new_minutes = (minutes+add_mins+min_carry)%60;
            int new_hours = (hours + add_hrs + hour_carry)%24;

            t.set_time (new_hours, new_minutes, new_seconds);

            return *this;    //Dereference this to return object.
    }
```

This operator may then be used as it would be with any of the inbuilt types.

Example

```
        time my_time;          //Defaults used. Time set to 00:00:00.
        my_time+=3700;         //3700s = 1h 1m 40s
                               //Time now set to 01:01:40.
```

Since an operator function is a function like any other, we may also use the normal syntax for a function call (i.e., function name, followed by argument list in brackets).

Example

```
        operator+=(my_time, 3700);
```

However, this is clearly less readable and defeats the whole purpose of using the inbuilt operators in the same way with our own classes as we would do with the inbuilt types.

11.3.2   Operator Functions Within Classes

In the preceding example, our operator function was able to make use of a member function to achieve its objective. If, however, the required access functions are not

to be made generally available by a class, then the operator function must be
declared a *member* of the class. In fact, it is often more convenient to do this
anyway (provided that it is our own class, of course!).

Example

```
class time
{
private:
     int hours, minutes, seconds;
public:
     ....................................
     ....................................
     time& operator+=(unsigned int add_secs);
     //Hidden argument this will automatically provide
     //first operand.
};

time& time::operator+=(unsigned int add_secs)
{
//This time, no need for local variables new_seconds,
// new_minutes and new_hours, since we can manipulate
//the instance variables directly.
     ....................................
     ....................................
     seconds = (seconds + add_secs)%60;
     int hour_carry = (minutes + add_mins + min_carry)/60;
     minutes = (minutes + add_mins + min_carry)%60;
     hours = (hours + add_hrs +hour_carry)%24;
     return *this;
     //No need to call set_time.
}
```

Once again, the operator may then be called via normal operator syntax.

Example

```
my_time+=3700;
```

There is one group of inbuilt operators which would appear to pose a problem for
overloading purposes, though — the increment and decrement operators. How are
we to distinguish between pre-increment and post-increment (or between pre-
decrement and post-decrement)? The solution built into the C++ language is a very
artificial one : the postfix form has a 'dummy' int argument, while the prefix form
has no argument. This dummy argument is not used and exists solely to distinguish
the postfix form from the prefix one.

Example
Suppose our *time* class holds a time only in seconds.

```
class time
{
private:
     int seconds;
public:
     ......................
     ......................
```

```
              time& operator++();     //Pre-increment.
              {
                  seconds++;  //Uses inbuilt definition for ints.
                  return *this;
              }
              time operator++(int);  //Post-increment.
              {
                  time temp_time = *this;   //To be returned.
                  //N.B.Can't return reference to a local variable.
                  seconds++; //Uses inbuilt definition for ints.
                  return temp_time;  //Value before increment.
              }
        };
```

Note that the dummy argument does not even require a name.

Assuming that *my_time* is again an object of type *time*, each of the following would then be legitimate :

```
        my_time++;
        ++my_time;
```

11.3.3   The Input and Output Operators

The input and output operators (>> and << respectively) provide good examples of inbuilt operator overloading. Before looking at an example declaration of such overloading, recall from Section 2.1 that all I/O in C++ is *stream-orientated*. This I/O is provided by a hierarchy of stream classes, the most important of which are **ostream** (the 'output stream' class) and **istream** (the 'input stream' class). cout (the standard output stream) is an object of class *ostream*, while cin (the standard input stream) is an object of class *istream*. The declaration of << for the inbuilt types has the following form :

```
        ostream& operator<<(ostream&, <type>);
```

Thus, the first operand of << is a reference to an output stream and the second operand is the value to be placed on this output stream.

Example
The declaration of << for int values :

```
        ostream& operator<<(ostream&, int);
```

The return value is a reference to the output stream which appears as the first argument. Since the output operator (a) always returns a reference to its first operand and (b) is left associative (i.e., when there are multiple occurrences of it, the leftmost one is executed first, with execution moving along to the right), we can 'chain' occurrences of the output operator.

Example
```
        cout<<100<<'\n';
```

This is equivalent to :

```
(cout<<100)<<'\n';
```

This first causes100 to be placed on the standard output stream, with a reference to the stream being returned for use by the second output operator :

```
cout<<'\n';      //Newline character now placed on stream.
```

This is the kind of thing we have used on a large number of occasions, of course, but it wasn't until now that it was appropriate to explain what was happening in the background.

The declaration of the input operator for the inbuilt types has a form which is analogous to that for the output operator :

```
istream& operator>>(istream&, <type>);
```

Example
```
istream& operator>>(istream&, int);
//For placing an int onto an input stream.
```

For reasoning similar to that given for the output operator, we are also able to chain together occurrences of the input operator.

Example
```
cin>>num1>>num2;
```

We can further overload the input and output operators so that they work with objects of our own classes. The syntax for doing so is the same as that used for the inbuilt types, except that (as usual) we should supply a reference argument for a class object.

Example
```
//emps.h
//Employee class hierarchy.

#ifndef EMPS_H
#define EMPS_H

class employee
{
protected:
    char name [30];
    long int payroll_number;
public:
    ................................
    char* get_name() {return name;}
    ................................
};

class manager:public employee
{
protected:
```

```
        long int salary;
    public:
        ...............................
        float pay() {return salary;}  //(Implicit typecast.)
        ...............................
    };

    ostream& operator<<(ostream&, manager&);
    //Standalone function prototype.
    ........................................
    ........................................

    #endif
```

```
    //emps.cpp
    //Implementation file for employee class hierarchy.

    #include "emps.h"
    ....................................
    ....................................
    ostream& operator<<(ostream& ostrm, manager& boss)
    {
        ostrm<<"\nManager : "<<boss.get_name()<<'\n';
        ostrm<<"Salary :  £"<<boss.pay()<<"\n\n";
        return ostrm;
    }
    ...............................
    ...............................
```

```
    //emp_prog.cpp
    //Demonstrates use of employee class hierarchy.

    #include "emps.h"
    ....................................
    ....................................
    main()
    {
        manager boss("Graham Turner", 127438L, 36250L);

        cout<<boss;
        //Standard output stream passed as first argument.
        return 0;
    }
```

The output from the above program would be as shown below.

```
    Manager :  Graham Turner
    Salary :  £36250
```

Note that we can define the meaning of output for objects of our classes to be
whatever we choose it to be, simply by using the inbuilt definitions of the output
operator within our own definition. In the above example, for instance, we used the
inbuilt definition for outputting a character string and that for outputting a float. We
can do the same thing with the input operator.

Example

```
//rat_nums.h
//Class of rational numbers.

#ifndef RAT_NUMS_H
#define RAT_NUMS_H

class rational_num
{
private:
    int numerator;
    int denominator;
public:
    rational_num(int num = 1, int denom = 1)
    {
        numerator = num;
        denominator = denom;
    }

    void set_value(int num, int denom);

    void get_value(int& num, int& denom)
    {
        num = numerator;
        denom = denominator;
    }
    .................................
    .................................
};

istream& operator>>(istream&, rational_num&);
ostream& operator<<(ostream&, rational_num&);

#endif

-----------------------------------------------------------

//rat_nums.cpp
//Implementation file for rational number class.

#include <iostream.h>
#include <stdlib.h>
//Above needed for exit function.

#include "rat_nums.h"

void rational_num::set_value(int num, int denom)
{
    .................................
    .................................
}
.................................
.................................

istream& operator>>(istream& istrm,rational_num& rat_num)
{
    int num, denom;

    istrm>>num>>'/'>>denom;
```

```
            rat_num.set_value(num, denom);
            return istrm;
      }

      ostream& operator<<(ostream& ostrm,rational_num& rat_num)
      {
            int num, denom;

            rat_num.get_value(num,denom);
            ostrm<<num<<"/"<<denom;
            return ostrm;
      }

------------------------------------------------------------

//rational.cpp

#include <iostream.h>
#include "rat_nums.h"

main()
{
      rational_num rat_num;            //Defaults used.

      cout<<"\nEnter a rational number in the form n/d ";
      cout<<(e.g., 2/5) : ";
      cin>>rat_num;
      //Standard input stream used as first argument.

      cout<<"\nValue entered : "<<rat_num<<"\n\n";
      return 0;
}
```

Sample output from this program is shown below.

```
      Enter a decimal number in the form n/d (e.g., 2/5) :   3/4

      Value entered :   3/4
```

N.B. The operator functions for << and >> **cannot** be declared members of a class, since the automatic inclusion by the system of the this operator as the first argument of a member function causes a conflict with the internal specification of an ostream/istream object as the first argument of the operator function for output/input. Consequently, if the required access functions are not to be provided by a class's public interface (as they were in the preceding example), then the operator functions for << and >> must be declared **friends** of the class.

Example

```
//rat_nums.h
//Rational number class.

#ifndef RAT_NUMS_H
#define RAT_NUMS_H

class rational_num
{
private:
```

```
            int numerator;
            int denominator;
        public:
            rational_num(int num = 1, int denom = 1)
            {
                numerator = num;
                denominator = denom;
            }
            ....................................
            ....................................
            friend istream& operator>>(istream&, rational_num&);
            friend ostream& operator<<(ostream&, rational_num&);
        };

        #endif

        ------------------------------------------------------------

        //rat_nums.cpp
        //Implementation file for rational number class.

        #include "rat_nums.h"

        ....................................
        ....................................
        istream& operator>>(istream& istrm,rational_num& rat_num)
        {
            istrm>>rat_num.numerator>>'/'>>rat_num.denominator;
            //Friend has access to instance variables.
            return istrm;
        }

        ostream& operator<<(ostream& ostrm,rational_num& rat_num)
        {
            ostrm<<rat_num.numerator<<'/'<<rat_num.denominator;
            return ostrm;
        }
```

(The above functions could easily have been inline, of course.)

11.3.4   Multiple Overloading of Operator Functions

Sometimes, we may wish to use the same operator in more than one way with the
same class.

<u>Example</u>
As well as adding a number of seconds to a *time* object, we may wish to add one
time object to another. (As usual, of course, the compiler will be able to distinguish
between the two definitions by the different argument lists.)

```
        //timclass.h
        //Class holding time in hours, minutes and seconds
        //on the 24-hour clock.

        #ifndef TIMCLASS_H
        #define TIMCLASS_H
```

```
class time
{
private:
    int hours, minutes, seconds;
public:
    time(unsigned int hrs=0, unsigned int mins=0,
                               unsigned int secs=0)
    {
        set_time(hrs, mins, secs);
    }

    void get_time(int& hrs, int&mins, int& secs);

    void set_time(unsigned int hrs, unsigned int mins,
                                 unsigned int secs);
    time& operator+=(unsigned int add_secs);
    time& operator+=(time& add_time);
};

#endif
```

```
//timclass.cpp
//Implementation file for class time.

#include "timclass.h"

....................................
....................................

time& time::operator+=(unsigned int add_secs)
{
    //Defined as before.
}

time& time::operator+=(time& add_time)
{
    int min_carry = (seconds + add_time.seconds)/60;
    //Member function of class has access to instance
    //variables of other objects of same class.

    seconds = (seconds + add_time.seconds)%60;
    int hour_carry =
            (minutes + add_time.minutes + min_carry)/60;
    //0 or 1, as for min_carry.

    minutes = (minutes+add_time.minutes+min_carry)%60;
    hours = (hours + add_time.hours + hour_carry)%24;
    return *this;
}
```

```
//timedemo.cpp
//Demonstrates use of time class.

#include <iostream.h>
#include <iomanip.h>
//Above included for use of setfill
```

```
//and setw.

#include "timclass.h"

main()
{
    time time1(14,35,40), time2(16,40,25);

    time1+=time2;
    int hrs, mins, secs;
    time1.get_time(hrs, mins, secs);

    cout<<"\n\nFirst time is now  "<<setfill('0');
    //Specifies character used to fill/pad out field
    //to width specified by setw.

    cout<<setw(2)<<hrs<<':'<<setw(2)<<mins;
    cout<<':'<<setw(2)<<secs<<"\n\n";
    //Field width must be specified for each
    //value output.

    return 0;
}
```

The output from this program is as shown below.

```
First time is now 07:16:05
```

Note that the combination of *setw(2)* and *setfill('0')* has ensured that each field comprises exactly two digits (with a leading zero added, if necessary).

11.3.5   The Assignment Operator

The easiest way to carry out assignments between objects is to let C++ do a memberwise copy, which is what it will do by default. In the majority of cases, this is precisely what we want to happen. However, there are times when a memberwise copy is inadequate. In particular, default memberwise assignment is undesirable in cases involving dynamic allocation of memory.

Example

```
//person.h

#ifndef PERSON_H
#define PERSON_H

class person
{
private:
    char* name;  //No memory allocated.
                 //Will need to be allocated dynamically.
    int age;
    float height;
    float weight;
public:
    person(char* name_in,int age_in,int ht_in,int wt_in);
```

```
.....................................
.....................................
    ~person() {delete[] name;}
};
#endif
```

```
//person.cpp
//Implementation file for person class.

#include <string.h>
#include "person.h"

person::person(char* name_in, int age_in, float ht_in,
float wt_in)
{
    name = new char[strlen(name_in) + 1];
    //Address copied.

    strcpy(name, name_in);         //Data copied.
    age = age_in;
    height = ht_in;
    weight = wt_in;
}
.....................................
.....................................
```

```
//prsndemo.cpp
//Demonstrates use of person class.

#include <iostream.h>
#include "person.h"

main()
{
    person   person1("Bill Robertson", 35, 1.80, 82.4),
             person2("Sally Jones", 33, 1.65, 53.5);

    person1 = person2;
    //Equivalent to :
    //      person1.name = person2.name;
    //      person1.age = person2.age;
    //      person1.height = person2.height;
    //      person1.weight = person2.weight;
.....................................
.....................................
    return 0;
}
```

There is nothing at all wrong with the last three member assignments. However, the first assignment involves the copy of a **pointer**, rather than the string itself. This results in two problems :

- the string originally pointed to by *person1.name* is no longer accessible, and so cannot be freed by the programmer;

- when the destructor is called for *person1* and *person2, delete*
  will be used twice for the same memory, thereby corrupting
  the heap!

Solution

Overload the assignment operator to work with *person* objects, ensuring that it
handles deallocation of dynamic memory :

```
class person
{
private:
      ......................
      ......................
public:
      ....................................
      ....................................
      person& operator=(person& human);
      //Returns current object, to allow 'chaining'
      //of assignments.
};
....................................
....................................

person& person::operator=(person& human)
{
      delete[] name;          //Free old space.
      name = new char[strlen(human.name) + 1];

      strcpy(name, human.name);
      age = human.age;
      height = human.height;
      weight = human.weight;

      return *this;
      //Returns current object, by dereferencing this.
      //Alternatively :        return human;
}
```

Note that, because of the return of the current object by this operator function, we
can chain occurrences of the assignment operator for our class objects in the same
way that we can for the inbuilt types.

Example

```
person person1, person2;
person person3("Andrew Paul Thomas", 27, 1.79, 79.6);
//Defaults used for first two.
....................................
....................................
person1 = person2 = person3;
```

If the return type had been void, the assignment *person2 = person3* would have
returned void, leading to an attempted invalid assignment to *person1*.

11.3.6   Assignment v Initialisation

As was mentioned at the start of Section 2.9.1, assignment and initialisation are **different operations**, even though they use the same symbol ('='). They are distinguishable in appearance by the fact that an initialisation specifies a type name, whereas an assignment doesn't.

<u>Example</u>

```
int number = 65;     //Initialisation.
total = 0;           //Assignment.
```

For variables of the inbuilt types, the difference between these two operations will be of no significance. However, when a class object is initialised, the initialisation is carried out by a *copy constructor*, and this *can* have implications for the programmer. If an object is passed to a function by value or returned from a function by value, a copy constructor is called and initialisation takes place. (To cater for the first of these, we should always pass a class object as a **reference** argument.) If no copy constructor has been defined for the class, then the system carries out a memberwise copy. As a consequence of this, the *person* class from the previous section has another flaw in it. Since it has no copy constructor, a memberwise copy will take place if one *person* object is initialised with another. Once again, this will result in a **pointer** being copied for the *name* field, not the string itself. To overcome this problem, we should define a copy constructor for the *person* class, as shown below.

```
class person
{
    ...................................
    ...................................
    person(person& human);
    ...................................
    ...................................
}

-----------------------------------------------------------

//Within implementation file...

person::person(person& human)
{
    name = new char[strlen(human.name) + 1];
    strcpy(name, human.name);
    age = human.age;
    height = human.height;
    weight = human.weight;
}
```

We have had to do this because of the difference between assignment and initialisation. Since the two operations are different, it is **not** the assignment operator which is used in an object initialisation.

Exercises

1. Using the *date* class from Section 7.7.2, but omitting the first constructor function, replace function *add_day* with an overloaded increment operator (++) which works with *date* objects. Write a simple program which accepts five dates individually from the user and, for each date entered, outputs the following day (as a date). [You needn't bother encoding the *leap_year* function. Simply set its body to either '*return FALSE;*' or '*return TRUE;*'.]

2. Again using the *date* class from Section 7.7.2, define operator functions for <= and > which will allow two *date* objects to be compared and define operator functions for >> and << which will allow dates to be input and output in the form dd/mm/yyyy (e.g., 12/09/1998).
[You will need to place the manipulator *dec* on the input stream, in order for days/months with leading zeroes not to be interpreted as octal numbers. This is done as follows :   cin>>dec>>...]
Then write a program which will allow the user to enter as many pairs of dates as he/she wishes (employing your definition of the input operator). For each pair which is entered, use your relational operator functions to determine the correct chronological ordering for the dates and then use your overloaded output operator to output the dates in order.

3. Using the *time* class from Section 11.3, overload operators ++, << and >> to work with objects of this class. [The easy way to deal with the first of these will be to have the function make use of the operator function for +=. For overloading of the output operator, you could adapt the code from the function *main* in the example in Section 11.3.4.] Allow the user to enter a series of five times, each individually. As each time is entered, output the time which is one second later. Times should be input and output via the overloaded >> and << operators in the form hh:mm:ss, so *dec* will need to be used again, in order to force decimal interpretation for numbers with leading zeroes.

4. Using the *rational_num* class from Section 7.5, provide operators for addition, subtraction, multiplication, division, comparison (==, <, >), input and output.
N.B. None of the arithmetic should affect a stored rational number. The result should simply be returned through the operator function's return type (as a **value** argument, not as a reference argument, since you cannot return a reference to a local variable, which is what will need to be used within each function for storing the result of arithmetic). You should find it convenient to make use of *this in several places.
Allow the user to input five pairs of rational numbers. For each pair entered, output the results of all arithmetic and comparison operations between the numbers (in their lowest terms).

Example
Input
            12/15
            3/5

Output

```
12/15 + 3/5 = 7/5
12/15 - 3/5 = 1/5
12/15 * 3/5 = 12/25
(12/15) / (3/5) = 4/3
12/15 >3/5
```

Chapter 12   File Handling

Aims

- To introduce the syntax for file declarations and associated specification of open modes.
- To familiarise the reader with the processing of such files under serial access.
- To demonstrate the mechanism for using command line parameters with executable files.
- To familiarise the reader with the processing of files under random access.

12.1   File Streams

As was noted in Chapter 11, input and output (I/O) in C++ is provided by a hierarchy of stream classes. Those classes which provide file I/O are *ifstream* ('input file stream'), *ofstream* ('output file stream') and *fstream* ('file stream'). They are used for input, output and both input and output respectively. Since *fstream* allows both input and output, *fstream* alone will be used for the majority of this chapter. To access the facilities offered by the *fstream* class, a program must include the file *fstream.h*. Since this header file itself includes *iostream.h*, there is no need to specify the latter as well (though it will do no harm to do so).

12.2   Opening and Closing Files

There are two methods for opening a file in C++ :

- create an unattached *fstream* object and then use an explicit *open* function to attach this stream to a particular file;
- create an *fstream* object and pass its constructor the name of the file to be associated with the stream.

These techniques are very similar in appearance and, in many cases, it is probably a matter of personal preference which one is used. If, however, a serial file is to be closed and reopened in the same program, the first method should be used. The next two sub-sections will explain the syntax which is required for each.

12.2.1   Creating an Unattached Stream

If this method is used, the stream must then be explicitly attached to a file by means of the member function *open*, the prototype for which is :

```
void open(const char* filename, int mode);
```

Here, the first argument specifies the external file name to be associated with the stream, while the second argument specifies the mode under which the file is to be opened.

The possible modes under which a file may be opened are shown in the table below. Since these modes are declared within an enumerated type inside class *ios*, each must be preceded by the qualifier *ios::* when used.

Mode	Description
in	Open for reading.
out	Open for writing.
ate	Seek to end of file upon opening.
app	Open in append mode.
trunc	Truncate file on open if it exists.
nocreate	File must exist on open, or open fails.
noreplace	File must be new on open, or open fails.

If a file is opened explicitly, then it should be closed explicitly by the member function *close*. If this is not done, then there is a danger of losing data from the file buffer if there is a program crash. Function *close* ensures that the buffer is flushed.

Example

```
#include <fstream.h>
main()
{
    fstream test_file;

    testfile.open("test.dat", ios::out)
    //Open for output.

    if (test_file)
    //If in a good state, it's open.
    {
        test_file<<"This is a test.\n";
        //N.B. Output operator used with an fstream
        //object in exactly same way as it is with cout
        //(or any other stream object).
```

```
            test_file.close();
      }
      return 0;
}
```

If this code is run and the file 'test.dat' then examined using a text editor, it will be found to hold the specified message. Note that the state of the stream can be ascertained simply by using 'if' with the stream name. This is because the name is a pointer to the stream. If an error occurs when an attempt is made to open the file, then this pointer will hold the value *NULL*. Since *NULL* is equivalent to 0 ('FALSE'), it indicates a faulty stream.

Note also that the mode constants may be combined by means of the bitwise OR operator ('|').

Example

```
      test_file.open("test.dat", ios::in|ios::out);
      //Opens file for both input and output.
```

Now for the second method of opening a file...

12.2.2   Creating an Attached Stream

With this method, the *fstream* constructor takes two arguments and has the following syntax :

```
      fstream(const char* filename, int mode);
```

The arguments have the same meaning as those used with function *open* in the previous method. Note that, since the file is opened by a constructor, it will be closed implicitly by the destructor (so that there is no explicit *close* function).

Example

```
      //Produces same result as first example in 12.2.1.

      #include <fstream.h>

      main()
      {
          fstream test_file("test.dat", ios::out);
          if (test_file)
          {
              test_file<<"This is a test.\n";
          }
          return 0;
      }
```

Since the default open mode for an *ostream* object is *out* and the file in the above example was used only for output, then its declaration could have been simplified to :

```
      ofstream  test_file("test.dat");
```

(In a similar way, the default open mode for an *ifstream* object is *in*.)

12.3   Writing and Reading Lines To/From a Text File

As was seen in Chapter 6, a full line of text may be obtained from the keyboard by use of the member function *getline*. Since *getline* is a member function of all stream objects, it may also be used to read lines back from a text file. The only modification which needs to be made is the insertion of a newline character at the end of each line sent to and retrieved from the file, since this character is stripped away from each line transferred. We also need some means of determining when the end of the file has been reached, of course. This is provided by the member function *eof*.

Example

```
//txtlines.cpp
//Accepts 3 lines of text from the keyboard, writes them
//to a text file and then reads them back, re-displaying
//them on the screen.

#include <iostream.h>
#include <stdlib.h>
//Above file included for exit function.

main()
{
    fstream line_file;
    char line[80];

    line_file.open("lines.dat", ios::out);

    if (!line_file) //Stream faulty.
    {
        cout<<"*** File cannot be opened! ***\n";
        exit(1);                //Quit the program.
    }

    for (int count=0; count<3; count++)
    {
        cout<<"Enter line  "<<(count+1)<< " : ";
        cin.getline(line, 80, '\n');
        line_file<<line<<'\n';    //Add newline.
    }

    line_file.close();
    line_file.open("lines.dat", ios::in);

    while (!line_file.eof())
    {
        line_file.getline(line, 80, '\n');
        cout<<line<<'\n';
    }

    line_file.close();
    return 0;
}
```

Note that it is not at all uncommon for errors to occur when attempting to open a file, so the state of the associated stream must **always** be checked before any attempt is made to process the file.

12.4   Character-Level I/O

Occasionally, it may be necessary to deal with file I/O on an individual character basis. The member functions which allow this are shown in the table below.

Prototype	Effect
ostream& put(char);	Inserts character onto input stream. Returns output stream.
istream& get(char&);	Extracts next character from input stream. Returns input stream.
int peek();	Returns next character from input stream without extracting it. (Provides a 'look ahead' facility.) An EOF is returned upon end of input.
istream& putback(char);	Pushes character back onto input stream. Returns input stream.

Example
The 'while' loop at the end of the example in the previous section may be replaced by the code below, with exactly the same output resulting.

```
char one_char;
test_file<<resetiosflags(ios::skipws);
//Must suppress the stripping of whitespace characters!
//(Function resetiosflags is used to disable the
//formatting flags.)

while (!test_file.eof())
{
    test_file.get(one_char);
    cout<<one_char;
}
```

Another member function which may occasionally be of use in combination with these single-character functions is *gcount*, which returns the number of characters in the last extraction. Its prototype is :

```
        int gcount();
```

Example

```
        //countcom.cpp
        //Counts number of comment lines in a file
        //and number of characters in those lines.
        //N.B. newline characters are counted!

        #include <fstream.h>
        #include <stdlib.h>

        const int MAX_CHARS = 500; //Should be plenty!

        main()
        {
            char one_char;
            int num_comments = 0, num_chars = 0;
            fstream test_file("test.dat",ios::in);

            if (!test_file)          //Stream faulty.
            {
                cout<<"*** Unable to open file! ***";
                exit(1);
            }

            while (!test_file.eof())
            {
                test_file.get(one_char);
                if ((one_char=='/') && (test_file.peek()=='/'))
                {
                    test_file.get(one_char);
                    //Get rid of second '/',

                    num_comments++;
                    test_file.ignore(MAX_CHARS, '\n');
                    char_count+=test_file.gcount();
                }
            }

            cout<<"\n\nNumber of comment lines : "
                <<num_comments;
            cout<<"\n\nNumber of comment characters : "
                <<num_chars<<"\n\n";
            return 0;
        }
```

12.5   cin **and** cout **as Files**

Though cin and cout are normally associated with the keyboard and monitor respectively, they may be associated explicitly with named disc files, as will be seen very shortly. Before that, though, it is worth pointing out that cin, in particular, may be treated as an input file without any change in its association.

Example

```
        char line[80];
        while (cin.eof())
```

```
      {
            cin.getline(line, 80, '\n');
            cout<<line<<'\n';
            //Simply outputs line entered.
      }
```

However, how can we signal the end of an input file when entering data from the keyboard? The simple answer is that we enter a special control character. Unfortunately, the character to be used will depend upon whether we are operating under MS-DOS/Windows or under Unix. For a DOS/Windows environment, the character is <Ctrl-Z>; for a Unix environment, the character is <Ctrl-D>.

In order to associate cin and cout explicitly with named disc files, we must use the redirection operators '<' and '>' on the command line after the name of an executable file.

Examples

    (i)   `testprog<infile`
              (Associate cin with *infile*.)

    (ii)   `testprog>outfile`
              (Associate cout with *outfile*.)

    (iii)   `testprog<infile>outfile`
              (Combine (i) and (ii).)

Such redirection will cause any program input/output associated with cin/cout to be read from/written to the named file(s).

12.6   Using Command Line Parameters

It is sometimes desirable for executable files to be supplied with parameters on the command line (i.e., on the same line as that on which the name of the executable file is entered from the keyboard). Nowadays, of course, this command line would be entered via the *Run* option of the *File* menu on a Windows PC. For file-handling programs, it can be convenient to pass the names of files via this mechanism.

Example
```
      filecopy source dest
```

Here, an executable file called *filecopy* (*filecopy.exe* on PCs) is supplied with two command-line parameters (presumably, the name of a file to copy from and the name of a file to copy to). In C++, these parameters are received by function main. Though main has been used exclusively without parameters so far, it has an overloaded form which takes two arguments :

```
      void main(int arg_count, char* arg[]);
```

The first argument specifies the number of parameters/arguments which are to be received from the command line (*including the name of the executable file itself*), while the second argument is an array of strings holding the names of the actual arguments (the first of which, element 0, will be the name of the executable file itself).

Example

```
//filecopy.cpp
//Copies contents of file named in command line parameter
//1 to file named in command line parameter 2.

#include <fstream.h>
#include <stdlib.h>

main(int arg_count, char* arg[])
{
    ifstream infile;
    ofstream outfile;

    if (arg_count < 3)
    {
        cout<<"\n\n*** Fewer than 2 files! ***\n\n";
        exit(1);
    }

    infile.open(arg[1]);   //For input, by default.

    if (!infile)
    {
        cout<<"\n\n*** Error opening input file ";
        cout<<arg[1]<< "! ***\n\n";
        exit(1);
    }

    outfile.open(arg[2]); //For output, by default.

    if (!outfile)
    {
        cout<<"\n\n*** Error opening output file ";
        cout<<arg[2]<< "! ***\n\n";
        exit(1);
    }

    char one_char;
    while (!infile.eof())
    {
        infile.get(one_char);
        outfile.put(one_char);
    }

    infile.close();
    outfile.close();
    return 0;
}
```

12.7   Random Access

12.7.1   The File Pointer

Though normally used for stream-orientated I/O (which is inherently **serial**), *fstream* objects may also be used for random (i.e., direct) access. A file pointer (specifying the current character/byte position in the file) is maintained by the system and may be both retrieved and modified by the programmer. There are two functions for retrieving the current position of the file pointer : `tellg` and `tellp`. These names are short for 'tell get' (retrieve current position prior to reading or 'getting' data) and 'tell put' (retrieve position prior to writing or 'putting' data). They return values of type `streampos` (which is simply a synonym for `long int`) and their prototypes are :

```
streampos tellg();
streampos tellp();
```

Example
```
streampos filepos = myfile.tellg();
```

The position at which reading or writing is to commence may be specified relative to the beginning of the file, relative to the current position or relative to the end of the file. (For the last option, a *negative* argument must be supplied if accessing existing file contents.) These three possibilities are specified by the values of an enumerated type called `seek_dir`, which is declared in class `ios`. The values are :

beg	(seek relative to beginning of file);
cur	(seek relative to current position);
end	(seek relative to end of file).

Since these values are declared within class `ios`, they must be preceded by `ios::` when used.

The file pointer may be moved by the programmer via functions `seekg` ('seek get') and `seekp` ('seek put'), which will be followed by reading or writing respectively.
Prototypes :

```
istream& seekg(long offset, seek_dir mode);
ostream& seekp(long offset, seek_dir mode);
```

Examples

```
(i)   myfile.seekg(20, ios::cur);
      //Move on 20 characters/bytes from current position,
      //prior to reading.

(ii)  myfile.seekp(-35, ios::end);
      //Move back 35 characters/bytes from end of file,
      //prior to writing.
```

12.7.2   Reading and Writing

It is perfectly possible to use the input and output operators (>> and <<) for random access as well as for serial access, but this is unlikely to be of much use, since there would be no way of telling where a particular item started or finished in the file, and so no way of positioning the file pointer to the required location. In order for random access to be feasible, characters need to be stored in fixed-size blocks. For example, a file holding a list of names might have exactly thirty characters allocated for each name. An individual name is unlikely to occupy the full thirty character positions (leading to some wasted space), but the programmer will know that names start at positions 0, 30, 60, ... (i.e., at position (n-1) x 30 for name n) and can position the file pointer accordingly. Thus, for instance, he/she will move the file pointer to position (10-1) x 30 = 270 in order to read the tenth name. There are two member functions designed to read and write characters/bytes in fixed-size blocks. Surprisingly, these have the rather obvious names read and write!
Prototypes :

```
istream& read(char* data, int num_bytes);
ostream& write(char* data, int num_bytes);
```

N.B. **All** data is written/read as a character sequence, even numeric data!
Note also that, if reading and writing are to be used on the same file without that file being closed between reading and writing, the member function flush should be used to empty the file's output buffer (and thereby ensure that the file is up to date) before reading is attempted.

Example

```
//stokfile.cpp
//Writes 5 stock records to a random access file and then
//retrieves and displays the third record.

#include <fstream.h>
#include <string.h>
#include <ctype.h>

main()
{
    char code[11], level[5];  //Includes null character.
                       //Max. stock level = 9999 (4 digits).
    fstream stock_file("stock.dat", ios::in|ios::out);

    for (int count=0; count<5; count++)
    {
        cout<<"\n\nEnter stock code : ";
        cin>>code;
        stock_file.write(code,10);
        cout<<"\nEnter stock level (0-9999) : ";
        cin>>level;
        stock_file.write(level,4);
        stock_file.flush();       //File is updated.
    }

    stock_file.seekg(28, ios::beg);
    //Record size = 10+4 = 14.   (3-1) x 14 = 28.
```

```
            stock_file.read(code,10);
            stock_file.read(level,4);
            cout<<"\n\nStock item 3 : "<<code;
            cout<<"\n\nStock level : "<<level<<"\n\n";
            return 0;
      }
```

It is not absolutely necesary to use character strings for all the original data, since *typecasting* may be employed (for both reading and writing).

<u>Examples</u>

```
      (i)     int num = 23;
              myfile.write((char*)num, 2);

      (ii)    int value;
              myfile.read((char*)value, 2);
```

12.7.3   Testing for End of File

With a random access file, function eof returns TRUE (i.e., a non-zero value) **not** when the last item has been read, but when an attempt is made to read beyond this item. As a consequence of this, we cannot really use a loop which starts off with *while (!<filename>.eof())*, unless we have a read preceding the loop body.

<u>Example</u>
```
            stock_file.read(code,10);
            while(!stock_file.eof())
            .......................
```

If we do not have a prior read, then there will be an extra iteration of the loop. If we are simply searching the file for a particular item, then this is of no great consequence. However, if we are displaying the contents of the file, then the last record will be displayed twice! As an alternative to having an extra read before the loop body, we can use a 'never-ending' do loop from out of which we break if an attempt is made to read beyond the end of the file.

<u>Example</u>
```
      //getnames.cpp
      //Reads surnames from a random access file
      //and displays them on screen.

      #include <fstream.h>

      main()
      {
            fstream namefile;
            char name[16];  //15 characters + '\0'.

            namefile.open("NAMES.DAT", ios::in);

            do
            {
```

```
        namefile.read(name, 15);
        if (namefile.eof()) break;    //Get out of loop.
        cout<<name<<'\n';
    }while (1);                        //'Infinite' loop.

    namefile.close();
    return 0;
}
```

Exercises

Single-file programs may be used for these exercises.

1. Accept a set of ten surnames from the user, writing these names to a serial file. Then read back the contents of the file, displaying the names on screen.

2. Reopen the file above and append five further names to the file, again displaying the full contents of the file afterwards.

3. Extend the first program so that, after the file of names has been created, it is reopened for input and its contents written to a separate file. Your program should ensure that the first character of each name is in upper case before it is sent to the second file. Once all names have been transferred, the new file's contents should be displayed as a check. When you run the program, be sure to enter some names without capital letters.

4. Modify the above program so that the file names are supplied as command line parameters/arguments.

5. Create a random access file holding six names and telephone numbers. Allow the user to retrieve the telephone number for any person whose name he/she enters. This should be repeated as many times as the user wishes.

6. Create a random access file of six stock items and associated stock levels. Allow the user to retrieve or change the level of any item whose stock code he/she enters (as many times as he/she wishes).

Chapter 13   Templates

Aims

- To give the reader an appreciation of the rationale behind the use of templates.
- To introduce and illustrate the mechanism for creating and using generic/template functions.
- To introduce and illustrate the mechanism for creating and using parameterised types.

13.1   Introduction

It is widely recognised that the same algorithms are often required for different types of data. For instance, a particular sorting algorithm may be of use with integers, real numbers, characters, dates, etc. It is also widely recognised that the same fundamental data structures may be used to hold many different types of data. For instance, a linked list will have the same basic structure, regardless of the type of data held in an individual node (and will require the same basic operations). In order to avoid the 'reinventing of the wheel' which has traditionally taken place when implementing such standard algorithms and data structures, templates were introduced into the C++ language. They are intended to promote further code reusability, via template libraries. For most implementations of the language, they are a fairly recent innovation. Unfortunately, there is significant variation in the way in which templates are implemented, but this variation is likely to be reduced considerably over the next few years.

Templates are intended to facilitate what is called *generic* ('typeless') programming. As their name suggests, templates provide code frameworks which the programmer can employ with his/her own types, simply by supplying the templates with the names of those types. The templates themselves specify 'placeholders' for the types which the programmer must supply.

As noted at the start of this introduction, the principle applies to both algorithms (implemented as functions in C++) and data structures (implemented as either inbuilt or programmer-defined types/classes). The next two sections examine these two categories in turn.

13.2   Template Functions ('Generic Functions')

In conventional programming, we design functions to work with specific types of parameter. For example, we might design a Shellsort function to work with integers.

If we subsequently wished to use a Shellsort function to sort floating point numbers or strings, then we would have to change the source code for the function. Using a *template*, though, we can make the function *generic* (i.e., type-independent). In order to do this, we need to specify a list of required parameters. This is done by placing the following syntax before the function declaration :

```
template <param1, param2, ...>
```
[Note that the angle brackets are *literals* here, and **not** part of BNF syntax.]

In general, a template may have two categories of parameter : *types* and *constants*. However, it is difficult to see how the use of a template constant with a function could be justified, since the constant could simply be supplied as an ordinary function argument. Consequently, neither the Borland Implementation nor the Sun Unix implementation which the author used for testing purposes will allow the use of template constants with functions. (They *are* allowed with classes, however, as will be seen in the next section.)

The parameters in the template list for a function, then, will all be *types*. Each type is denoted by prefixing the parameter name with the keyword class. Misleading though it might seem, this does **not** mean that only types created via the class construct can be used. *Any* valid type (int, float, struct, etc.) may be used.

Examples
```
template <class TYPE>
template <class DATA1, class DATA2>
```

It is not, of course, necessary to use capitals for the names of template types, but doing so does assist in picking out their occurrences within a particular generic function.
N.B. Unlike other functions, *a template function does not have external linkage*, and so *its definition (not just its declaration) usually resides in a header file*.

Example
As a simple illustration of the technique, suppose we wish to convert a function designed to swap the values of two integers into a generic function which can be used to swap the contents of any two identifiers of the same type (whether an inbuilt type or our own type/class). The definition of the original function is shown below.

```
void swap(int& val1, int& val2)
{
    int temp_val = num1;

    val1 = val2;
    val2 = temp_val;
}
```

In order to make this function generic (i.e., able to work on any type), we must place before it a template which specifies any types which can vary when the algorithm is used on variables of another type. There is only one such type : int, the type of the two elements being swapped. Note that there are three places within the original function definition where the type of the elements to be swapped is specified : twice in the argument list and once (implicitly) in the declaration of the temporary variable. Each of the three references to int within the function definition must be preceded by the specified placeholder, as shown below.

N.B. This is one of those situations in which the #ifndef/#define/#endif combination mentioned in Section 4.4 **must** be used! If this is not done, then multiple declaration error messages are likely to be generated.

```
//swap.h
//Full definition in header file!

#ifndef STOCK_H
#define STOCK_H
//Above mandatory with templates.

template <class T>
void swap(T& val1, T& val2)
{
    T temp_val = val1;
    val1 = val2;
    val2 = temp_val;
}

#endif
```

However, there are some hidden assumptions here which will prevent this function from being used with our own classes, unless we ensure that those assumptions are valid. The assumptions are :

- that *either* an object of type T has a copy constructor *or* a default memberwise copy is adequate to initialise an object of type T (so that *temp_val* may be created);
- the assignment operator is defined for objects of type T.

For other generic functions, of course, it may be that different operators are required for use on the template type(s). For example, a sorting algorithm would probably need to have the > (or <) operator defined for any class which made use of it. It is the responsibility of the template designer to ensure that documentation is provided to specify clearly the requirements which must be satisfied for a class to make use of the template. Once these requirements have been satisfied, the generic/template function may easily be used with other types.

Examples

```
(i)    float num1, num2;
       ...........................
       swap(num1, num2);   //Used with another inbuilt type.

(ii)   employee   emp1("Sarah Reynolds", 235726L),
                  emp2("Kenneth Dalton", 187294L);
       ..............................
       swap(emp1, emp2);
       //Used with programmer-supplied class.
       //Assumes existence of copy constructor
       //and definition of assignment operator.
```

When the compiler meets one of these calls to the template function, it first looks for an exactly matching prototype and doesn't find one. It then looks for a template which will work and finds that template parameter T, if replaced by float/employee (as appropriate), will allow the function to have the correct prototype for the call. It then proceeds to *instantiate* the template, which means producing a copy of the template function with the placeholder replaced by the specific type. This function is then treated like any other function. Thus, there is no saving at all in terms of code size. The only saving is in the programmer's time.

Now let's extend the previous example so that our *swap* function is used on objects of our own class...

Example

```
//stock.h
//Declaration of stock class.

#ifndef STOCK_H
#define STOCK_H

#include <string.h>

class stock
{
private:
    char* stock_name;
    unsigned int current_level;
public:
    stock(char* name, unsigned int level);

    stock(stock& stock_item);
    //Copy constructor. Needed for initialisation of
    //local stock object in swap function.

    stock& operator=(stock& stock_item);
    ~stock() {delete[] stock_name;}
    friend ostream& operator<<(ostream& ostrm,
                               stock& stock_item);
};

#endif

------------------------------------------------------------

//stock.cpp
//Implementation of stock class.

#include <iostream.h>
#include "stock.h"

stock::stock(char* name, unsigned int level)
{
    stock_name = new char[strlen(name)+1];
    //(Allow space for null character.)

    strcpy(stock_name name);
    current_level = level;
}
```

```
stock::stock(stock& stock_item)
{
    stock_name=new char[strlen(stock_item.stock_name)+1];
    strcpy(stock_name, stock_item.stock_name);
    current_level = stock_item.current_level;
}

stock& operator=(stock& stock_item)
{
    delete[] stock_name;    //Deallocate dynamic memory.
    stock_name=new char[strlen(stock_item.stock_name)+1];
    strcpy(stock_name, stock_item.stock_name);
    current_level = stock_item.current_level;
}

ostream& operator<<(ostream& ostrm, stock& stock_item)
//Output a stock item's code and current level.
{
    ostrm<<"\n\nStock item : "<<stock_name;
    ostrm<<"\nCurrent level : "<<current_level<<"\n\n";
    return ostrm;
}

------------------------------------------------------------

//stokswap.cpp
//Demonstrates use of generic swap function on
//stock objects.

#include <iostream.h>
#include "swap.h"
#include "stock.h"

main()
{
    stock item1("A4 notepad", 100), item2("Staples", 50);

    cout<<"Original contents of item 1 : "<<item1;
    cout<<"Original contents of item 2 : "<<item2;
    swap(item1,item2);
    cout<<"\n\nFinal contents of item 1 : "<<item1;
    cout<<"\n\nFinal contents of item 2 : "<<item2;
    cout<<"\n\n";
    return 0;
}
```

If a generic function definition is separated from its declaration (which must still be in the same header file), then the definition must be preceded by the same template as that which preceded the function declaration.

Example

```
template <class T>
void swap(T&, T&);
.........................
.........................
template <class T>
void swap(T& val1, T& val2)
{
    .........................
```

```
        . . . . . . . . . . . . . . . . . . . . . . .
}
```

Occasionally, it is not possible to make a template function work with all possible types. For example, suppose we define a generic sort function as follows :

```
template <class T>
void gen_sort(T* array, int num_vals)
{
        . . . . . . . . . . . . . . . . . . . . . . . . . . . . . . . .
        if (array[count1] < array[count2])
        . . . . . . . . . . . . . . . . . . . . . . . . . . . . . . . .
        . . . . . . . . . . . . . . . . . . . . . . . . . . . . . . . .
}
```

Now, the operator < is defined for the inbuilt types int, float, char and double and can be redefined for our own types, so there should be no problem in using this function with any of these types. However, if used with values of type char* (i.e., strings), it will compare *pointers* and not the strings themselves. In such circumstances, we must *override* the template function by defining a sort function of the same name which will work specifically with strings. The central comparison statement in this new definition will be :

```
if (strcmp(array[count1],array[count2])< 0)
```

Since the compiler looks for an exactly matching prototype before it examines any templates, it will find the string-sorting prototype first and use that whenever *gen_sort* is called to sort an array of strings.

13.3   Parameterised Types ('Generic Types')

As noted in 13.1, templates may be used with *classes*, as well as with functions. When used with classes, the generic types which are created are sometimes called *parameterised types*. The syntax for template declarations used with classes is the same as that for template declarations used with functions, except that it is possible to include **constant** parameters as well as type parameters. As before, placeholders for type parameters are preceded by the word class. Placeholders for constants are preceded by their type specifiers (int, float, etc.).

Examples

```
template <class TYPE, int NUM_VALUES>
template <class NODE_DATA, float MIN_SIZE, float MAX_SIZE>
```

As a simple illustration, suppose we wish to create a generic *stack* class which is capable of holding nodes of any specified type.
[For the benefit of the reader who is unfamiliar with this data structure, a stack comprises a sequence of nodes which may be accessed at only one end (usually called the 'top'). When an element is added to the stack, it is said to be *pushed* onto

the stack (at the top); when an element is removed, it is said to be *popped* off the
stack (from the top). A stack is usually implemented as a linked list.]

Though a stack is usually implemented as a linked list, we shall first implement the
stack as a fixed-size structure, employing a constant parameter in the stack template
to specify the stack size. The only structural variation in our stack class will be in
the type of data which it may hold. This will be expressed via a type parameter in
our template. The code for this generic stack class is shown below.

```cpp
//genstack.h
//Holds template and class definition for a generic
//stack class.

#ifndef GENSTACK_H
#define GENSTACK_H

#include <iostream.h>
#include <stdlib.h>

template <class TYPE, int SIZE>
class stack
{
private:
    TYPE data[SIZE];
    //Stack implemented as an array (fixed size).

    int top;  //Current location of top of stack (0-SIZE).
              //This is always one position 'above' last
              //element placed on stack.
public:
    stack() {top = 0;}
    void push(const TYPE& value);
    TYPE& pop();
};

template <class TYPE, int SIZE>
//Each function definition will need to be preceded by
//the same template as that which preceded the class
//declaration.
void stack<TYPE, SIZE>::push(CONST TYPE& value)
{
    if (top == SIZE)
    {
        cout<<"*** STACK OVERFLOW! ***\n";
        exit(1);
    }
    data[top++] = value;
}

template <class TYPE, int SIZE>
TYPE& stack<TYPE, SIZE>::pop()
{
    if (top == 0)
    {
        cout<<"*** STACK UNDERFLOW! ***\n";
        exit(1);
    }
    return (data[--top]);
}
```

```
#endif
```

Once a parameterised type has been defined, we may create specific types from it and declare variables of these types. In order to specify a particular type, we must use the template class name, followed (in angle brackets) by the actual parameter(s) to be used.

<u>Examples</u>

```
node<int> int_node;
//Declares int_node as a node object holding a
//single integer.

node<staff> staff_node;
//Declares staff_node as a node object holding a
//staff object.

list<employee, 20> dept_list;
//declares dept_list as a list object holding 20
//employee objects (assuming the existence of a
//parameterised type list).
```

As was the case for template functions, each of these declarations will cause a template to be instantiated.

As a simple demonstration of the use of our parameterised stack type, the program shown below declares a stack which is capable of holding ten characters. It then pushes the letters 'A' - 'J' onto the stack and immediately pops them off again, displaying the letters as they are removed.

```
//stakdem1.cpp
//Demonstrates use of generic stack class.

#include <iostream.h>
#include "genstack.h"

main()
{
    stack<char, 10> my_stack;

    for (char letter='A'; letter<'K'; letter++)
        my_stack.push(letter);

    for (int count=0; count<10; count++)
        cout<<my_stack.pop()<<"          ";

    return 0;
}
```

Since a stack is a LIFO (Last In First Out) data structure, the letters are output in reverse order :

J   I   H   G   F   E   D   C   B   A

Now let's consider a more extensive and realistic implementation of a generic stack, employing a generic *node* class and dynamic memory management...

Our generic node may hold data of any type (int, float, struct, class object, etc.). Regardless of the type of data to be held, the node must hold a pointer to the next node in the stack (the one 'below' it) and should also have a constructor. The only structural variation in our node object is in the type of data which it may hold, so this is expressed via a template parameter, as shown below.

```
template <class DATA>
class node
{
private:
    DATA contents;
    node* next_node;
public:
    node(DATA& contents_in) {contents = contents_in;}
    //N.B. Assignment operator must be defined for type
    //DATA (unless memberwise assignment is adequate).
};
```

This node class is not of much use to our stack class at present, since a stack class will not have access to the private members of the corresponding node class. In order to make our parameterised node type useful, we must modify its declaration by declaring class stack to be a *friend* of it. However, if *node<DATA>* is our node type, only a stack made up of nodes containing the same type of data can be a friend. This is expressed as *stack<DATA>* and can be seen in the modified declaration of class *node* in the example below. Since dynamic memory management is now being employed, of course, we must provide a destructor for our *stack* class which will deallocate memory for nodes in the stack.

Example
This example defines and makes use of parameterised types *node* and *stack* to create a stack holding three *stock_item* objects. After creating the stack, the program terminates, causing the stack destructor to display the data contents of each node as the node is destroyed.

```
//nodestak.h
//Holds templates and class definitions for node and
//stack of nodes.

#ifndef NODESTAK_H
#define NODESTAK_H

#include <iostream.h>
#include <stdlib.h>

template <class DATA>
class node
{
private:
    DATA contents;
    node* next_node;
public:
    node(DATA& contents_in) {contents = contents_in;}
    //Assignment operator must be defined for type DATA!
```

```
            friend class stack<DATA>;
     };

     template <class DATA>
     class stack
     {
     private:
         node<DATA>* top;
     public:
         stack() {top = NULL;};   //Creates empty stack.

         void push(node<DATA>*& new_node)
         {
             new_node->next_node = top;
             top = new_node;
         }

         DATA pop();

         ~stack();
     };

     template <class DATA>
     DATA stack<DATA>::pop()
     {
         if (top==NULL)
         {
             cout<<"\n\n*** Stack empty! ***\n\n";
             exit(1);
         }
         DATA contents = top->contents;
         node<DATA>* old_top = top;
         top = top->next_node;
         delete old_top;
         return contents;
     }

     template <class DATA>
     stack<DATA>::~stack()
     {
        while (top!=NULL)
        {
            node<DATA>* old_top = top;
            cout<<"\nRemoving node holding :  ";

            cout<<top->contents<<"\n\n";
            //Output operator must be defined for type DATA!

            top = top->next_node;
            delete old_top;
        }
     }

     #endif

-----------------------------------------------------------

//stokitem.h

#ifndef STOKITEM_H
```

```
#define STOKITEM_H

struct stock_item
{
    unsigned long code;
    char description[20];
    unsigned int level;

    stock_item& operator=(stock_item& item);
    friend ostream& operator<<(ostream& ostrm,
                                    stock_item& item);
};

#endif
```

```
//stokitem.cpp
//Implementation of functions for stock_item.

#include <iostream.h>
#include "stokitem.h"

stock_item& stock_item::operator=(stock_item& item)
{
    code = item.code;
    strcpy(description, item.description);
    level = item.level;
    return *this;    //Allows 'chaining' of operator.
}

ostream& operator<<(ostream& ostrm, stock_item& item)
{
    ostrm<<"\tItem "<<item.code<<"\t\tLevel ";
    ostrm<<item.level <<'\n';
    //Recall that '\t' is the tab character.

    return ostrm;    //Allows 'chaining of operator.
}
```

```
//stakdemo.cpp
#include <iostream.h>
#include "nodestak.h"
#include "stokitem.h"

main()
{
    stack<stock_item> my_stack;
    //Creates (empty) stack capable of holding nodes of
    //type node<stock_item>.

    stock_item item[3]= { {123456L,"Pencil",3000},
                    {111111L,"A4 Ring Binder",250},
                    {999999L, "Eraser", 745} };
    //Creates array of 3 stock_item objects and
    //initialises objects with data.

    node<stock_item> stock_node[3] =
```

```
                            {  node<stock_item>(item[0]),
                               node<stock_item>(item[1]),
                               node<stock_item>(item[2]) };
    //Creates array of 3 stock_item nodes and uses
    //constructor to initialise nodes with data from
    //the stock_item array.

    for (int count=0; count<3; count++)
    {
        my_stack.push(&stock_node[count]);
        //Pushes each node onto stack.
    }
    return 0;
}
```

When run, the above program produces the output shown below.

```
Removing node holding :    Item 999999    Level 745
Removing node holding :    Item 11111     Level 250
Removing node holding :    Item 123456    Level 3000
```

Exercises

1. Define a generic function *maximum* which will return the largest element in an array. The array may contain elements of any type, whether a simple type or a class type. (For this function to be used with a class, the operator > must be defined for that class.) The template used must specify the base/component type of the array (which will also be the return type of the function). The function itself will take two arguments : the name of the array and its size.
Write a program which declares three *account* objects and outputs details of the largest account. The structure of an *account* object should be as shown below.

```
class account
{
private:
    unsigned long int account_no;
public:
    account(unsigned long acct_no, float bal)
    {
        account_no = acct_no;
        balance = bal;
    }

    int operator>(account& acct)
    {
        if (balance>acct.balance) return 1;
        else return 0;
    }

    friend ostream& operator<<(ostream& ostrm,
                                          account& acct)
    {
        ostrm<<"Account no. "<<acct.account_no<<'\n';
        ostrm<<"Balance        "<<acct.balance<<'\n';
        return ostrm;
    }
}
```

2. Convert function *bubble_sort* shown below into a generic sort function, making use of the generic function *swap* from Section 13.2. Using class *time* from Section 11.3 and overloading operator > for this class, write a program which declares an array of five (initialised) *time* objects and use the function *bubble_sort* to put them into ascending sequence. Then, as a check, output the contents of the array (making use of the overloaded output operator from Exercise 3 at the end of Chapter 11).

```
void bubble_sort(int value[], int num_values)
{
    int upper_limit = num_values-1;

    for (int outer=upper_limit; outer>=0; outer---)
        for (int inner=0; inner<outer; inner++)
            if (value[inner] > value[inner+1])
                swap(value[inner], value[inner+1]);
}
```

3. Define a linked list class as a parameterised type which is capable of holding any specified node type. Use this parameterised type to create and process two different unordered linked lists, the first of which holds surnames and examination marks (one per name) and the second of which holds account numbers and balances. Once each list has been created, a destructor should display the contents of each node. (This will require a destructor to be defined in each node type.)   A list of the required files and their contents is shown below.

(i)   *listtemp.h*
         Header file for linked list parameterised type.
         Holds following items :
                  •   body of parameterised list class;
                  •   definition of list destructor;
                  •   definition of function **add_node**
                         (which adjusts pointers to insert a node into the list).

(ii)   *examnode.h*
         Header file for examination nodes.
         Holds structure declaration for an examination node and prototype for function **create_exam_list**.

(iii)   *examnode.cpp*
         Implementation file for examination nodes.

(iv)   *acctnode.h*
         Header file for account nodes.
         Holds structure declaration for an account node and prototype for function **create_acct_list**.

(v)   *acctnode.cpp*
         Implementation file for account nodes.

(vi)   *template.cpp*
         Creates two linked lists with differing structures, using the same template.
         The code is provided below.

```
#include "examnode.h"
#include "acctnode.h"

main()
{
    list<exam_node> exam_list;
    list<account_node> acct_list;

    create_exam_list(exam_list);
    create_acct_list(acct_list);

    return 0;
}
```

Appendix A   Exception Handling

There are certain circumstances under which program execution must not be allowed to proceed normally. Examples include such things as attempted division by zero and exhaustion of the heap when allocating memory dynamically. Such events are called *exceptions* and need to be *handled* (i.e., processed or dealt with) by routines built into the software which is being executed. C++ formalises this procedure by providing a special exception handling mechanism based on the keywords try, catch and throw. The use of each of these keywords is described below.

- try

This keyword immediately precedes the block of code which is to be subject to the exception handling mechanism.

- catch (<type>)

This keyword immediately precedes a *handler*, a set of statements to be executed if a value of the specified type is received when an exception has occurred. There may be more than one handler for the same block of code, each preceded by the word *catch* and each capable of receiving and responding to a different type. These handlers must be located immediately below the block of code which is to be monitored for an exception (a block preceded by the word *try*).

- throw <value>

When an exception occurs, this keyword sends ('throws') a value to be received ('caught') by a handler, which will then take the appropriate action.

Example

```
//xceptdemo.cpp

#include <iostream.h>
#include <iomanip.h>
#include <stdlib.h>

main()
{
    int numerator, denominator;

    try
    {
        cout<<"Enter numerator and denominator : ":
        cin>>numerator>>denominator;
        if (denominator==0) throw 1;
    }

    catch(int i)
```

```
        {
            cout<<"\n\n\a*** Division by zero! ***\n\n";
            exit(1);
        }

        cout<<setiosflags(ios::fixed|ios::showpoint);
        cout<<setprecision(2)<<"\n\nDecimal value : ";
        cout<<float(numerator)/float(denominator)<<"\n\n";
        return 0;
    }
```

If 0 is entered for the denominator above, then a value of 1 is sent by throw and received by the catch following the try block (since this catch expects to receive an integer). In this example, the value received by catch is not used in the handler, making argument *i* redundant. Consequently, we can omit the argument name and specify the type only, as follows :

```
        catch(int) {........................}
```

As noted earlier, the same try block may have more than one exception handler (each one designed to handle a different type of exception). It may also be the case that, having handled an exception, the handler allows program execution to continue. In this case, execution will continue from the first statement following all the handlers for the particular try block.

Example
```
    //xceptdemo.cpp

    #include <iostream.h>
    #include <iomanip.h>
    #include <stdlib.h>

    main()
    {
        int numerator, denominator;

        try
        {
            cout<<"Enter numerator and positive denominator: ";
            cin>>numerator>>denominator;
            if (denominator == 0) throw 'X';
            //Could be any character.

            if (denominator < 0) throw denominator;
        }

        catch(char)
        {
            cout<<"\n\n\a*** Division by zero! ***\n\n";
            exit(1);
        }

        catch(int denom)
        {
            cout<<"\n\n"<<denom<<" entered for denominator.\n";
            cout<<"Will be converted to  "<<(-denom)<<"\n\n";
        }
```

```
         if (denominator<0) denominator = -denominator;
         //N.B. Has no effect if done inside handler!

         cout<<setiosflags(ios::fixed|ios::showpoint);
         cout<<setprecision(2)<< "\n\nDecimal value : ";
         cout<<float(numerator)/float(denominator)<< "\n\n";
         return 0;
}
```

Note that the types received by the handlers must be different. If we wish, we can define our own classes and use these as the types to be 'thrown' and 'caught'.

Appendix B   Platform Variations

The two common platforms for C++ are Windows-based PCs and Unix workstations. On PCs, there are currently two major implementations of the language : *Borland C++* and Microsoft's *Visual C++*. All the software in this book has been tested using *Borland C++ for Windows (Version 4.51)*.

B.1   Borland C++

B.1.1 Creating and Running a Program

Borland's IDE (Integrated Development Environment) provides a very flexible and user-friendly environment for software development. For a multi-file program under this implementation, it is necessary to create a *project* which will hold all the files making up the program. This is done by selecting *New* from the *Project* menu. It is advisable to give the project the same name as that of your main file, since a file with that name (and a .cpp extension) will automatically be added to the *project tree* (a diagrammatic representation of the structure of your project which is shown at the bottom of the screen on leaving the project creation screen). Before leaving this screen, though, it is necessary to specify the *Target Type* (the type of application program you wish to create), the *Platform* to be used and the *Target Model* (the memory model appropriate to the program's memory requirements). The selection made will depend upon your precise requirements and system, but a commonly used combination is *EasyWin* under *Windows 3.x (16)* with a *Large* memory model.

Upon leaving the project creation screen (by clicking on *OK* or pressing *<Return>*) , you will need to add your other .cpp file(s) to the project tree. The easiest way to do this is to click on the project icon (the one at the top of the tree) with the *rightmost* mouse button. This will bring up a menu from which you can select *Add node*. Upon selecting this, you will be prompted to enter the name of the file.

You do not need to attach your header file(s) to the project tree, but doing so will do no harm, provided that you have used the #ifndef/#define/#endif combination. (See Section 4.4 if you require an explanation of the use of these directives.) If you do this by mistake, simply right-click on the unwanted icon and select *Delete node* from the menu which appears.

Once a project has been created, it may be compiled and/or executed, either by use of a speedbar button or by selecting one of the options from the *Project* menu.

The other major PC implementation of C++, Microsoft's Visual C++, has similar facilities for creating and running a project file.

B.1.2   Single-Key Input

For the user's convenience, it is often desirable to accept his/her response to a question as a single keypress (i.e., without the user pressing <Return> afterwards). This is achieved by use of one of the functions getch and getche, each of which takes no arguments and accepts a single keypress, returning the character whose key was pressed. Prototypes :

```
char getch();
char getche();
```

The difference between these two functions is that getche echoes the character to the screen, while getch does not. This means that getch is more appropriate when we are not interested in the actual character whose key was pressed (e.g., when prompting the user to press any key to continue), whereas getche is more appropriate when we *are* interested in the actual character entered.

These functions are amongst a number of screen-handling functions which are implementation-dependent. [See the next section for details of other such functions.] In the Borland implementation, the screen-handling functions are declared within *conio.h*.

<u>Example</u>

```
//one_key.cpp
//'Skeleton' code showing the use of single-key input.

#include <iostream.h>
#include <conio.h>
//Above file provides access to the required function.

main()
{
    char reply;
    .......................
    .......................
    do
    {
        .......................
        .......................
        cout<<"Do you wish to quit? (y/n) : ";
        reply = getche();
    } while (reply != 'y');
    //Above 2 lines may be replaced with :
    //      } while (getche() != 'y');
    return 0;
}
```

The reader may feel a little uneasy about the reliance upon the user entering his/her response in lower case in this example. Of course, one should not really rely upon entry of either upper or lower case in any program. One way around this would be to make the following compound test :

```
while ((reply != 'y') && (reply != 'Y'));
```

A more elegant way of achieving the same end is to convert the user's input into either upper or lower case. This is achieved by functions `toupper` and `tolower` respectively. These functions are declared within the standard library header file **ctype.h** and have the following prototypes :

```
char toupper(char char_in);
//Returns upper case equivalent of char_in.

char tolower(char char_in);
//Returns lower case equivalent of char_in.
```

The loop test in the previous example would then become :

```
}while (tolower(reply) != 'y');
```

B.1.3   Screen-Handling

As noted in the previous section, the screen-handling functions for the Borland implementation of C++ are declared within *conio.h*. In addition to `getch`, there are two such functions which are very useful : `clrscr` and **gotoxy**. Their prototypes are shown below.

```
void clrscr();                //Clears the screen.
void gotoxy(int x, int y);    //Positions cursor at (x,y).
```

Example

```
//scrndemo.cpp
//Simple demonstration of Borland screen-handling.

#include <iostream.h>
#include <conio.h>

main()
{
    char name[16];

    clrscr();        //Clear screen.
    gotoxy(25,10);//Put cursor at position 25 on line 10.
    cout<<"What is your first name? ";
    cin>>name;
    gotoxy(25,15); //Position 25 on line 15.
    cout<<"Goodbye, "<<name<<"!\n\n";
    return 0;
}
```

B.2   Unix Implementations

B.1.1 Compiling and Running a Program

A C++ source program is created using any available text editor and then compiled and linked from the command line. There are two categories of C++ compiler on Unix systems : native code compilers (such as the Gnu gcc compiler from the Free Software Foundation) and C front-ends (such as Unix System Laboratories' CC compiler). The description which follows applies specifically to SunPro's native code SPARCompiler (Version 4.1), but the details are similar for all Unix implementations.

The SPARCompiler is invoked from a Shell tool via the command **CC**. Since Unix is case-sensitive, it is very important that CC be entered in upper case. For a single-file program, CC will be followed by the name of the source code file, which will have the suffix .cc (or .c, on some systems).

Example

```
CC  myprog.cc
```

By default, the executable file created (assuming successful compilation) will be given the name *a.out*. This should normally be changed to something more meaningful by means of the *-o* flag ('o' for object file name).

Example

```
CC  myprog.cc   -o myprog
```
(The executable file is given the name *myprog* here.)

For a program made up of several source files, the files may be compiled and linked by supplying the names of all .cc files on the command line.

Example

```
CC  myprog.cc  subord.cc   -o myprog
```
(The order of the files is not significant.)

Header files *iostream.h* and *stdlib.h* will be linked automatically, if included in the source files by means of *#includes*. If other library files are to be linked, however, the linker must be told about them explicitly on the command line by means of the *-l* ('library file') flag. In particular, if a program is to use screen-handling, the linker must be told to link **curses.h** and **termcap.h** (the latter of which holds a database of terminal capabilities).

Example

```
CC  myprog.cc  subord.cc   -o myprog   -l curses   -l termcap
```

Either or both of the above source files may be compiled separately, by use of the *-c* flag.

Example
```
CC    -c subord.cc
```

This will result in the creation of an object file called *subord.o*, which may then be linked with the main file.

Example
```
CC    subord.o myprog.cc  -o myprog  -l curses  -l termcap
```
(Again, the order of the files is not significant.)

Once a file has been compiled successfully, it may be executed simply by entering its name.

Example
```
myprog
```

B.2.2   Unix Screen-Handling

Unix screen-handling functions are declared within **curses.h**. The equivalents of Borland's clrscr and gotoxy are clear and move respectively, the prototypes for which are shown below.

```
void clear();
void move (int y, int x);  //N.B. y coordinate first!
```

However, in order for these functions to work and for screen output to be achieved, four more screen-handling functions must be employed : initscr, refresh, flush and endwin. These functions, none of which takes any arguments, should be used according to the rules stated below.

(i)   At the start of main, the following call must be made :   initscr();
       This call initialises *curses*, obtaining terminal-specific characteristics.

(ii)   After each occurrence of either clear or move, a call to function refresh must be made, in order to update the screen display.

Example
```
move(12,30);          //Position 30 on line 12.
refresh();
```

(iii) Whenever cout is used, output should be ensured by use of the manipulator function flush.

Example
```
cout<<"An example.\n\n"<<flush;
```
[It is possible that this will not be required by some Unix implementations, but it was found to be necessary on the Sun workstations used by the author for testing.]

(iv)   At the end of main, the following call must be made :   endwin();

This restores normal terminal I/O mode and performs other cleanup activities.
N.B. Failure to include this function may leave your terminal pretty unusable!

<u>Example</u>
This is the Unix equivalent of the example program from Section B.1.3.

```
//scrndemo.cc
//Simple demonstration of Unix screen-handling.

#include <iostream.h>
#include <curses.h>

main()
{
    char name[16];

    initscr();
    clear();
    refresh();
    move(10,25);        //Remember that y value comes first.
    refresh();
    cout<<"What is your first name? "<<flush;
    cin>>name;
    move(15,25);
    refresh();
    cout<<"Goodbye, "<<name<<"!\n\n";
    endwin();
    return 0;
}
```

Note that function getch is also available via *curses.h*.

Appendix C   Stream Formatting

Each stream in C++ has a *formatting state* which determines the formatting to be used for that stream. This stream is stored as a series of bit flags, defined by an enumerated type in class *ios*. These flags are shown in the table below.

Label	Action
skipws	Skip white space on input.
left	Left justify output.
right	Right justify output.
internal	Use padding after sign or base indicator.
dec	Use decimal conversion.
oct	Use octal conversion.
hex	Use hexadecimal conversion.
showbase	Use base indicator on output.
showpoint	Always show decimal point and trailing zeros on floating point output.
uppercase	Use uppercase for hex output.
showpos	Add '+' to positive integers on output.
scientific	Use exponential notation on floats.
fixed	Use fixed point notation on floats.
unitbuf	Flush all streams after output.
stdio	Flush cout and cerr after output.

Though the stream operators are overloaded with default formats for all the inbuilt types and these default values are adequate for many situations, there are times when the programmer needs to modify the default formatting. This is achieved by setting or clearing flags from the table above. When referring to one of these flags, it must be preceded by ios::.

Example

        ios::showpoint

However, it is not necessary to use explicit bitwise manipulation, since the *ios* class provides a set of high-level functions for setting and resetting the formatting flags. These functions, called *manipulators*, allow the formatting state of a stream to be altered during I/O. The table below shows the available manipulators.

Manipulator	I/O	Action
dec	I/O	Sets base to decimal.
oct	I/O	Sets base to octal.
hex	I/O	Sets base to hexadecimal.
ws	I	Extracts white space chars.
endl	O	Inserts a newline and flushes stream.
ends	O	Inserts a null byte.
flush	O	Flushes a stream.
setbase (int b)	I/O	Sets conversion base(0/8/10/16). (Base 0 means use base 10 for output and C parsing rules for integer literals on input.)
setiosflags (long f)	I/O	Sets specified bits.
resetiosflags(long f)	I/O	Clears specified bits.
setfill (char c)	O	Sets fill character.
setprecision (int n)	O	Sets precision to n digits after decimal point.
setw (int w)	I/O	Sets total field width.

Example

    cout<<setw(6)<<number;
    //Output *number,* using a field width of *c.*

To use any of the manipulator functions which take arguments, it is necessary to include the header file *iomanip.h*. For manipulators without arguments, including *iostream.h* is sufficient.

Model Solutions to Programming Exercises

Chapter 2

1.
```
//hello.cpp
//Accepts user's initials and
//displays greeting.

#include <iostream.h>

main()
{
    char init1, init2;

    cout<<"\n\nWhat are your initials? ";
    cin>>init1>>init2;
    cout<<"\n\nHello, "<<init1<<'.'<<init2<<".\n\n";
    return 0;
}
```

2.
```
//pythag.cpp
//Accepts lengths of 2 shortest sides of a right-
//angled triangle and displays length of hypotenuse
//(to nearest whole number).

#include <iostream.h>
#include <math.h>

main()
{
    int side1, side2;

    cout<<"\n\n\nEnter the lengths (in cm) of the "
        <<"two shortest sides\n
        <<"of a right-angled triangle :   ";
    cin>>side1>>side2;
    cout<<"\n\nLength of hypotenuse "
        <<"(to nearest whole number) = ";
        <<int(sqrt(side1*side1 + side2*side2) + 0.5)
        <<" cm\n\n";
    return 0;
}
```

```
3.
//mean.cpp
//Accepts 3 integers and displays their arithmetic
//mean (to 1 dec. place).

#include <iostream.h>
#include <iomanip.h>

main()
{
    int int1, int2, int3;

    cout<<"Enter 3 integers, separated by spaces: ";
    cin>>int1>>int2>>int3;
    cout<<"\n\nMean (to 1 d.p.) = ";
    cout<<setiosflags(ios::fixed)<<setprecision(1);
    cout<<float(int1 + int2 + int3) / 3<<"\n\n";

    return 0;
}



4.
//ascii.cpp
//Uses ASCII codes and increment/decrement operators to
//display 3 consecutive letters in both ascending and
//descending sequence.

#include <iostream.h>

main()
{
    char letter = 65;

    cout<<++letter<<"   ";
    cout<<++letter<<"   ";
    cout<<++letter<<'\n';
    cout<<letter<<"   ";
    cout<<--letter<<"   ";
    cout<<--letter<<"\n\n";

    return 0;
}
```

Chapter 3

```
1.
//largest.cpp
//Accepts 3 integers and outputs the largest one.

#include <iostream.h>

main()
{
    int num1, num2, num3, largest;

    cout<<"Enter 3 integers, separated by spaces: ";
    cin>>num1>>num2>>num3;
    largest = (num1>num2)?num1:num2;
    largest = (num3>largest)?num3:largest;
    //Could have used 'nested' ifs above.

    cout<<"\nLargest value entered is "<<largest".\n\n";

    return 0;
}


2.
//digits.cpp
//Accepts a single digit and outputs
//its text name ('zero'...'nine').

#include <iostream.h>

main()
{
    char one_char;

    cout<<"Enter a single digit (0-9) :  ";
    cin>>one_char;
    cout<<"\n\n";
    switch (one_char)
    {
        case '0' :   cout<<"Zero"; break;
        case '1' :   cout<<"One"; break;
        case '2' :   cout<<"Two"; break;
        case '3' :   cout<<"Three"; break;
        case '4' :   cout<<"Four"; break;
        case '5' :   cout<<"Five"; break;
        case '6' :   cout<<"Six"; break;
```

```
        case '7'  :   cout<<"Seven"; break;
        case '8'  :   cout<<"Eight"; break;
        case '9'  :   cout<<"Nine"; break;
        default   :   cout<<"\a*** Not an integer! ***";
    }
    cout<<"\n\n";
    return 0;
}



3.
//oddcount.cpp
//Accepts a series of positive integers (terminated
//by zero) and outputs number of odd values entered.

#include <iostream.h>

main()
{
    int number, odd_count=0;

    cout<<"Enter positive integer (or 0 to quit): ";
    cin>>number;
    while (number>0)
    {
        if (number%2 == 1)
            odd_count++;
        cout<<"\nEnter next positive integer ";
        cout<<"(or 0 to quit) :   ";
        cin>>number;
    }
    cout<<"\n\nNumber of odd integers entered :   ";
    cout<<odd_count<<"\n\n";

    return 0;
}



4.
//fctorial.cpp
//Waits for an integer in the range 2-7 and then
//outputs its factorial value.

#include <iostream.h>

main()
{
    int number, factorial=1;
```

```
        do
        {
            cout<<"Enter an integer in the range 2-7: ";
            cin>>number;
            cout<<"\n\n";
            if ((number<2)||(number>7))
            {
                cout<<"\aNumber must be in range 2-7. ";
                cout<<Try again...\n\n";
            }
        }while ((number<2)||(number>7));
        for (int count=2; count<=number; count++)
            factorial*=count;
        cout<<"\n\n"<<number<<"! = "<<factorial<<"\n\n";
        return 0;
}


5.
//primetst.cpp
//Accepts an integer and determines
//whether or not it is prime.

#include <iostream.h>
#include <math.h>

enum boolean {FALSE, TRUE};

main()
{
    int entry, root, count;
    boolean is_prime = TRUE;

    do
    {
        cout<<"\n\n\n";
        cout<<"Enter an integer greater than 1 :   ";
        cin>>entry;
        if (entry < 2)
        {
            cout<<"\n\n\n";
            cout<<"*** Invalid entry. Try again! ***";
        }
    }while (entry < 2);

    root = sqrt(entry);
    //Decimal part removed by truncation.
    //Could use entry/2, but would not be
```

```
    //as efficient.

    if ((entry%2 == 0) && (entry != 2))
    //An even number > 2.
        is_prime = FALSE;
    else
        count = 3;
    while ((is_prime) && (count <= root))
    {
        if (entry%count == 0)
            is_prime = FALSE;
        else
            count = count+2;
        //Step through odd integers.
    }
    cout<<"\n\n\n";
    if (is_prime)
        cout<<entry<<" IS prime.";
    else
        cout<<entry<<" is NOT prime.";

    return 0;
}
```

Chapter 4

```
1.
//maxfunc.h
//Holds prototype for function to return
//largest of its 3 arguments.


#ifndef MAXFUNC_H
#define MAXFUNC_H

int max(int num1, int num2, int num3);

#endif
--------------------------------------------------------

//maxfunc.cpp
//Holds definition for function which returns
//largest of 3 integers.

#include "maxfunc.h"
```

```
int max(int num1, int num2, int num3)
{
    int largest = (num1>num2)?num1:num2;
    largest = (num3>largest)?num3:largest;
    return largest;
}
```

```
//largest.cpp
//Accepts 3 integers and outputs the largest one.

#include <iostream.h>
#include "maxfunc.h"

main()
{
    int num1, num2, num3;

    cout<<"Enter 3 integers, separated by spaces: ";
    cin>>num1>>num2>>num3;
    cout<<"\n\nLargest value entered is ";
    cout<<max(num1, num2, num3)<<".\n\n";
    return 0;
}
```

```
2.
//showtabl.h
//Holds prototype for function to display
//a multiplication table.

#ifndef SHOWTABL_H
#define SHOWTABL_H

void show_table(int);

#endif
```

```
//showtabl.cpp
//Holds definition of function to display a
//multiplication table.

#include <iostream.h>
#include "showtabl.h"

void show_table(int multiplier)
{
    cout<<'\n';
```

```
    for (int count=1; count<13; count++)
    {
        cout<<"          "<<count<<" x "<<multiplier<<" = ";
        cout<<"          "<<(count*multiplier)<<'\n';
    }
}
```

```
//mlttable.cpp
//Displays the multiplication table
//for any integer in the range 2-12.

#include <iostream.h>
#include "showtabl.h"

main()
{
    int number;

    cout<<"Enter an integer in the range 2-12 ";
    cout<<"(or any other value to quit) :  ";
    cin>>number;
    while ((number>1) && (number<13))
    {
        show_table(number);
        cout<<"\n\nEnter an integer in range 2-12 ";
        cout<<"(or any other value to quit) :   ";
        cin>>number;
    }
    return 0;
}
```

```
3.
//fact.h
//Holds prototype for function to return
//factorial n for any integer in the range 2-7.

#ifndef FACTN_H
#define FACTN_H

int factorial(int);

#endif
```

```
//factn.cpp
//Holds definition of function to return
//factorial n for any integer in the range 2-7.
```

```
#include "factn.h"

int factorial(int number)
{
    int result=1;

    for (int count=2; count<=number; count++)
        result*=count;
    return result;
}
```

```
//fctorial.cpp
//Waits for an integer in the range 2-7 and then
//outputs its factorial value.

#include <iostream.h>
#include "factn.h"

main()
{
    int number;

    do
    {
        cout<<"Enter an integer in the range 2-7: ";
        cin>>number;
        cout<<"\n\n";
        if ((number<2)||(number>7))
            cout<<"\aNumber must be in range 2-7.\n\n"
    }while ((number<2)||(number>7));
    cout<<"\n\n"<<number<<"! = ";
    cout<<factorial(number)<<"\n\n";
    return 0;
}
```

```
4.
//prime.h
//Holds prototype for function to determine
//whether an integer is prime.

#ifndef PRIME_H
#define PRIME_H

enum boolean {FALSE, TRUE};

boolean is_prime(int entry);
```

```
#endif
------------------------------------------------------


//prime.cpp
//Holds definition of function to determine
//whether an integer is prime.

#include <math.h>
#include "prime.h"

boolean is_prime(int entry)
{
    boolean prime_num = TRUE;

    int count, root = sqrt(entry);
    //Decimal part removed by truncation.

    if ((entry%2 == 0) && (entry != 2))
    //An even number > 2.
        prime_num = FALSE;
    else
        count = 3;
    while ((prime_num) && (count <= root))
    {
        if (entry%count == 0)
            prime_num = FALSE;
        else
            count = count+2;
        //Step through odd integers.
    }
    return prime_num;
}
------------------------------------------------------


//primetst.cpp
//Accepts an integer and determines whether or not
//it is prime.

#include <iostream.h>
#include "prime.h"

main()
{
    int entry;

    do
    {
        cout<<"\n\n\n";
        cout<<"Enter an integer greater than 1 :   ";
```

```
            cin>>entry;
            if (entry < 2)
            {
                cout<<"\n\n\n";
                cout<<"\a*** Invalid entry. Try again! ***"
            };
        }while (entry < 2);

        cout<<"\n\n\n";
        if (is_prime(entry))
            cout<<entry<<" IS prime.";
        else
            cout<<entry<<" is NOT prime.";
        return 0;
}
```

5.
```
//gcdfunc.h
//Holds prototype for function to return greatest
//common divisor of any 2 positive integers.

#ifndef GCDFUNC_H
#define GCDFUNC_H

int gcd(int, int);

#endif
-------------------------------------------------------

//gcdfunc.cpp
//Holds definition of function which returns greatest
//common divisor of any 2 positive integers.

#include "gcdfunc.h"

enum boolean{FALSE, TRUE};

int gcd(int n1, int n2)
{
    if ((n1<=0) || (n2<=0)) return 0;
    //Mustn't depend upon application program
    //carrying out this check!

    if (n1%n2 == 0) return n2;
    //n1 a multiple of n2.

    if (n2%n1 == 0) return n1;
```

```
    //n2 a multiple of n1.

    int max_divisor;
    //Variable declarations can occur anywhere
    //within a C++ program.

    if (n1<n2)
        max_divisor = n1/2;
        //Start with highest possible value.
    else
        max_divisor = n2/2;      //(Integer division)

    boolean divisor_found = FALSE;
    do
    {
        if ((n1%max_divisor == 0)
                        && (n2%max_divisor ==0))
            divisor_found = TRUE;
        else
            max_divisor--;
    }while(!divisor_found);
    //Loop must terminate, since both numbers
    //will at least be divisible by 1.

    return max_divisor;
}
------------------------------------------------------


//find_gcd.cpp
//Accepts pairs of integers and, for each pair,
//returns the greatest common divisor.

#include <iostream.h>
#include "gcdfunc.h"

main()
{
    int num1, num2;
    char reply;

    do
    {
        do
        {
            cout<<"Enter 2 positive integers, ";
            cout<<"separated by spaces :   ";
            cin>>num1>>num2;
            if ((num1<=0) || (num2<=0))
                cout<<"\a\n\nNumbers must be > zero!\n\n";
```

```
        }while ((num1<=0) || (num2<=0));
        cout<<"\nGreatest common divisor of ";
        cout<<num1<<" and "<<num2;
        cout<<" is "<<gcd(num1,num2);
        cout<<"\n\nDo this again?(y/n) :   ";
        cin>>reply;
        cout<<"\n\n";
    } while ((reply=='y') || (reply=='Y'));
    return 0;
}
```

Chapter 5

```
1.
//swapfnc1.h
//Holds prototype for function to swap contents
//of 2 integers,using pointers.

#ifndef SWAPFNC1_H
#define SWAPFNC1_H

void swap(int*, int*);

#endif
```

```
//swapfnc1.cpp
//Holds definition of function to swap contents
//of 2 integers, using pointers.

#include "swapfnc1.h"

void swap(int* int1, int* int2)
{
    int temp;

    temp = *int1;
    *int1 = *int2;

    *int2 = temp;
}
```

```
//numorder.cpp
//Accepts 3 integers and employs a function to sort them
```

```
//into ascending order, using pointers.

#include <iostream.h>
#include "swapfnc1.h"

void rearrange(int* int1, int* int2, int* int3);
//Unlikely to be reusable for specifically
//3 values, so not in header file.

main()
{
    int first, second, third;

    cout<<"Enter 3 integers :   ";
    cin>>first>>second>>third;
    rearrange(&first, &second, &third);
    cout<<"\n\nAscending sequence :   ";
    cout<<first<<"   "<<second<<"   "<<third<<"\n\n";
    return 0;
}

void rearrange(int* int1, int* int2, int* int3)
{
    if (*int1 > *int2) {swap(int1,int2);}
    if (*int2 > *int3) {swap(int2,int3);}
    if (*int1 > *int2) {swap(int1,int2);}
}


2.
//swapfnc2.h
//Contains prototype for function to swap contents
//of 2 integers, using references.

#ifndef SWAPFNC2_H
#define SWAPFNC2_H

void swap(int&, int&);

#endif
-----------------------------------------------------

//swapfnc2.cpp
//Contains definition of function to swap contents
//of 2 integers, using references.

#include "swapfnc2.h"

void swap(int& int1, int& int2)
```

```
{
    int temp;

    temp = int1;
    int1 = int2;
    int2 = temp;
}
```

```
//numorder.cpp
//Accepts 3 integers and employs a function to put them
//into ascending order, using references.

#include <iostream.h>
#include "swapfnc2.h"

void rearrange(int& int1, int& int2, int& int3);

main()
{
    int first, second, third;

    cout<<"Enter 3 integers :   ";
    cin>>first>>second>>third;
    rearrange(first, second, third);
    cout<<"\n\nAscending sequence :   ";
    cout<<first<<"   "<<second<<"   "<<third<<"\n\n";

    return 0;
}

void rearrange(int& int1, int& int2, int& int3)
{
    if (int1 > int2) {swap(int1,int2);}
    if (int2 > int3) {swap(int2,int3);}
    if (int1 > int2) {swap(int1,int2);}
}
```

```
3.
//exmfuncs.h
//Contains prototypes for functions to process
//exam results.

#ifndef EXMFUNCS_H
#define EXMFUNCS_H

#include <iostream.h>
#include <iomanip.h>
```

```cpp
void get_data(int, char[][15],int[][3],float[3]);
void show_results(int, char[][15],int[][3],float[3]);

#endif
```

```cpp
//exmfuncs.cpp
//Contains implementation of functions to process
//exam results.

#include "exmfuncs.h"
#include <iomanip.h>

const char* exam[3] = {"English","Maths","French"};
//Convenient for naming specific subject
//on each loop iteration.

void get_data(int num_pupils, char name[][15],
                        int mark[][3], float average[3])
{
    for (int pupil_num=0; pupil_num<num_pupils;
                                        pupil_num++)
    {
        cout<<"Enter name of pupil ";
        cout<<(pupil_num+1)<<" : ";
        cin>>name[pupil_num];
        cout<<'\n';
        for (int exam_num=0; exam_num<3; exam_num++)
        {
            cout<<'\n';
            cout<<"Enter "<<exam[exam_num]<<" mark:";
            cin>>mark[pupil_num][exam_num];
            average[exam_num]+= mark[pupil_num][exam_num];
        }
        cout<<"\n\n\n";
    }
    for (int exam_num=0; exam_num<3; exam_num++)
    {
        average[exam_num] /= num_pupils;
    }
}

void show_results(int num_pupils, char name[][15],
                        int mark[][3], float average[3])
{
    cout<<"Name"<<"                English   Maths";
    cout<<"     French\n";
    cout<<"----"<<"                -------   -----";
```

```
    cout<<"      ------\n\n";
    for (int pupil_num=0; pupil_num<num_pupils;
                            pupil_num++)
    {
        cout<<name[pupil_num]<<"     ";
        for (int exam_num=0; exam_num<3; exam_num++)
            cout<<"       "<<mark[pupil_num][exam_num];
        cout<<'\n';
    }
    cout<<"\nAverage : ";
    cout<<setiosflags(ios::fixed)<<setprecision(1);
    for (int exam_num=0; exam_num<3; exam_num++)
        cout<<"       "<<average[exam_num];
    cout<<"\n\n";
}
```

```
//exams.cpp
//Accepts the names and exam marks of 4 school
//pupils and then displays the results in a table.

#include "exmfuncs.h"

main()
{
    const int NUM_PUPILS = 4;
    char name[NUM_PUPILS][15];
    int mark[NUM_PUPILS][3];
    float average[3]= {0.0,0.0,0.0};

    get_data(NUM_PUPILS, name,mark,average);
    show_results(NUM_PUPILS, name,mark,average);
    return 0;
}
```

```
4.
//strfuncs.h
//Contains prototypes for 2 string-handling functions
//and prototypes for functions to demonstrate the use
//of those string-handling functions.

#ifndef STRFUNCS_H
#define STRFUNCS_H

int strpos(const char*, const char);

char* strcat(char*, const char*);
```

```
void strpos_demo();

void strcat_demo();

#endif
------------------------------------------------------------

//strfuncs.cpp
//Implementation of 2 string-handling functions
//and demonstration functions.

#include <iostream.h>
#include "strfuncs.h"

int strpos(const char* s, const char c)
{
    for (int count=0; s[count]; count++)
    {
        if (s[count] == c) return (count+1);
    }
    return 0;
}

char* strcat(char* s1, const char* s2)
{
    for (int count1=0; s1[count1]; count1++)
        ;
    //Nothing in body of loop.
    //Exit when null character found.

    for (int count2=0; s2[count2]; count2++,count1++)
    {
        s1[count1] = s2[count2];
    }
    s1[count1] = '\0';
    return s1;
}

void strpos_demo()
{
    char string1[20], string2[20];
    char char_in[2];

    cout<<"Demonstration of strpos function\n";
    cout<<"-------------- -- ------ --------\n\n";
    cout<<"Enter test string :  ";
    cin>>string1;
    cout<<"\nEnter 2 characters, one of which is in ";
```

```
        cout<<"string\n and the other of which is not :    ";
        cin>>char_in[0]>>char_in[1];
        cout<<"\n\n";

    for (int count=0; count<2; count++)
    {
        cout<<"Character "<<(count+1);

        int char_pos = strpos(string1,char_in[count]);

        if (char_pos)
        {
            cout<<" occurs at position "<<char_pos;
            cout<<" in string "<<string1;
        }
        else
        {
            cout<<" is not in string "<<string1;
        }
        cout<<".\n\n\n";
    }
}

void strcat_demo()
{
    char string1[20], string2[20];

    cout<<"\nDemonstration of strcat function\n";
    cout<<"------------- -- ------ --------\n\n";
    cout<<"Enter test string 1 :   ";
    cin>>string1;
    cout<<"\nEnter test string 2 :   ";
    cin>>string2;
    cout<<"\n\nConcatenation of strings :    ";
    cout<<strcat(string1,string2)<<"\n\n\n";
}
//----------------------------------------------------

//strdemo.cpp
//Demonstrates operation of 2 string-handling
//functions.

#include "strfuncs.h"

main()
{
    strpos_demo();
    strcat_demo();
```

```
      return 0;
}
```

Chapter 6

```
1.
//exmfncs1.h
//Contains prototypes for functions to process
//examination results.

#ifndef EXMFNCS1_H
#define EXMFNCS1_H

#include <iostream.h>
#include <iomanip.h>

void get_data(intnum_pupils, char name[][15],
                 int mark[][3],float average[3]);
void show_results(intnum_pupils, char name[][15],
                 int mark[][3], float average[3]);

#endif
-------------------------------------------------------

//exmfncs1.cpp
//Contains implementation of functions to
//process examination results.

#include "exmfncs1.h"

const char* exam[3] = {"English","Maths","French"};
//Convenient for naming specific subject
//on each loop iteration.

void get_data(int num_pupils, char name[][15],
                 int mark[][3], float average[3])
{
    for (int pupil_num=0; pupil_num<num_pupils;
                                    pupil_num++)
    {
        cout<<"Enter name of pupil ";
        cout<<(pupil_num+1)<<" : ";
        cin>>name[pupil_num];
        for (int exam_num=0; exam_num<3; exam_num++)
        {
            cout<<"\nEnter "<<exam[exam_num]<<" mark : ";
```

```
                cin>>mark[pupil_num][exam_num];
                average[exam_num]+=mark[pupil_num][exam_num];
        }
        cout<<"\n\n\n";
    }
    for (int exam_num=0;exam_num<3;exam_num++)
    {
        average[exam_num] /= num_pupils;
    }
}

void show_results(int num_pupils, char name[][15],
                        int mark[][3], float average[3])
{
    cout<<setw(22)<<setiosflags(ios::left);
    cout<<"Name"<<"     English     Maths";
    cout<<"     French\n";
    cout<<setw(22)<<"----"<<"      -------    ";
    cout<<"-----      ------\n\n";
    for (int pupil_num=0;pupil_num<num_pupils;
                                        pupil_num++)
    {
        cout<<setiosflags(ios::left);
        cout<<setw(22)<<name[pupil_num];
        cout<<setiosflags(ios::right);
        for (int exam_num=0; exam_num<3; exam_num++)
        {
            cout<<setw(9);
            cout<<mark[pupil_num][exam_num]<< '\n';
        }
    }
    cout<<setiosflags(ios::left)<<setw(26)<<"Average : ";
    cout<<setw(5)<<setiosflags(ios::fixed);
    cout<<setprecision(1);
    for (int exam_num=0;exam_num<3;exam_num++)
    {
        cout<<setw(9)<<average[exam_num]<<" ";
    }
    cout<<"\n\n";
}
-----------------------------------------------------

//exams1.cpp
//Accepts the surnames and examination marks of 4 school
//pupils and then displays the results in a table.

#include "exmfncs1.h"
```

```
main()
{
    const int NUM_PUPILS = 4;
    char name[NUM_PUPILS][15];
    int mark[NUM_PUPILS][3];
    float average[3]= {0.0,0.0,0.0};

    get_data( NUM_PUPILS, name,mark,average);
    show_results(NUM_PUPILS, name,mark,average);
    return 0;
}
```

2.
```
//exmfncs2.h
//Contains prototypes for functions to process
//examination results.

#ifndef EXMFNCS2_H
#define EXMFNCS2_H

#include <iostream.h>
#include <iomanip.h>

void get_data(intnum_pupils, char name[][15],
              int mark[][3],float average[3]);
void show_results(intnum_pupils,
              char name[][15],int mark[][3],
              float average[3]);

#endif
```

```
//exmfncs2.cpp
//Contains implementation of functions to process
//examination results.

#include "exmfncs2.h"

const char* exam[3] = {"English","Maths","French"};

void get_data(intnum_pupils, char name[][15],
              int mark[][3],float average[3])
{
    for (int pupil_num=0; pupil_num<num_pupils;
                                      pupil_num++)
    {
        cout<<"Enter name of pupil ";
```

```
        cout<<(pupil_num+1)<<" : ";
        cin.getline(name[pupil_num], 30, '\n');
        cout<<'\n';
        for (int exam_num=0; exam_num<3; exam_num++)
        {
            cout<<"\nEnter "<<exam[exam_num];
            cout<<" mark : ";
            cin.ignore(80, '\n');
            average[exam_num]+=mark[pupil_num][exam_num];
        }
        cout<<"\n\n\n";
    }
    for (int exam_num=0; exam_num<3; exam_num++)
    {
            average[exam_num] /= num_pupils;
    }
}


void show_results(int num_pupils,char name[][15],
                  int mark[][3], float average[3])
{
    cout<<setw(22)<<setiosflags(ios::left);
    cout<<"Name"<<"      English   Maths French\n";
    cout<<setw(22)<<"----"<<"      -------   ";
    cout<<"-----     ------\n\n";
    for (int pupil_num=0;pupil_num<num_pupils;
                                        pupil_num++)
    {
        cout<<setiosflags(ios::left)<<setw(22);
        cout<<name[pupil_num];
        cout<<setiosflags(ios::right);
        for (int exam_num=0; exam_num<3; exam_num++)
        {
            cout<<setw(11);
            cout<<mark[pupil_num][exam_num]<<'\n';
        }
        cout<<setiosflags(ios::left)<<setw(30);
        cout<<"Average : ";
        cout<<setw(5)<<setiosflags(ios::fixed);
        cout<<setprecision(1);
        for (int exam_num=0; exam_num<3; exam_num++)
        {
            cout<<setw(11)<<average[exam_num];
        }
        cout<<"\n\n";
    }
}
--------------------------------------------------------
```

```
//exams2.cpp
//Accepts the full names and examination marks of
//4 school pupils and then displays the results
//in a table.

#include "exmfncs2.h"

main()
{
        const int NUM_PUPILS = 4;
        char name[NUM_PUPILS][26];
        int mark[NUM_PUPILS][3];
        float average[3]= {0.0,0.0,0.0};

        get_data( NUM_PUPILS, name,mark,average);
        show_results(NUM_PUPILS, name,mark,average);
        return 0;
}
```

```
3.
//stokctrl.h
//Holds prototypes for functions to accept stock
//details and retrieve stock levels.

#ifndef STOKCTRL_H
#define STOKCTRL_H


void enter_stock(unsigned int num_items, char code[][8],
                                unsigned int level[])

int level(unsigned int num_items, char code[][8],
                unsigned int level[],char code_in[])

#endif
--------------------------------------------------------

//stokctrl.cpp
//Holds definitions of functions to accept stock
//details and retrieve stock levels.

#include <iostream.h>
#include <string.h>
#include "stokctrl.h"

enum boolean{FALSE, TRUE};

void enter_stock(unsigned int num_items, char code[][8],
```

```
                                          unsigned int level[])
{
    for (int count=0; count<num_items; count++)
    {
        cout<<"Stock code for item ";
        cout<<(count+1)<<" : ";
        cin>>code[count];
        cout<<"Stock level for item ";
        cout<<(count+1)<<" :   ";
        cin>>level[count] <<"\n\n";
    }
}

int level(unsigned int num_items, char code[][8],
             unsigned int level[],char code_in[])
{
    boolean item_found = FALSE;
    int count = 0;

    while ((!item_found) && (count < num_items))
    {
        if (strcmp(strupr(code_in),
                        strupr(code[count]))==0)
            item_found = TRUE;
        else
            count++;
    }
    if (item_found) return level[count];
    else return -1;
}
-------------------------------------------------------

//stoktest.cpp
//Accepts codes and current levels of 10 items of stock.
//Then allows user to retrieve levels of any items whose
//codes are entered.

#include <iostream.h>
#include <string.h>
#include <ctype.h>
#include "stokctrl.h"

main()
{
    const int NUM_ITEMS = 10;
    char stock_code[NUM_ITEMS][8];
    unsigned int stock_level[NUM_ITEMS];
    char code_in[8];
    int level_out;
```

```cpp
    char reply;

    enter_stock(NUM_ITEMS, stock_code, stock_level);
    do
    {
        cout<<"Enter stock code for required item :   ";
        cin>>code_in;
        cout<<"\n\n";
        level_out = level(NUM_ITEMS, stock_code,
                                    stock_level, code_in);
        if (level_out == -1)
            cout<<"\a*** Invalid stock code! ***\n\n "
        else
            cout<<"Current level : "<<level_out<<"\n\n";
        cout<<"Retrieve another level? (y/n) :   ";
        cin>>reply;
    }while (tolower(reply) == 'y');
    return 0;
}



4.
//numbases.cpp
//Accepts numbers in bases 8, 10 and 16 and displays
//each in the other 2 bases.

#include <iostream.h>
#include <iomanip.h>

main()
{
    int  oct_num, dec_num, hex_num;

    cout<<"\nEnter an octal integer : ";
    cin>>oct>>oct_num;
    cout<<"Enter a decimal integer : ";
    cin>>dec>>dec_num;
    cout<<"\nEnter a hexadecimal integer : ";
    cin>>hex>>hex_num;

    cout<<"\n\n\n"<<oct<<oct_num;
    cout<<" in decimal is "<<dec<<oct_num;
    cout<<"\n"<<oct<<oct_num;
    cout<<" in hex is "<<hex<<oct_num;

    cout<<"\n\n\n"<<dec<<dec_num;
    cout<<" in octal is "<<oct<<dec_num;
    cout<<"\n"<<dec<<dec_num;
    cout<<" in hex is "<<hex<<dec_num;
```

```
    cout<<"\n\n\n"<<hex<<hex_num;
    cout<<" in decimal is "<<dec<<hex_num;
    cout<<"\n"<<hex<<hex_num;
    cout<<" in octal is "<<oct<<hex_num;
    cout<<"\n\n\n";

    return 0;
}
```

5.
```
//fmtreals.cpp
//Accepts 5 real numbers and then displays them
//in a column, using a field width of 10, 2 decimal
//places and a fill character of '*'.

#include <iostream.h>
#include <iomanip.h>

main()
{
    float real_num[5];

    for (int count=0; count<5; count++)
    {
        cout<<"Enter a real number :   ";
        cin>>real_num[count];
        cout<<"\n\n";
    }
    cout<<"\n\n";
    cout<<setiosflags(ios::fixed|ios::showpoint);
    cout<<setprecision(2)<<setfill('*');
    for (count=0; count<5; count++)
    {
        cout<<setw(10)<<real_num[count]<<'\n';
    }

    return 0;
}
```

Chapter 7

1.
```
//stkfuncs.h
//Header file for stock processing functions.
```

```cpp
#ifndef STKFUNCS_H
#define STKFUNCS_H

#include <string.h>

struct stock_item
{
   char name[30];
   unsigned int level;
};

const int ERROR = -1;

void get_details(stock_item&);

int get_level(char[30], stock_item[], int);
//arg1: stock item;  arg2: array;  arg3: current level.

#endif
```

```cpp
//stkfuncs.cpp
//Implementation of stock processing functions.

#include <iostream.h>
#include "stkfuncs.h"

void get_details(stock_item& item)
{
   cout<<"\n\nEnter name of item :   ";
   cin>>item.name;
   cout<<"\nEnter stock level :   ";
   cin>>item.level;
}

int get_level(char name_in[30], stock_item list[],
                              int num_items)
{
   for (int count=0; count<num_items; count++)
   {
      if (strcmp(list[count].name, name_in) == 0)
      {
          return list[count].level;
      }
   }
   return ERROR;      //Indicates 'not found'.
}
```

```
//stock.cpp
//Accepts names and stock levels of a pre-
//determined number of items and then allows user
//to retrieve stock levels of specified items.

#include <iostream.h>
#include <ctype.h>
#include "stkfuncs.h"

const int NUM_ITEMS = 6;

stock_item stock_list[NUM_ITEMS];

main()
{
    char name_in[30];
    int level_out;
    char reply;

    for (int count=0; count<NUM_ITEMS; count++)
    {
        get_details(stock_list[count]);
    }

    do
    {
        cout<<"\n\n\n\n Name of required item? ";
        cin>>name_in;
        level_out = get_level(name_in, stock_list,
                                          NUM_ITEMS);
        if (level_out != ERROR)
        {
            cout<<"\nStock level for this item is ";
            cout<<level_out<<"\n\n";
        }
        else
        {
            cout<<"\nThis item does not exist!\n\n";
        }
        cout<<"\nAnother stock level?(y/n) :   ";
        cin>>reply;
    } while (tolower(reply) == 'y');
    return 0;
}


2.
//robot.h
//Header file for robot class.
```

```cpp
#ifndef ROBOT_H
#define ROBOT_H

#include <iostream.h>
#include <string.h>
#include <iomanip.h>

enum direction {NORTH, SOUTH, EAST, WEST};

class robot
{
private:
   int x_dist,y_dist;
   direction curr_direction;
public:
   robot(int x=0, int y=0, direction dir=NORTH)
   {
       x_dist=x; y_dist=y; curr_direction=dir;
   }
   void move(int distance);
   void left_face();
   void right_face();
   int x_pos() {return x_dist;}
   int y_pos() {return y_dist;}
   direction orientation() {return curr_direction;}
};

void process_command(char, robot&);

char* string_dir(direction);
//Returns current direction as a string.

#endif
```

```cpp
//robot.cpp
//Implementation of robot class.

#include "robot.h"

void robot::move(int dist)
{
    switch (curr_direction)
    {
        case NORTH : y_dist += dist; break;
        case SOUTH : y_dist -= dist; break;
        case EAST  : x_dist += dist; break;
        case WEST  : x_dist -= dist;
```

```
    }
}

void robot::left_face()
{
    switch (curr_direction)
    {
        case NORTH : curr_direction = WEST; break;
        case SOUTH : curr_direction = EAST; break;
        case EAST  : curr_direction = NORTH; break;
        case WEST  : curr_direction = SOUTH;
    }
}

void robot::right_face()
{
    switch (curr_direction)
    {
        case NORTH : curr_direction = EAST; break;
        case SOUTH : curr_direction = WEST; break;
        case EAST  : curr_direction = SOUTH; break;
        case WEST  : curr_direction = NORTH;
    }
}

void process_command (char cmd, robot& rob)
{
    switch (cmd)
    {
        case 'l' :  rob.left_face(); break;
        case 'r' :  rob.right_face(); break;
        case 'd' :  int distance;
                    cout<<"Enter distance :  ";
                    cin>>distance;
                    rob.move(distance);
                    break;
        case 'q' :  break;
        default  :  cout<<"Invalid command!\n\n";
    }
    cout<<"\n\nThe robot is currently at location";
    cout<<'('<<rob.x_pos()<<', ';
    cout<<rob.y_pos()<<") and is facing ";
    cout<<string_dir(rob.orientation())<<".\n\n";
}

char* string_dir(direction dir)
{
    switch (dir)
    {
```

```
        case    NORTH : return "North";
        case    SOUTH : return "South";
        case    EAST  : return "East";
        case    WEST  : return "West";
    }
}
```

```
//robotest.cpp
//Demonstrates use of robot class.

#include <iostream.h>
#include <ctype.h>
#include "robot.h"

void display_info(robot& rob);

main()
{
    robot robby;
    //Default values used by constructor.

    char cmd;

    display_info(robby);
    do
    {
        cout<<"\n\nEnter a command (l/r/d/q) :   ";
        cin>>cmd;
        cmd = tolower(cmd);
        process_command(cmd, robby);
    }while (cmd != 'q');
    return 0;
}

void display_info(robot& rob)
{
    cout<<"\n\n      Robot demonstration Program\n";
    cout<<"      ----- ------------- -------\n\n";
    cout<<"           l = left-turn\n";
    cout<<"           r = right-turn\n";
    cout<<"           d = distance to move\n";
    cout<<"           q = quit\n\n";
    cout<<"The robot is currently at location (";
    cout<<rob.x_pos()<<","<<rob.y_pos();
    cout<<") and is facing ";
    cout<<string_dir(rob.orientation())<<".\n\n";
}
```

```
3.
//shapes.h
//Holds classes 'point' and 'triangle'.

#ifndef SHAPES_H
#define SHAPES_H

#include <iostream.h>

//All functions inline.

class point
{
private:
    float x,y;
public:
    point(float x_val, float y_val)
    {
        x = x_val;
        y = y_val;
        cout<<"\nPoint ("<<x<<','<<y<<") created.\n\n";
    }
    ~point()
    {
        cout<<"\nPoint ("<<x<<','<<y;
        cout<<") going out of scope.\n\n";
    }
};

class triangle
{
private:
    point vertex1, vertex2, vertex3;
public:
    triangle(int x1,int y1,int x2,int y2,int x3,int y3)
    : vertex1(x1,y1), vertex2(x2,y2), vertex3(x3,y3)
    {
        cout<<"\nTriangle created.\n\n";
    }

    ~triangle()
    {
        cout<<"\nTriangle going out of scope.\n\n";
    }
};

#endif
```

```
//tripoint.cpp
//Gives a simple demonstration of the execution of
//constructors and destructors for classes point
//and triangle.

#include "shapes.h"

main()
{
    triangle tri(0,0,2,5,-3,10);
    return 0;
}
```

Chapter 8

1.
```
//linklst1.h
//Header file for unordered linked list class.
//Each node in list holds a student's name and
//exam mark.

#ifndef LINKLST1_H
#define LINKLST1_H

const int NAMESIZE = 16;
//15 for name + 1 for null terminator.

struct node
{
    char name[NAMESIZE];
    short unsigned int mark;
    node* next_node;
};

class linked_list
{
private:
    node* head;
public:
    linked_list(){head = NULL;}
    void add_node(node* new_node);
    int delete_node(char* name_in);
    short unsigned int find_mark(char* name_in);
    void display_list();
    ~linked_list();
};
```

```
#endif
---------------------------------------------------------

//linklst1.cpp
//Implementation of unordered linked list class of
//examination results.

#include <iostream.h>
#include <iomanip.h>
#include <string.h>
#include "linklst1.h"

enum boolean{FALSE, TRUE};

void linked_list::add_node(node* new_node)
{
    new_node->next_node=head;
    head = new_node;
}

int linked_list::delete_node(char* search_name)
{
    node* before_node = head;
    node* this_node = head;
    boolean found = FALSE;

    while ((this_node!=NULL) && (!found))
    //Not at end of list and name not found.
    {
        if (strcmp(this_node->name, search_name)==0)
            found = TRUE;
        else
        {
            before_node = this_node;
            this_node = this_node->next_node;
        }
    }
    if (found)
    {
        if (this_node == head)
        {
            node* old_head = head;
            head = head->next_node;
            delete old_head;
        }
        else
        {
            before_node->next_node = this_node->next_node;
            delete this_node;
```

```
        }
        return 1;     //Node deleted.
    }
    return 0;
    //End of list reached without finding name.
}

short unsigned int linked_list
::find_mark(char* search_name)
{
    node* this_node = head;

    while (this_node!=NULL)    //Not at end of list.
    {
        if (strcmp(this_node->name, search_name)==0)
            return (this_node->mark);
        else
            this_node = this_node->next_node;
    }
    return -1;
    //End of list reached without name being found.
}

void linked_list::display_list()
{
    node* this_node = head;
    char any_key;

    cout<<"              Name                  Mark\n";
    cout<<"              ----                  ----\n\n";
    while (this_node != NULL)
    //Not at end of list.
    {
        cout<<"          "<<setiosflags(ios::left);
        cout<<setw(20)<<this_node->name;
        cout<<setiosflags(ios::right)<<setw(3);
        cout<<this_node->mark<<"\n";
        this_node = this_node->next_node;
    }
    cout<<"\n\n\nPress any key to continue ... ";
    cin>>any_key;
}

linked_list::~linked_list()
{
    node* old_head = head;

    while (head != NULL)
```

```
        //Until end of list reached.
        {
            old_head = head;
            head = head->next_node;
            delete old_head;
        }
        cout<<"\n\n*** List deleted ***\n\n";
}
-----------------------------------------------------

//examlst1.cpp
//Creates and processes an unordered linked list
//holding names and examination marks.

#include <iostream.h>
#include <iomanip.h>
#include "linklst1.h"

//Top-level functions. Might have been placed in header.
void display_menu();
void do_add_node();
void do_find_mark();
void do_delete_node();

linked_list list;
char any_key;

main()
{
    char option;

    do
    {
        display_menu();
        cout<<"Enter your choice (1-5) :   ";
        cin>>option;
        cout<<"\n\n";
        switch (option)
        {
            case '1' :     do_add_node();
                           break;

            case '2' :     do_delete_node();
                           break;

            case '3' :     do_find_mark();
                           break;

            case '4' :     list.display_list();
```

```
                              break;

          case '5' :        break;          //'Quit' option.

          default   :       cout<<"\nInvalid option!\n";
                            cout<<"Press any key... ";
                            cin>>any_key;
      }
   }while (option!='5');
   cout<<"\n\n\n";
   return 0;
}

void display_menu()
{
   cout<<"\n\n\n  Linked List Program\n";
   cout<<"  ------ ---- -------\n\n\n";
   cout<<"  1. Add a node to the list.\n\n";
   cout<<"  2. Delete a node from the list.\n\n";
   cout<<"  3. Find a student's mark.\n\n";
   cout<<"  4. Display the contents of the list.\n\n";
   cout<<"  5. Quit.\n\n\n\n";
}

void do_add_node()
{
   node* new_node = new node;

   cout<<"Enter name :   ";
   cin>>new_node->name;
   cout<<"\nEnter mark :   ";
   cin>>new_node->mark;
   list.add_node(new_node);
}

void do_find_mark()
{
   char search_name[NAMESIZE];
   short int mark;

   cout<<"\nEnter name :   ";
   cin>>search_name;
   mark = list.find_mark(search_name);
   if (mark!=-1)
   {
       cout<<"\n\nMark for "<<search_name;
       cout<<" is "<<setw(2)<<mark<<"\n\n\n";
   }
   else
```

```
            cout<<"\n\nName not in list.\n\n\n";
     cout<<"Press any key to continue ... ";
     cin>>any_key;
}


void do_delete_node()
{
    char search_name[NAMESIZE];

    cout<<"Enter name for node to be deleted :   ";
    cin>>search_name;
    if (list.delete_node(search_name))
        cout<<"\n\nNode deleted.\n\n";
    else
        cout<<"\n\nName not in list.\n\n\n";
    cout<<"Press any key to continue ... ";
    cin>>any_key;
}



2.
//linklst2.h
//Header file for unordered linked list class.
//Each node in list holds a student's name and
//examination mark.
//Memory for names is allocated dynamically.

#ifndef LINKLST2_H
#define LINKLST2_H

struct node
{
    char* name;
    short unsigned int mark;
    node* next_node;
};

class linked_list
{
private:
    node* head;
public:
    linked_list(){head = NULL;}
    void add_node(node* new_node);
    int delete_node(char* name_in);
    short unsigned int find_mark(char* name_in);
    void display_list();
    ~linked_list();
};
```

```
#endif
-------------------------------------------------------

//linklst2.cpp
//Implementation of unordered linked list class of
//examination results.
//Memory for names allocated dynamically.

#include <iostream.h>
#include <iomanip.h>
#include <string.h>
#include "linklst2.h"

enum boolean{FALSE, TRUE};

void linked_list::add_node(node* new_node)
{
    new_node->next_node=head;
    head = new_node;
}

int linked_list::delete_node(char* search_name)
{
    node* before_node = head;
    node* this_node = head;
    boolean found = FALSE;

    while ((this_node!=NULL) && (!found))
    //Not at end of list and name not found.
    {
        if (strcmp(this_node->name, search_name)==0)
            found = TRUE;
        else
        {
            before_node = this_node;
            this_node = this_node->next_node;
        }
    }
    if (found)
    {
        if (this_node == head)
        {
            node* old_head = head;
            head = head->next_node;

            delete old_head->name;
            //Deallocate space for name.
```

```
            delete old_head;
            //Deallocate space for node.
        }
        else
        {
            before_node->next_node = this_node->next_node;
            delete this_node;
        }
        return 1;    //Node deleted.
    }
    return 0;
    //End of list reached without finding name.
}

short unsigned int linked_list
::find_mark(char* search_name)
{
    node* this_node = head;

    while (this_node!=NULL)    //Not at end of list.
    {
        if (strcmp(this_node->name, search_name)==0)
            return (this_node->mark);
        else
            this_node = this_node->next_node;
    }
    return -1;
    //End of list reached without name being found.
}

void linked_list::display_list()
{
    node* this_node = head;
    char any_key;

    cout<<"              Name                    Mark\n";
    cout<<"              ----                    ----\n\n";
    while (this_node!=NULL)  //Not at end of list.
    {
        cout<<"           "<<setiosflags(ios::left);
        cout<<setw(20)<<this_node->name;
        cout<<setiosflags(ios::right)<<setw(3);
        cout<<this_node->mark<<'\n';
        this_node = this_node->next_node;
    }
    cout<<"\n\n\nPress any key to continue ... ";
    cin>>any_key;
}
```

```
linked_list::~linked_list()
{
    node* old_head = head;

    while (head != NULL)
    //Until end of list reached.
    {
        old_head = head;
        head = head->next_node;

        delete old_head;
        //Deallocate space for node.
    }
    cout<<"*** List deleted ***\n\n";
}
```

```
//examlst2.cpp
//Creates and processes an unordered linked list
//holding names and examination marks.
//Memory for names allocated dynamically.

#include <iostream.h>
#include <iomanip.h>
#include <string.h>
#include "linklst2.h"

//Top-level functions.
void display_menu();
void do_add_node();
void do_find_mark();
void do_delete_node();

const int NAMESIZE = 16;
//15 for name + 1 for null terminator.

linked_list list;
char any_key;

main()
{
    char option;

    do
    {
        display_menu();
        cout<<"Enter your choice (1-5) :   ";
        cin>>option;
        cout<<"\n\n";
```

```
        switch (option)
        {
            case '1' :      do_add_node();
                            break;

            case '2' :      do_delete_node();
                            break;

            case '3' :      do_find_mark();
                            break;

            case '4' :      list.display_list();
                            break;

            case '5' :      break;          //'Quit' option.

            default  :      cout<<"\nInvalid option!\n";
                            cout<<"Press any key... ";
                            cin>>any_key;
        }
    }while (option!='5');
    cout<<"\n\n\n";
    return 0;
}

void display_menu()
{
    cout<<"\n\n\n  Linked List Program\n";
    cout<<"   ------ ---- -------\n\n\n";
    cout<<"  1. Add a node to the list.\n\n";
    cout<<"  2. Delete a node from the list.\n\n";
    cout<<"  3. Find a student's mark.\n\n";
    cout<<"  4. Display the contents of the list.\n\n";
    cout<<"  5. Quit.\n\n\n\n";
}

void do_add_node()
{
    char name_in[MAX_NAMESIZE];
    node* new_node = new node;

    cout<<"Enter name :   ";
    cin>>name_in;

    new_node->name = new char[strlen(name_in)+1];
    //Address copied.
    strcpy(new_node->name, name_in);
    //Contents copied.
```

```
    cout<<"\nEnter mark :   ";
    cin>>new_node->mark;
    list.add_node(new_node);
}

void do_find_mark()
{
    char search_name[MAX_NAMESIZE];
    short int mark;

    cout<<"\nEnter name :   ";
    cin>>search_name;
    mark = list.find_mark(search_name);
    if (mark!=-1)
    {
        cout<<"\n\nMark for "<<search_name<<" is ";
        cout<<setw(2)<<mark<<"\n\n\n";
    }
    else
        cout<<"\n\nName not in list.\n\n\n";
    cout<<"Press any key to continue ... ";
    cin>>any_key;
}

void do_delete_node()
{
    char search_name[MAX_NAMESIZE];

    cout<<"Enter name for node to be deleted :   ";
    cin>>search_name;
    if (list.delete_node(search_name))
        cout<<"\n\nNode deleted.\n\n";
    else
        cout<<"\n\nName not in list.\n\n\n";
    cout<<"Press any key to continue ... ";
    cin>>any_key;

}


3.
//ordllist.h
//Header file for alphabetically ordered linked
//list class.
//Each node in list holds a student's full name and
//examination mark.
//Memory for names allocated dynamically.

#ifndef ORDLLIST_H
```

```
#define ORDLLIST_H

struct node
{
    char* surname;
    char* first_name;
    short unsigned int mark;
    node* next_node;
};

class linked_list
{
private:
    node* head;
    void find_pos(char*, char*, node*&, node*&);
    //Used by 'add_node' to find insertion position.
    //Arguments 1 and 2 : surname + first_name.
    //Argument 3 : node before insertion pos.
    //Argument 4 : node after insertion pos.
public:
    linked_list(){head = NULL;}
    void add_node(node*);
    int delete_node(char*, char*);
    short unsigned int find_mark(char*, char*);
    void display_list();
    ~linked_list();
};

#endif
```

```
//linklst3.cpp
//Implementation of alphabetically ordered linked list
//class of examination results.
//Memory for names allocated dynamically.

#include <iostream.h>
#include <iomanip.h>
#include <string.h>
#include "linklst3.h"

enum boolean{FALSE, TRUE};

void linked_list::find_pos(char* sname, char* fname,
                node*& before_node, node*& after_node)
{
    before_node = head;
    after_node = head;
    boolean pos_found = FALSE;
```

```
    int surname_diff;

    while ((after_node!=NULL) && (!pos_found))
    {
        surname_diff =
            strcmp(sname, after_node->surname);
        if ((surname_diff<0) ||
          ((surname_diff==0)
                 &&
          (strcmp(fname,after_node->first_name)<0)))
        {
            pos_found = TRUE;
        }
        else
        {
            before_node = after_node;
            after_node = after_node->next_node;
        }
    }
}

void linked_list::add_node(node* new_node)
{
    node* before_node;
    node* after_node;

    find_pos(new_node->surname, new_node->first_name,
                            before_node, after_node);
    if (after_node == head)
    {
        new_node->next_node=head;
        head = new_node;
    }
    else
    {
        before_node->next_node = new_node;
        new_node->next_node = after_node;
    }
}

int linked_list::delete_node(char* sname, char* fname)
{
    node* before_node = head;
    node* this_node = head;
    boolean found = FALSE;
    int surname_diff;

    while ((this_node!=NULL) && (!found))
    //Not at end of list and name not found.
```

```
    {
        surname_diff = strcmp(sname, this_node->surname);
        if ((surname_diff < 0) ||
          ((surname_diff == 0)
                &&
        (strcmp(fname, this_node->first_name) < 0)))
        {
            found = TRUE;
        }
        else
        {
            before_node = this_node;
            this_node = this_node->next_node;
        }
    }
    if (found)
    {
        if (this_node == head)
        {
            node* old_head = head;
            head = head->next_node;

            delete old_head->surname;
            //Deallocate space for surname.

            delete old_head->first_name;
            //Deallocate space for  first name.

            delete old_head;
        //Deallocate space for node.
        }
        else
        {
            before_node->next_node = this_node->next_node;
            delete this_node;
        }
        return 1;   //Node deleted.
    }
    return 0;
    //End of list reached without finding name.
}

short unsigned int linked_list
::find_mark(char* sname, char* fname)
{
    node* this_node = head;
    int surname_diff, firstname_diff;

    while (this_node!=NULL)  //Not at end of list.
```

```
    {
        surname_diff = strcmp(sname, this_node->surname);
        firstname_diff =
                strcmp(fname, this_node->first_name);
        if ((surname_diff==0)&&(firstname_diff==0))
            return (this_node->mark);
        else if (surname_diff < 0)
            return -1;
        else if ((surname_diff==0) &&(firstname_diff<0))
            return -1;
        else
            this_node = this_node->next_node;
    }
    return -1;
    //End of list reached without name being found.
}


void linked_list::display_list()
{
    node* this_node = head;
    char full_name[32];
    char any_key;

    cout<<"       Name                      Mark\n";
    cout<<"       ----                      ----\n\n";
    while (this_node!=NULL)    //Not at end of list.
    {
        cout<<"       "<<setiosflags(ios::left);
        cout<<setw(32);
        strcpy(full_name,
                strcat(this_node->first_name, " "));
        strcpy(full_name,
            strcat(full_name, this_node->surname));
        cout<<full_name;

        cout<<setiosflags(ios::right)<<setw(3);
        cout<<this_node->mark<<'\n';
        this_node = this_node->next_node;
    }
    cout<<"\n\n\nPress any key to continue ... ";
    cin>>any_key;
}


linked_list::~linked_list()
{
    node* old_head = head;

    while (head != NULL)
    //Until end of list reached.
```

```
    {
        old_head = head;
        head = head->next_node;

        delete old_head->surname;
        //Deallocate space for surname.

        delete old_head->first_name;
        //Deallocate space for first name.

        delete old_head;
        //Deallocate space for node.
    }
    cout<<"\n\n*** List deleted ***\n\n";
}
--------------------------------------------------

//examlst3.cpp
//Creates and processes an unordered linked list
//holding names and examination marks.
//Memory for names allocated dynamically.

#include <iostream.h>
#include <iomanip.h>
#include <string.h>
#include "linklst3.h"

//Top-level functions.
void display_menu();
void do_add_node();
void do_find_mark();
void do_delete_node();

linked_list list;
const int MAX_NAMESIZE = 16;
//15 characters + '\0'.

main()
{
    char option, any_key;

    do
    {
        display_menu();
        cout<<"Enter your choice (1-5) :  ";
        cin>>option;
        cout<<"\n\n";
        switch (option)
        {
```

```
           case '1' :    do_add_node();
                         break;

           case '2' :    do_delete_node();
                         break;

           case '3' :    do_find_mark();
                         break;

           case '4' :    list.display_list();
                         break;

           case '5' :    break;       //'Quit' option.

           default  :    cout<<"\nInvalid option!\n";
                         cout<<"Press any key... ";
                         cin>>any_key;
        }
    }while (option!='5');
    cout<<"\n\n\n";
    return 0;
}

void display_menu()
{
    cout<<"\n\n\n  Linked List Program\n";
    cout<<"  ------ ---- -------\n\n\n";
    cout<<"  1. Add a node to the list.\n\n";
    cout<<"  2. Delete a node from the list.\n\n";
    cout<<"  3. Find a student's mark.\n\n";
    cout<<"  4. Display the contents of the list.\n\n";
    cout<<"  5. Quit.\n\n\n\n";
}

void do_add_node()
{
    char surname_in[MAX_NAMESIZE];
    char first_name_in[MAX_NAMESIZE];
    node* new_node = new node;

    cout<<"Enter surname :  ";
    cin>>surname_in;

    new_node->surname = new char[strlen(surname_in)+1];
    //Address copied.
    strcpy(new_node->surname, surname_in);
    //Contents copied.
```

```
    cout<<"\nEnter first name :   ";
    cin>>first_name_in;

    new_node->first_name =
                    new char[strlen(first_name_in)+1];
                    //Address copied.
    strcpy(new_node->first_name, first_name_in);
    //Contents copied.

    cout<<"\nEnter mark :   ";
    cin>>new_node->mark;
    list.add_node(new_node);
}

void do_find_mark()
{
    char    search_sname[MAX_NAMESIZE],
            search_fname[MAX_NAMESIZE]
            any_key;
    short int mark;

    cout<<"\nEnter surname :   ";
    cin>>search_sname;
    cout<<"\nEnter first name :   ";
    cin>>search_fname;
    mark = list.find_mark(search_sname, search_fname);
    if (mark!=-1)
    {
        cout<<"\n\nMark for "<<search_fname;
        cout<<' '<<search_sname;
        cout<<" is "<<setw(2)<<mark<<"\n\n\n";
    }
    else
        cout<<"\n\nName not in list.\n\n\n";
    cout<<"Press any key to continue ... ";
    cin>>any_key;
}

void do_delete_node()
{
    char    search_sname[MAX_NAMESIZE],
            search_fname[MAX_NAMESIZE],
            any_key;

    cout<<"Surname for node to be deleted :   ";
    cin>>search_sname;
    cout<<"\nFirst name for node to be deleted :   ";
    cin>>search_fname;
    if (list.delete_node(search_sname,search_fname))
```

```
        cout<<"\n\nNode deleted.\n\n";
    else
        cout<<"\n\nName not in list.\n\n\n";
    cout<<"Press any key to continue ... ";
    cin>>any_key;
}
```

Chapter 9

1.   [Code supplied.]

```
2.
//staff.h
//Header file for employee hierarchy of classes.

#ifndef STAFF_H
#define STAFF_H

#include <iostream.h>
#include <iomanip.h>
#include <string.h>

class employee
{
protected:
    char name[30];
    unsigned long start_date;
    unsigned long emp_number;
    char dept[20];
public:
    employee(char*, unsigned long, unsigned long, char*);
    ~employee()
    {
        cout<<'\n'<<name<<"\n\n";
    }
    char* get_name() {return name;}
    unsigned long get_start_date()
    {
        return start_date;
    }
    unsigned long get_emp_no() {return emp_number;}
    char* get_dept() {return dept;}
    void change_name(char* new_name)
    {
```

```
            strcpy(name, new_name);
    }
};

class manager : public employee
{
private:
    unsigned long salary;
public:
    manager(char*, unsigned long, unsigned long, char*,
                            unsigned long sal=35000L);
    ~manager(){cout<<"\n\n\n*** Manager ***\n";}
    unsigned long get_salary() {return salary;}
    void change_salary(unsigned long sal)
    {
        salary = sal;
    }
};

class staff : public employee
{
private:
    float hours_per_wk;
    float hourly_rate;
public:
    staff(char*, unsigned long, unsigned long, char*,
                            float, float hours = 40);
    ~staff(){cout<<"\n\n\n*** Staff member ***\n";}
    void change_hours(float hours)
    {
        hours_per_wk = hours;
    }
    void change_rate(float rate)
    {
        hourly_rate = rate;
    }
    unsigned long get_wage()
    {
        return (hours_per_wk * hourly_rate);
    }
};

#endif
```

```
//staff.cpp
//Implementation of employee class hierarchy.

#include "staff.h"
```

```
employee::employee(char* person, unsigned long date,
              unsigned long emp_no, char* dept_name)
{
    strcpy(name, person);
    start_date = date;
    emp_number = emp_no;
    strcpy(dept, dept_name);
}

manager::manager(char* person,unsigned long date,
unsigned long emp_no,char* dept_name,unsigned long sal)
:employee(person, date, emp_no, dept_name)
{
    salary = sal;
}

staff::staff(char* person, unsigned long date, unsigned
long emp_no, char* dept_name, float rate, float hours)
:employee(person,date,emp_no,dept_name)
{
    hourly_rate = rate;
    hours_per_wk = hours;
}
-------------------------------------------------------

//employee.cpp
//Uses the employee class hierarchy to create 3
//managers, 5 staff and 3 departments, after which
//their details are displayed in a table.

#include "staff.h"

main()
{
    const short int NUM_MGRS = 3;
    const short int NUM_STAFF = 5;

    manager boss[NUM_MGRS] =
    {   manager("Michael Jones", 12051973L, 123456L,
                          "Sales", 32000),
        manager("Julie Fisher", 9121980L, 234567L,
              "Despatch"),  // Default salary
        manager("James Cotton", 18071962L, 102102L,
                      "Finance",41500L) };

    staff subord[NUM_STAFF] =
        {staff("Linda Reynolds",14031959L,101307L,
                          "Finance", 15.5, 37.5),
        staff("Harold Perkins", 27101968L, 121121L,
```

```
                                  "Despatch", 12),//Default rate
            staff("Dean Thompson", 6111989L, 234234L,
                                       "Sales", 9.5, 48),
            staff("Paula Burton", 11081975L, 134567L,
                                       "Sales",10, 35),
            staff("Susan Porter", 31081991L, 144578L,
                           "Despatch", 15) };//Default rate

    cout<<"\n\n\n                      Employee Details\n";
    cout<<"                     --------- -------\n\n";
    cout<<"Name                          Start Date    ";
    cout<<"Emp. No.     Salary/Wage\n";
    cout<<"----                          ----------    ";
    cout<<"--------     -----------\n\n";

    for (int count=0; count<NUM_MGRS; count++)
    {
        cout<<setiosflags(ios::left)<<setw(24);
        cout<<boss[count].get_name();
        cout<<setiosflags(ios::right);
        cout<<setw(8)<<boss[count].get_start_date();
        cout<<setw(12)<<boss[count].get_emp_no();
        cout<<setw(15)<<boss[count].get_salary()<<"\n";
    }

    for (count=0; count<NUM_STAFF; count++)
    {
        cout<<setiosflags(ios::left)<<setw(24);
        cout<<subord[count].get_name();
        cout<<setiosflags(ios::right);
        cout<<setw(8)<<subord[count].get_start_date();
        cout<<setw(12)<<subord[count].get_emp_no();
        cout<<setw(15)<<subord[count].get_wage()<<"\n";
    }
    return 0;
}
```

Chapter 10

```
1.
//account.h
//Header file for account class hierarchy.

#ifndef ACCOUNT_H
#define ACCOUNT_H
```

```cpp
class account
{
protected:
    unsigned long int acct_num;
    double balance;
public:
    account(unsigned long acct_no,
                double balance_in = 0.0)
    {
        acct_num = acct_no;
        balance = balance_in;
    }
    virtual ~account();
};

class savings_account : public account
{
protected:
    double rate;
public:
    savings_account(unsigned long acct_no,
    float rate_in, double balance_in = 0.0)
    : account(acct_no, balance_in)
    {
        rate = rate_in/100;
    }
    virtual ~savings_account();
};

class current_account : public account
{
protected:
    double limit;
    double charge;
public:
    current_account(unsigned long acct_no,
    double balance_in = 0.0, double limit_in = 0.0,
    double charge_in = 0.75)
    : account(acct_no, balance_in)
    {
        limit = limit_in;
        charge = charge_in;
    }
    virtual ~current_account();
};

#endif
```

```
//account.cpp
//Implementation of account classes.

#include "account.h"
#include <iomanip.h>

account::~account()
{
    cout<<"Final balance for account no. ";
    cout<<acct_num;
    cout<<setiosflags(ios::fixed|ios::showpoint);
    cout<<setprecision(2)<<" :   £"<<balance<<'\n';
}

savings_account::~savings_account()
{
    cout<<"\nCurrent rate for account no. ";
    cout<<acct_num<<" :   ";
    cout<<setiosflags(ios::fixed|ios::showpoint);
    cout<<setprecision(2)<<rate<<"%\n";
}

current_account::~current_account()
{
    cout<<"\nCurrent limit for account no. ";
    cout<<acct_num;
    cout<<setiosflags(ios::fixed|ios::showpoint);
    cout<<setprecision(2)<<" :   £"<<limit<<'\n';
    cout<<"Current charge for account no. ";
    cout<<acct_num;
    cout<<setiosflags(ios::fixed|ios::showpoint);
    cout<<setprecision(2)<<" :   £"<<charge<<'\n';
}
//----------------------------------------------------

//acctdemo.cpp
//Creates and destroys a savings_account object
//and a current_account object.

#include "account.h"

main()
{
    savings_account save_acct(123456L, 237.59, 2.75);
    current_account curr_acct(999999L, 5394.72, 1000);
    //Default charge assumed.
    return 0;
}
```

2.
```
//shapes.h
//Holds declaration of shape class hierarchy.

#ifndef SHAPES_H
#define SHAPES_H

#include <iostream.h>
#include <iomanip.h>

const float PI = 3.142;

class shape
{
protected:
    float x, y;
    static int num_shapes;
public:
    shape(float x_val, float y_val);
    virtual float area() {}  //Empty in base class.
    virtual ~shape();
};

class circle : public shape
{
protected:
    float radius;
public:
    circle(float x_val, float y_val,
    float rad):shape(x_val, y_val)
    {
        radius = rad;
    }
    virtual float area()
    {
        return (PI*radius*radius);
    }
    virtual ~circle();
};

class rectangle : public shape
{
protected:
    float length, breadth;
public:
    rectangle(float x_val, float y_val, float len,
    float width): shape(x_val, y_val)
    {
        length = len;
```

```
        breadth = width;
    }
    virtual float area() {return (length*breadth);}
    virtual ~rectangle();
};

#endif
```

```
//shapes.cpp
//Implementation of shape class hierarchy.

#include <iostream.h>
#include <iomanip.h>
#include "shapes.h"

int shape::num_shapes = 0;

shape::shape(float x_val, float y_val)
{
    x = x_val;
    y = y_val;
    num_shapes++;
}

shape::~shape()
{
    num_shapes--;
    cout<<"\n\nNumber of shapes remaining :   ";
    cout<<num_shapes<<"\n\n";
}

circle::~circle()
{
    cout<<"\n\nCircle with area ";
    cout<<setiosflags(ios::fixed)<<setprecision(1);
    cout<<area()<<" going out of scope.\n";
}

rectangle::~rectangle()
{
    cout<<"\n\nRectangle with area ";
    cout<<setiosflags(ios::fixed)<<setprecision(1);
    cout<<area()<<" going out of scope.\n";
}
```

```
//shapedem.cpp
//Creates up to 6 shape objects (circles and/or
```

```
//rectangles), using dynamic memory management.

#include <iostream.h>
#include <ctype.h>
#include "shapes.h"

void create_circle(shape*&);
void create_rectangle(shape*&);
void remove_shapes(shape**, int);

main()
{
    char reply;
    int shape_count = 0;
    shape* shape_ptr[6];

    do
    {
        do
        {
            cout<<"\n\n\nCircle or rectangle?(c/r):";
            cin>>reply;
            reply = tolower(reply);
            if ((reply!='c') && (reply!='r'))
            {
                cout<<"\a\n\n*** Invalid entry! ";
                cout<<"Try again...***\n\n";
            }
        }while ((reply!='c') && (reply!='r'));

        if (reply=='c')
            create_circle(shape_ptr[shape_count]);
        else
            create_rectangle(shape_ptr[shape_count]);
        shape_count++;

        if (shape_count==6) break;
        cout<<"\n\nCreate another shape? (y/n) :  ";
        cin>>reply;
    }while (tolower(reply) == 'y');
    remove_shapes(shape_ptr, shape_count);
    return 0;
}

void create_circle(shape*& one_shape)
{
    float x_val, y_val, rad;

    cout<<"\n\nEnter reference point coordinates, ";
```

```
        cout<<"separated by space(s) :   ";
        cin>>x_val>>y_val;
        cout<<"\nEnter radius :   ";
        cin>>rad;
        one_shape = new circle(x_val, y_val, rad);
}

void create_rectangle(shape*& one_shape)
{
        float x_val, y_val, len, width;

        cout<<"\n\nEnter reference point coordinates, ";
        cout<<"separated by space(s) :   ";
        cin>>x_val>>y_val;
        cout<<"\nEnter length and breadth, ";
        cout<separated by space(s) :   ";
        cin>>len>>width;
        one_shape=new rectangle(x_val,y_val,len,width);
}

void remove_shapes(shape** shape_ptr, int num_shapes)
{
        for (int count=0; count<num_shapes; count++)
            delete shape_ptr[count];
}


3.
//carparts.h
//Header file for classes in stock hierarchy.

#ifndef CARPARTS_H
#define CARPARTS_H

#include <iostream.h>
#include <string.h>
#include <iomanip.h>

const unsigned short MAX_MODEL = 20;

class stock
{
protected:
    unsigned int current_level;
    float price;
public:
    stock(unsigned int level, float price_in)
    {
        current_level = level;
```

```
        float price = price_in;
    }

    unsigned int get_level() {return current_level;}

    virtual void change_level(unsigned new_level)
    {
        current_level = new_level;
    }

    void change_price(float new_price)
    {
        price = new_price;
    }

    virtual ~stock()
    //Called after destructor for derived classes.
    {
        cout<<"\n\nNo. in stock :  "<<current_level;
    }
};

class part : public stock
{
private:
    unsigned int reorder_level;
    char part_num[4];
public:
    part(unsigned int curr_level, float price_in,
    unsigned int order_level,char part_no[4])
    : stock(curr_level, price_in)
    {
        reorder_level = order_level;
        strcpy(part_num,part_no);
    }

    char* get_partnum() {return part_num;}

    void set_reorder(unsigned int new_level)
    {
        reorder_level = new_level;
    }

    virtual ~part()
    {
        cout<<"\n\n\nPart number "<<part_num;
        cout<<" has been deleted...";
    }
    //Destructor for base class then called to
```

```
        //display stock level.
};

class car : public stock
{
private:
    char model[MAX_MODEL+1];
    float engine_size;
    unsigned short int max_speed;
public:
    car(unsigned int level, float price, char* model_in,
                            float size, unsigned speed);
    char* get_model() {return model;}
    virtual ~car()
    {
        cout<<"\n\n\nCar model "<<model;
        cout<<" has been deleted...";
    }
};

#endif
```

```
//carparts.cpp
//Implementation of stock hierarchy.

#include <string.h>
#include "carparts.h"

car::car(unsigned int level, float price,
char* model_in, float size, unsigned short speed)
: stock(level, price)
{
    strcpy(model, model_in);
    engine_size = size;
    max_speed = speed;
}
```

```
//stoklist.h
//Declaration of heterogeneous linked list class of
//parts and cars.

#ifndef STOKLIST_H
#define STOKLIST_H

#include "carparts.h"

struct stock_node
```

```
{
    stock* stock_ptr;
    char stock_type;      //'p' or 'c'.
    stock_node* next_node;
};

class stock_list
{
private:
    stock_node* head_ptr;
public:
    stock_list() {head_ptr = NULL;}

    void insert_stock(stock_node*& new_stock);
    //Inserts new node at head of list.

    stock_node* find_part(char part_no[4]);

    stock_node* find_car(char model[MAX_MODEL+1]);

    void display_list();

    ~stock_list();
    //Deallocates memory used for nodes.
};

void insert_part(stock_list&);

void insert_car(stock_list&);

void change_stock_level(stock_list&, char);

void query_part_level(stock_list&);

void generate_part_error();

#endif
--------------------------------------------------------

//stoklist.cpp
//Implementation of heterogeneous linked list class of
//parts and cars.

#include <iostream.h>
#include "stoklist.h"

void stock_list::insert_stock(stock_node*& new_node)
{
    new_node->next_node = head_ptr;
```

```
    //Place node at head of list.

    head_ptr = new_node; //Update head_ptr.
}

void stock_list::display_list()
{
    if (head_ptr == NULL)
    {
        cout<<"\n\n          ***\a List empty! ***";
        return;
    }

    stock_node* current_node = head_ptr;
    part* part_ptr;
    car* car_ptr;

    cout<<"Stock Item (Part/Model)    Current Level\n";
    cout<<"-----------------------    -------------\n\n";
    do
    {
        cout<<setw(15)<<setiosflags(ios::left);
        cout<<setw(28);
        if (current_node->stock_type == 'p')
        {
            part_ptr = (part*)(current_node->stock_ptr);
            cout<<part_ptr->get_partnum();
        }
        else
        {
            car_ptr = (car*)(current_node->stock_ptr);
            cout<<car_ptr->get_model();
        }
        cout<<setw(8)<<setiosflags(ios::right);
        cout<<current_node->stock_ptr->get_level();
        current_node = current_node->next_node;
    }while (current_node != NULL);
    cout<<"\n\n";
}

stock_list::~stock_list()
{
    stock_node* old_head;


    while (head_ptr!=NULL)
    {
        old_head = head_ptr;
        head_ptr = head_ptr->next_node;
```

```
        delete old_head;
    }
}

void insert_part(stock_list& slist)
{
    char part_num[4];
    unsigned int current_level, reorder_level;
    float price;

    cout<<"\n\n";
    cout<<"Enter part no. (1 letter + 2 digits) : ";
    cin>>part_num;

    cout<<"\nPrice :   ";
    cin>>price;

    cout<<"\nCurrent level :   ";
    cin>>current_level;

    cout<<"\nReorder level :   ";
    cin>>reorder_level;

    part* new_part =
    new part(current_level,price,reorder_level,part_num);
    stock_node* new_node = new stock_node;
    new_node->stock_ptr = new_part;
    new_node->stock_type = 'p';
    slist.insert_stock(new_node);
}

enum boolean{FALSE,TRUE};

stock_node* stock_list::find_part(char part_num[])
{
    stock_node* snode_ptr = head_ptr;
    part* part_ptr;
    boolean found = FALSE;

    while ((snode_ptr!=NULL) && (!found))
    {
        if (snode_ptr->stock_type == 'p')
        {
            part_ptr = (part*)(snode_ptr->stock_ptr);
            if (strcmp(part_ptr->get_partnum(),part_num)
                                                == 0)
                return snode_ptr;
        }
        snode_ptr = snode_ptr->next_node;
```

```
    }
    return NULL;
}

stock_node* stock_list::find_car(char model[])
{
    stock_node* snode_ptr = head_ptr;
    car* car_ptr;
    boolean found = FALSE;

    while ((snode_ptr!=NULL) && (!found))
    {
        if (snode_ptr->stock_type == 'c')
        {
            car_ptr = (car*)(snode_ptr->stock_ptr);
            if (strcmp(car_ptr->get_model(), model) == 0)
                return snode_ptr;
        }
        snode_ptr = snode_ptr->next_node;
    }
    return NULL;
}

void insert_car(stock_list& slist)
{
    char model[MAX_MODEL+1];
    float engine_size;
    unsigned short int max_speed;
    unsigned int current_level;
    float price;

    cout<<"\n\n";
    cout<<"Enter model name :  ";
    cin>>model;

    cout<<"\nPrice :  ";
    cin>>price;

    cout<<"\nCurrent level :  ";
    cin>>current_level;

    cout<<"\nEngine size :  ";
    cin>>engine_size;

    cout<<"\nMaximum speed :  ";
    cin>>max_speed;

    car* new_car = new
```

```
        car(current_level,price,model,engine_size,max_speed);
        stock_node* new_node = new stock_node;
        new_node->stock_ptr = new_car;
        new_node->stock_type = 'c';
        slist.insert_stock(new_node);
}

void change_stock_level(stock_list& slist,char part_car)
{
        stock_node* snode_ptr;
        char part_num[4];
        unsigned level;
        char model[MAX_MODEL+1];

        if (part_car == 'p')
        {
            cout<<"Enter part no. (1 letter + 2 digits) :  ";
            cin>>part_num;
            snode_ptr = slist.find_part(part_num);
        }
        else
        {
            cout<<"Enter model name :  ";
            cin>>model;
            snode_ptr = slist.find_car(model);
        }
        if (snode_ptr == NULL)
            generate_part_error();
        else
        {
            cout<<"\nEnter new level :";
            cin>>level;
            snode_ptr->stock_ptr->change_level(level);
        }
}

void query_part_level(stock_list& slist)
{
        stock_node* snode_ptr;
        char part_num[4];
        char any_key;

        cout<<"\n\nEnter part no. (1 letter + 2 digits) :   ";
        cin>>part_num;
        snode_ptr = slist.find_part(part_num);
        if (snode_ptr == NULL)
            generate_part_error();
        else
        {
```

```
            cout<<"\nCurrent level :   ";
            cout<<snode_ptr->stock_ptr->get_level()<<"\n\n";
            cout<<"Press any key to continue...";
            cin>>any_key;
    }
}

void generate_part_error()
{
    cout<<"\n\n\n\a";
    cout<<"           *** Part not in list! ***";
}
-----------------------------------------------------

//mainstok.cpp
//Menu-driven program which creates and processes a
//heterogeneous linked list of parts and cars.
//N.B. 'getline' has not been used to accept car models,
//so replace spaces with underscores.
//E.g., 'Vauxhall_Cavalier'.

#include <iostream.h>
#include "stoklist.h"

void display_menu();
void await_keypress();

main()
{
    stock_list stoklist;
    char option;

    do
    {
        display_menu();
        cout<<"Enter your choice (1-7) :   ";
        cin>>option;
        cout<<"\n\n";
        switch (option)
        {
            case '1' :  insert_part(stoklist);
                        break;

            case '2' :  insert_car(stoklist);
                        break;

            case '3' :  change_stock_level
                                (stoklist, 'p');
                        break;
```

```
            case '4' :  change_stock_level
                                    (stoklist, 'c');
                        break;

            case '5' :  query_part_level(stoklist);
                        break;

            case '6' :  stoklist.display_list();
                        break;

            case '7' :  break;  //'Quit' option.

            default  :  cout<<"\n\n                    ***";
                        cout<<"Invalid option! ***\n\n";
        }
        if (option != '7')
            await_keypress();
    }while (option != '7');
    cout<<"\n\n\n";
    return 0;
}

void display_menu()
{
    cout<<"\n\n\n              Car Stock Program\n";
    cout<<"              --- ----- -------\n\n\n";
    cout<<"        1. Add a part.\n\n";
    cout<<"        2. Add a model.\n\n";
    cout<<"        3. Change level of a part.\n\n";
    cout<<"        4. Change no. of cars of a model.\n\n";
    cout<<"        5. Query current part level\n\n";
    cout<<"        6. Display full stock list.\n\n";
    cout<<"        7. Quit.\n\n\n\n";
}

void await_keypress()
{
    char any_key;

    cout<<"\n\nPress any key to continue...";
    cin>>any_key;
    cout<<"\n\n";
}
```

Chapter 11

```
1.
//dates1.h
//Declaration of 'date' class.

#ifndef DATES1_H
#define DATES1_H

enum boolean {FALSE, TRUE};

class date
{
private:
    int day, month, year;
    int max_day;         //365 or 366
    int max_feb_day;     //28 or 29

    int days_in_month(int month_in);
    //Returns no. of days in month_in.

    void set_max_days(int year_in);
    //Sets max_day and max_feb_day.

    boolean leap_year(int year_in);
    void check_date(int day_in, int month_in,
                                    int year_in);
    void quit_with_error();
    //Executed for invalid date.
public:
    date(int day_in, int month_in, int year_in);

    boolean set_date(int day_in, int month_in,
                                    int year_in);
    void get_date(int& day_out, int& month_out,
                                    int& year_out);
    void operator++(int);
};

#endif
```

```
//dates1.cpp
//Implementation of 'date' class.

#include <iostream.h>
#include <stdlib.h>
```

```
//Above header file included for 'exit' function.

#include "dates1.h"

int date::days_in_month(int month_in)
{
    int month_length[12] =
        {31,max_feb_day,31,30,31,30,31,31,30,31,30,31};

    return month_length[month_in-1];
    //Array elements numbered 0-11, not 1-12.
}

boolean date::leap_year(int year_in)
{
// ......................
// ......................
    return FALSE;
}

void date::set_max_days(int year_in)
{
    max_day = 365;
    max_feb_day = 28;

    if (leap_year(year_in))
    {
        max_day++;
        max_feb_day++;
    }
}

void date::check_date(int day_in, int month_in,
                                      int year_in)
{
    if ((day_in<1) || (day_in>31)
                   || (month_in<1) || (month_in>12))
    {
        quit_with_error();
    }

    //Otherwise, set max_day to 365/366 and max_feb_day
    //to 28/29 (as appropriate) :
    set_max_days(year_in);

    switch (month_in)
    //Check that day_in doesn't exceed last day
    //for a short month_in.
    {
```

```
        case 4:  case 6:          //April, June,
        case 9:  case 11:         //September, November
                 if (day_in==31)
                     quit_with_error();
                 break;
        case 2:  if (day_in>max_feb_day)
                     quit_with_error();
    }
}

void date::quit_with_error()
{
    cout<<"\n\n\n\a*** Invalid date! ***\n\n";
    exit(1); //Non-zero value indicates an error.
}

date::date(int day_in, int month_in, int year_in)
{
    set_date(day_in, month_in, year_in);
}

boolean date::set_date(int day_in, int month_in,
                                        int year_in)
{
    check_date(day_in, month_in, year_in);
    day = day_in;
    month = month_in;
    year = year_in;
}

void date::get_date(int& day_out, int& month_out,
                                    int& year_out)
{
    day_out = day;
    month_out = month;
    year_out = year;
}

void date::operator++(int)
{
    day++;
    if (day > month_days)
    {
        //Set date to first day of next month.
        day = 1;
        month++;
        if (month > 12) //New Year!
        {
            month = 1;
```

```
            year++;
        }
    }
}
```

```
//nextdate.cpp
//Accepts 5 dates and, for each one, outputs
//the date of the following day.

#include <iostream.h>
#include "dates1.h"

main()
{
    date my_date(1,1,97);
    int day, month, year;

    for (int count=0; count<5; count++)
    {
        cout<<"Enter a date as 3 integers ";
        cout<<" (e.g., 3 11 1998) :  ";
        cin>>day>>month>>year;
        my_date.set_date(day,month,year);
        my_date++;
        my_date.get_date(day,month,year);
        cout<<"\n\nDate of following day :  ";
        cout<<day<<' '<<month<<' '<<year<<"\n\n\n";
    }
    return 0;
}
```

```
2.
//dates2.h
//Declaration of 'date' class.

#ifndef DATES2_H
#define DATES2_H

enum boolean {FALSE, TRUE};

class date
{
private:
    int day, month, year;
    int max_day;          //365 or 366
    int max_feb_day;      //28 or 29
```

```
    int days_in_month(int month_in);
    //Returns no. of days in month_in.

    void set_max_days(int year_in);
    //Sets max_day and max_feb_day.

    boolean leap_year(int year_in);

    void check_date(int day_in,int month_in,int year_in);

    void quit_with_error();
    //Executed for invalid date.
public:
    date(int day_in, int month_in, int year_in);
    boolean set_date(int day_in, int month_in,
                                        int year_in);
    void get_date(int& day_out, int& month_out,
                                    int& year_out);
    void operator++(int);
    friend boolean operator<=(date& date1, date& date2);
    friend boolean operator>(date& date1, date& date2);
    friend ostream& operator<<(ostream& ostrm,
                                    date& date_out);
    friend istream& operator>>(istream& istrm,
                                    date& date_in);
};

#endif
------------------------------------------------------

//dates2.cpp
//Implementation of 'date' class.

#include <iostream.h>
#include <iomanip.h>
#include <stdlib.h>

#include "dates2.h"

int date::days_in_month(int month_in)
{
    int month_length[12] =
        {31,max_feb_day,31,30,31,30,31,31,30,31,30,31};

    return month_length[month_in-1];
    //Array elements numbered 0-11, not 1-12.
}

boolean date::leap_year(int year_in)
```

```
{
// ......................
// ......................
    return FALSE;
}

void date::set_max_days(int year_in)
{
    max_day = 365;
    max_feb_day = 28;
    if (leap_year(year_in))
    {
        max_day++;
        max_feb_day++;
    }
}

void date::check_date(int day_in, int month_in,
                                     int year_in)
{
    if ((day_in<1) || (day_in>31)
                 || (month_in<1) || (month_in>12))
    {
        quit_with_error();
    }

    //Otherwise, set max_day to 365/366 and max_feb_day
    //to 28/29 (as appropriate) :
    set_max_days(year_in);

    switch (month_in)
    //Check that day_in doesn't exceed last day
    //for a short month_in.
    {
        case 4:  case 6:        //April, June,
        case 9:  case 11:       //September, November
                 if (day_in==31)
                     quit_with_error();
                 break;
        case 2:  if (day_in>max_feb_day)
                     quit_with_error();
    }
}

void date::quit_with_error()
{
    cout<<"\n\n\n\a*** Invalid date! ***\n\n";
    exit(1);
    //Non-zero return value indicates an error.
```

```
}

date::date(int day_in, int month_in, int year_in)
{
    set_date(day_in, month_in, year_in);
}

boolean date::set_date(int day_in, int month_in,
                                   int year_in)
{
    check_date(day_in, month_in, year_in);
    day = day_in;
    month = month_in;
    year = year_in;
}

void date::get_date(int& day_out, int& month_out,
                                       int& year_out)
{
    day_out = day;
    month_out = month;
    year_out = year;
}

void date::operator++(int)
{
    day++;
    if (day > month_days)
    {
        //Set date to first day of next month.
        day = 1;
        month++;
        if (month > 12) //New Year!
        {
            month = 1;
            year++;
        }
    }
}

boolean operator<=(date& date1, date& date2)
{
    if (date1.year > date2.year) return FALSE;
    if (date1.month > date2.month) return FALSE;
    if (date1.day > date2.day) return FALSE;
    return TRUE;
}

boolean operator>(date& date1, date& date2)
```

```
{
    if (date1.year < date2.year) return FALSE;
    else if (date1.year >date2.year) return TRUE;
    if (date1.month < date2.month)  return FALSE;
    else if (date1.month >date2.month) return TRUE;
    if (date1.day <= date2.day)  return FALSE;
    return TRUE;
}

ostream& operator<<(ostream& ostrm, date& date_out)
{
    ostrm<<setfill('0');
    ostrm<<setw(2)<<date_out.day<<'/';
    ostrm<<setw(2)<<date_out.month<<'/';
    ostrm<<setw(2)<<date_out.year;
    return ostrm;
}

istream& operator>>(istream& istrm, date& date_in)
{
    int dd, mm, yy;

    cin>>dec>>dd>>'/'>>mm>>'/'>>yy;
    date_in.set_date(dd,mm,yy);
    return istrm;
}
//--------------------------------------------------------

//dateordr.cpp
//Accepts pairs of dates and outputs them in order.

#include <iostream.h>
#include <ctype.h>
#include "dates2.h"

main()
{
    date date1(1,1,97), date2(1,1,97);
    char reply;

    do
    {
        cout<<"Enter 2 dates in the form dd/mm/yy:";
        cin>>date1>>date2;
        cout<<"\n\n";

        if (date2>date1)
        {
            cout<<date1<<'\n';
```

```
            cout<<date2;
        }
        else
        {
            cout<<date2<<'\n';
            cout<<date1;
        }
        cout<<"\n\n\n";
        cout<<"Do this again? (y/n) :   ";
        cin>>reply;
        reply = tolower(reply);
        cout<<"\n\n\n";
    }while (reply=='y');
    return 0;
}
```

```
3.
//time.h
//Declaration of class time.

#ifndef TIME_H
#define TIME_H

#include <iostream.h>

class time
{
private:
    int hours, minutes, seconds;
public:
    time(unsigned hrs=0,unsigned mins=0,unsigned secs=0)
    {
        set_time(hrs, mins, secs);
    }

    void get_time(int& hrs, int& mins, int& secs);
    void set_time(unsigned hrs, unsigned mins,
                                    unsigned secs);
    time& operator+=(unsigned int add_secs);
    time& operator+=(time& add_time);

    time operator++() //Pre-increment.
    {
        time temp_time = *this;

        (*this)+=1; //Use second += operator.
        return temp_time;
    }
```

```
    friend ostream& operator<<(ostream& ostrm, time&);
    friend istream& operator>>(istream& istrm, time&);
};

#endif
--------------------------------------------------------

//time.cpp
//Implementation of class time.

#include <iomanip.h>
#include "time.h"

void time::get_time(int& hrs, int& mins, int& secs)
{
    hrs=hours;
    mins=minutes;
    secs=seconds;
}

void time::set_time(unsigned hrs, unsigned mins,
                                  unsigned secs)
{
    hours = hrs%24;
    minutes = mins%60;
    seconds = secs%60;
}

void time::operator+=(unsigned int add_secs)
{
    int add_hrs = (add_secs/3600)%24;
    int add_mins = (add_secs-add_hrs*3600)/60;
    add_secs%=60;

    int min_carry = (seconds+add_secs)/60;
    seconds = (seconds+add_secs)%60;
    int hour_carry = (minutes+add_mins+min_carry)/60;
    minutes = (minutes+add_mins+min_carry)%60;
    hours = (hours+add_hrs+hour_carry)%24;
}

void time::operator+=(time& add_time)
{
    int min_carry = (seconds+add_time.seconds)/60;

    seconds = (seconds+add_time.seconds)%60;

    int hour_carry =
```

```
                    (minutes+add_time.minutes+min_carry)/60;

    minutes = (minutes+add_time.minutes+min_carry)%60;
    hours = (hours+add_time.hours+hour_carry)%24;
}


ostream& operator<<(ostream& ostrm, time& time_out)
{
    ostrm<<dec<<setfill('0')<<setw(2);
    ostrm<<time_out.hours<<':';
    ostrm<<setw(2)<<time_out.minutes<<':';
    ostrm<<setw(2)<<time_out.seconds;
    return ostrm;
}


istream& operator>>(istream& istrm, time& time_in)
{
    istrm>>dec>>setfill('0')>>setw(2);
    istrm>>time_in.hours>>':';
    istrm>>setw(2)>>time_in.minutes>>':';
    istrm>>setw(2)>>time_in.seconds;
    return istrm;
}
-------------------------------------------------------

//timedemo.cpp
//Demonstrates use of operator functions
//with class time.

#include <iostream.h>
#include <iomanip.h>
#include "time.h"

main()
{
    time time_in;
    //Default time of 00:00:00 assumed.

    for (int count=0; count<5; count++)
    {
        cout<<"Enter a time the format 'hh:mm:ss':";
        cin>>time_in;
        ++time_in;
        cout<<"One second later :    ";
        cout<<time_in<<"\n\n";
    }
    return 0;
}
```

```
4.
//ratnums.h
//Header file for class of rational numbers.

#ifndef RATNUMS_H
#define RATNUMS_H

#include <iostream.h>

enum boolean {FALSE, TRUE};

int gcd(int m, int n);
//Returns greatest common divisor of its arguments.

class rational_num
{
private:
    int numerator;
    int denominator;
public:
    rational_num(int num=1, int denom=1)
    {
        numerator=num;
        denominator=denom;
    }

    rational_num(rational_num&);
    //Copy constructor.

    void set_val(int num, int denom);
    void get_val(int& num, int& denom);
    void get_lowest_terms(int& num, int& denom);
    rational_num operator+ (rational_num&);
    rational_num operator-(rational_num&);
    rational_num operator*(rational_num&);
    rational_num operator/(rational_num&);
    boolean operator==(rational_num&);
    boolean operator<(rational_num&);
    boolean operator>(rational_num&);
    friend istream& operator>>(istream&, rational_num&);
    friend ostream& operator<<(ostream&, rational_num&);
};

#endif
```

```
//ratnums.cpp
//Implementation file for class of rational
//numbers.
```

```
#include <stdlib.h>
#include "ratnums.h"

rational_num::rational_num(rational_num& r)
{
    numerator = r.numerator;
    denominator = r.denominator;
}

void rational_num::set_val(int num, int denom)
{
    if (denom == 0)
    {
        cout<<"\n\n\n\a*** Denominator of zero not ";
        cout<<"allowed! ***\n\n";
        exit(1); //Any non-zero value indicates an error.
    }
    if (denom<0)      //Only numerator may be signed.
    {
        numerator = -num;
        denominator = -denom;
    }
    else
    {
        numerator = num;
        denominator = denom;
    }
}

void rational_num::get_val(int& num, int& denom)
{
    num = numerator;
    denom = denominator;
}

void rational_num::get_lowest_terms(int& num,int& denom)
{
    int sign_adjuster = 1;
    if (numerator < 0)
    {
        sign_adjuster = -1;
        num = -numerator;
        //Must be positive for arithmetic which follows.
    }
    else
        num = numerator;
    denom = denominator;
    if (num%denom == 0)
    //Num exactly divisible by denom.
```

```
    {
        num = (num/denom) * sign_adjuster;
        denom = 1;
        return;
    }
    if (denom%num == 0)
    //Denom exactly divisible by num.
    {
        denom/=num;
        num = 1*sign_adjuster;
        return;
    }
    int greatest_divisor;
    //Will hold greatest possible common divisor.

    if (num < denom)
        greatest_divisor = num/2;
    else
        greatest_divisor = denom/2;

    int divisor_found = FALSE;
    while ((greatest_divisor>1)&&(!divisor_found))
    {
        if ((num%greatest_divisor == 0) &&
                        (denom%greatest_divisor == 0))
            divisor_found = TRUE;
        else
            greatest_divisor--;
    }
    num = (num/greatest_divisor) * sign_adjuster;
    denom/=greatest_divisor;
}

rational_num rational_num::operator+(rational_num& r)
{
    rational_num result(*this);

    result.denominator *= r.denominator;
    result.numerator = (numerator * r.denominator)
                    + (denominator * r.numerator);
    int num, denom;
    result.get_lowest_terms(num,denom);
    return rational_num(num,denom);
}

rational_num rational_num::operator-(rational_num& r)
{
    rational_num result(*this);
```

```
    result.denominator *= r.denominator;
    result.numerator = (numerator * r.denominator)
                    - (denominator * r.numerator);
    int num, denom;
    result.get_lowest_terms(num,denom);
    return rational_num(num,denom);
}

rational_num rational_num::operator*(rational_num& r)
{
    rational_num result(*this);

    result.numerator *= r.numerator;
    result.denominator *= r.denominator;

    int num, denom;
    result.get_lowest_terms(num,denom);
    return rational_num(num,denom);
}

rational_num rational_num::operator/(rational_num& r)
{
    rational_num result(*this);

    result.numerator *= r.denominator;
    result.denominator *= r.numerator;

    int num, denom;
    result.get_lowest_terms(num,denom);
    return rational_num(num,denom);
}

boolean rational_num::operator==(rational_num& r)
//Not actually used by demo program.
{
    return boolean((numerator == r.numerator) &&
                    (denominator == r.denominator));
    //Typecast into appropriate return type.
}

boolean rational_num::operator<(rational_num& r)
{
    int numerator1 = numerator * r.denominator;
    int numerator2 = r.numerator * denominator;

    return boolean(numerator1<numerator2);
}

boolean rational_num::operator>(rational_num& r)
```

```
{
    int numerator1 = numerator * r.denominator;
    int numerator2 = r.numerator * denominator;

    return boolean(numerator1 > numerator2);

}

istream& operator>>(istream& c, rational_num& r)
{
    c>>r.numerator>>'/'>>r.denominator;
    return c;
}

ostream& operator<<(ostream& c, rational_num& r)
{
    c<<r.numerator<<"/"<<r.denominator;
    return c;
}
-----------------------------------------------------

//rational.cpp
//Demonstrates operation of class rational_num.

#include <iostream.h>
#include "ratnums.h"

main()
{
    unsigned short count;
    rational_num ratnum1, ratnum2;
    int num, denom;

    for (count=0; count<5; count++)
    {
        cout<<"Enter first rational number of pair :  ";
        cin>>ratnum1;
        cout<<"Enter second rational number of pair :  ";
        cin>>ratnum2;
        cout<<ratnum1<<" + "<<ratnum2<<" = ";
        cout<<(ratnum1 + ratnum2)<<"\n";
        cout<<ratnum1<<" - "<<ratnum2<<" = ";
        cout<<(ratnum1 - ratnum2)<<"\n";
        cout<<ratnum1<<" x "<<ratnum2<<" = ";
        cout<<(ratnum1 * ratnum2)<<"\n";
        cout<<'('<<ratnum1<<") / ("<<ratnum2;
        cout<<") = "<<(ratnum1 / ratnum2)<<"\n";
        if (ratnum1 < ratnum2)
            cout<<ratnum1<<" < "<<ratnum2;
```

```
        else if (ratnum1 > ratnum2)
            cout<<ratnum1<<" > "<<ratnum2;
        else
            cout<<ratnum1<<" = "<<ratnum2;
        cout<<"\n\n";
    }
    return 0;
}
```

Chapter 12

1.
```
//names_io.cpp
//Accepts 10 surnames and writes them to a serial
//file. Then reads back contents of file,
//displaying them on screen.

#include <fstream.h>

main()
{
    fstream namefile;
    char name[16];  //Maximum of 15 chars + '\n'.

    namefile.open("NAMES.DAT", ios::out);
    for (int count=0; count<10; count++)
    {
        cout<<"Enter name "<<(count+1)<<" :   ";
        cin>>name;
        namefile<<name<<'\n';
    }
    namefile.close();
    cout<<"\n\n\n\n\n";
    namefile.open("NAMES.DAT",ios::in);
    while (!namefile.eof())
    {
        namefile>>name;
        cout<<name<<'\n';
    }
    namefile.close();
    return 0;
}
```

2.
```
//addnames.cpp
//Opens a serial file holding 10 surnames and
//appends a further 5 names. Then reads back
//contents of file, displaying them on screen.

#include <fstream.h>

main()
{
    fstream namefile;
    char name[16];  //Maximum of 15 chars + '\n'.

    namefile.open("NAMES.DAT",ios::app);
    for (int count=0; count<5; count++)
    {
        cout<<"Enter name "<<(count+1)<<" :   ";
        cin>>name;
        namefile<<name<<'\n';
    }
    namefile.close();
    cout<<"\n\n\n\n\n";
    namefile.open("NAMES.DAT",ios::in);
    while (!namefile.eof())
    {
        namefile>>name;
        cout<<name<<'\n';
    }
    namefile.close();
    return 0;
}
```

3.
```
//copyfil1.cpp
//Creates a serial file of 10 names and then transfers
//file's contents to a second file, ensuring that the
//first letter of each name is a capital.

#include <fstream.h>
#include <ctype.h>

main()
{
    fstream namefile1, namefile2;
    char name[16];  //Maximum of 15 chars + '\n'.

    namefile1.open("NAMES1.DAT",ios::out);
    for (int count=0; count<10; count++)
```

```
    {
        cout<<"Enter name "<<(count+1)<<" :   ";
        cin>>name;
        namefile1<<name<<'\n';
    }
    namefile1.close();
    namefile1.open("NAMES1.DAT",ios::in);
    namefile2.open("NAMES2.DAT",ios::out);
    while (!namefile1.eof())
    {
        namefile1>>name;
        name[0]=toupper(name[0]);
        namefile2<<name<<'\n';
    }
    namefile1.close();
    namefile2.close();
    cout<<"\n\n\n\n\n";
    namefile2.open("NAMES2.DAT",ios::in);
    while (!namefile2.eof())
    {
        namefile2>>name;
        cout<<name<<'\n';
    }
    return 0;
}
```

4.
```
//copyfil2.cpp
//Creates a serial file of 10 names and then transfers
//the file's contents to a second file, ensuring that
//the first letter of each name is a capital.
//Accepts file names as command line parameters.

#include <fstream.h>
#include <ctype.h>
#include <stdlib.h>

main(int arg_count, char* arg[])
{
    fstream namefile1, namefile2;
    char name[16];   //Maximum of 15 chars + '\n'.

    if (arg_count < 3)
    {
        cout<<"\a*** Error : ";
        cout<<"fewer than 2 files! ***\n\n";
        exit(1);
    }
```

```
    namefile1.open(arg[1],ios::out);
    if (!namefile1)
    {
        cout<<"\a*** Error opening file ";
        cout<<arg[1]<<"! ***\n\n";
        exit(1);
    }
    namefile2.open(arg[2],ios::out);
    if (!namefile2)
    {
        cout<<"\a*** Error opening file ";
        cout<<arg[2]<<"! ***\n\n";
        exit(1);
    }
    for (int count=0; count<3; count++)
    {
        cout<<"Enter name "<<(count+1)<<" :   ";
        cin>>name;
        namefile1<<name<<'\n';
    }
    namefile1.close();
    namefile1.open(arg[1],ios::in);
    while (!namefile1.eof())
    {
        namefile1>>name;
        name[0]=toupper(name[0]);
        namefile2<<name<<'\n';
    }
    namefile1.close();
    namefile2.close();
    cout<<"\n\n\n\n\n";
    namefile2.open(arg[2],ios::in);
    while (!namefile2.eof())
    {
        namefile2>>name;
        cout<<name<<'\n';
    }
    return 0;
}
```

5.
```
//telnofil.cpp
//Creates a random access file holding 6 names and
//telephone numbers. Then allows the user to
//retrieve the telephone no. for any of the names.

#include <fstream.h>
```

```
#include <string.h>
#include <ctype.h>

void get_details(char* name, char* telnum);

enum boolean{FALSE,TRUE};

boolean find_number(fstream& file, char* name,
                                       char* telnum);


main()
{
    fstream phone_file;
    char name[31];
    char telnum[13];
    boolean name_found;
    char reply;

    phone_file.open("TELNUMS.DAT",ios::out);
    for (int count=0; count<6; count++)
    {
        get_details(name, telnum);
        phone_file.seekp(42*count,ios::beg);
        //Record length =
        //size of name field + size of telnum field
        //= 30 + 12 = 42

        phone_file.write(name,30);
        phone_file.write(telnum,12);
        cout<<"\n\n";
    }
    phone_file.close();
    do
    {
        cout<<"Enter name for required number : ";
        cin.getline(name,80,'\n');
        name_found = find_number(phone_file,name,telnum);
        cout<<'\n';
        if (name_found)
            cout<<"Telephone number :  "<<telnum;
        else
            cout<<"***\a Name not found! ***";
        cout<<"\n\n\n";
        cout<<"Repeat this? (y/n) :   ";
        cin>>reply;
        reply = tolower(reply);
        cout<<"\n\n";
    }while (reply=='y');
    phone_file.close();
```

```
      return 0;
}

void get_details(char* name, char* telnum)
{
      cout<<"Enter a name :   ";
      cin.getline(name,80,'\n');
      cout<<"\n\n";
      cout<<"Enter telephone number :   ";
      cin.getline(telnum,80,'\n');
}

boolean find_number(fstream& file, char* name,
                                        char* telnum)
{
    boolean found=FALSE;
    char name_read[31];

    file.open("TELNUMS.DAT",ios::in);
    while ((!file.eof()) && (!found))
    {
        file.read(name_read,30);
        file.read(telnum,12);
        if (strcmp(name_read,name)==0)
            found = TRUE;
    }
    file.close();
    return found;
}
```

6.
```
//stokfile.cpp
//Creates a random access file holding 6 stock items and
//associated levels. Then allows the user to retrieve or
//change stock level of any item.

#include <fstream.h>
#include <string.h>
#include <ctype.h>
#include <stdlib.h>

void get_details(char* item, char* level);

void get_choice(char& option);

enum boolean{FALSE,TRUE};

void get_or_change_level(fstream& file, char option);
```

```
streampos find_item(fstream& file, char* code,
                                        char* level);


main()
{
    fstream stock_file;
    char stock_code[9];
    //8 characters in code + '\0'.

    char stock_level[6];
    char option;

    stock_file.open("STOCK.DAT",ios::in|ios::out);
    for (int count=0; count<6; count++)
    {
        get_details(stock_code,stock_level);
        stock_file.write(stock_code,8);
        stock_file.write(stock_level,5);
        stock_file.flush();
        cout<<"\n\n";
    }
    do
    {
        get_choice(option);
        switch (option)
        {
            case 'r':
                get_or_change_level(stock_file,'r');
                break;
            case 'c' :
                get_or_change_level(stock_file,'c');
                break;
            case 'q' :
                //Nothing. (Quit option.)
                break;
            default :
                cout<<"\n\n";
                cout<<"\a*** Invalid option! ";
                cout<<"Press any key... ***";
                break;
        }
    }while (option!='q');
    stock_file.close();
    return 0;
}

void get_choice(char& option)
{
```

```cpp
    cout<<"           r. Retrieve a stock level.";
    cout<<"           c. Change a stock level.";
    cout<<"           q. Quit.";
    cout<<"\n          Enter your choice (r/c/q): ";
    cin>>option;
}

void get_details(char* code, char* level)
{
    cout<<"Enter stock code :  ";
    cin>>code;
    cout<<"\n\nEnter stock level :  ";
    cin>>level;
}

void get_or_change_level(fstream& file,char option)
{
    char code_in[9];
    streampos file_pos;
    char level[6],new_level[6];
    char any_key;

    cout<<"\n\n\nEnter stock code :  ";
    cin>>code_in;
    file_pos = find_item(file,code_in,level);
    //'file_pos' holds position of level.
    cout<<'\n';
    if (file_pos<0)
        cout<<"***\a Item not found! ***";
    else
    {
        cout<<"Current level :  "<<level<<"\n\n";;
        if (option=='c')
        {
            cout<<"Enter new level :  ";
            cin>>new_level;
            file.seekp(file_pos,ios::beg);
            file.write(new_level,5);
            file.flush();
        }
    }
    cout<<"\n\n\n";
    cout<<"Press any key to continue...";
    cin>>any_key;
}

streampos find_item(fstream& file,char* code,
                                    char* level)
{
```

```
        boolean found = FALSE;
        char code_read[9];
        streampos file_pos;

        file.seekg(0,ios::beg);
        while (!found)
        {
            file.read(code_read,8);
            if (file.eof()) break;
            file_pos = file.tellg();
            file.read(level,5);
            if (strcmp(code_read,code)==0)
                found = TRUE;
        }
        if (!found) {file_pos = -1;}
        return file_pos;
}
```

Chapter 13

```
1.
//account.h
//Holds declaration of account class (and also
//definition, since all functions are inline).

#ifndef ACCOUNT_H
#define ACCOUNT_H

class account
{
private:
    unsigned long int account_no;
    float balance;
public:
    account (unsigned long acct_no, float balance_in)
    {
        account_no = acct_no;
        balance = balance_in;
    }

    int operator>(account& acct)
    {
        if (balance > acct.balance) return 1;
        else return 0;
    }
```

```
        friend ostream& operator<<(ostream& ostrm,
                                   account& acct);
};

#endif
------------------------------------------------------


//account.cpp
//Holds definition of function to output
//an account class object.

#include <iostream.h>
#include <iomanip.h>
#include "account.h"

ostream& operator<<(ostream& ostrm, account& acct)
{
    ostrm<<"Account no. "<<acct.account_no<<'\n';
    ostrm<<setiosflags(ios::fixed|ios::showpoint);
    ostrm<<setprecision(2);
    ostrm<<"Balance        £"<<acct.balance<<'\n';
    return ostrm;
}
------------------------------------------------------


//max.h
//Holds declaration and definition of a generic function
//which returns the largest element in an array.

#ifndef MAX_H
#define MAX_H

template <class TYPE>
//Specifies base type of array.
TYPE maximum(TYPE* element, int size)
{
    TYPE temp = element[0];

    for (int count=1; count<size-1; count++)
    {
        if (element[count] > temp)
            temp = element[count];
    }
    return temp;
}

#endif
------------------------------------------------------
```

```
//maxdemo.cpp
//Declares 3 account objects and outputs the largest
//one, making use of the generic function 'maximum'.

#include <iostream.h>
#include "max.h"
#include "account.h"

main()
{
    account acct[3] = {  account(123456L,14759.28),
                         account(300300L,17648.35),
                         account(900900L,16508.95) };

    cout<<"Largest account :\n\n"<<maximum(acct,3);
    return 0;
}
```

2.
```
//swap.h
//Contains declaration and definition of generic
//swap function.

#ifndef SWAP_H
#define SWAP_H

template <class T>
void swap(T& val1, T& val2)
{
    T temp_val = val1;
    val1 = val2;
    val2 = temp_val;
}

#endif
```

```
//bubbsort.h
//Declares and defines a generic bubble sort function.

#ifndef BUBBSORT_H
#define BUBBSORT_H

template <class TYPE>
void bubble_sort(TYPE* value, int size)
{
```

```
    int upper_limit = size-1;
    for (int outer=upper_limit; outer>=0; outer--)
        for (int inner=0; inner<outer; inner++)
            if (value[inner] > value[inner+1])
                swap(value[inner],value[inner+1]);
}

#endif
```

```
//time.h
//Declaration of class time.

#ifndef TIME_H
#define TIME_H

#include <iostream.h>

enum boolean {FALSE, TRUE};

class time
{
private:
    int hours, minutes, seconds;
public:
    time(unsigned hrs=0,unsigned mins=0,unsigned secs=0)
    {
        set_time(hrs, mins, secs);
    }
    void get_time(int& hrs, int& mins, int& secs);
    void set_time(unsigned hrs,unsigned mins,
                                    unsigned secs);
    time& operator+=(unsigned add_secs);
    time& operator+=(time& add_time);

    time operator++();

    friend boolean operator>(time& time1, time& time2);
    friend ostream& operator<<(ostream& ostrm, time&);
    friend istream& operator>>(istream& istrm, time&);
};

#endif
```

```
//time.cpp
//Implementation of class time.
```

```cpp
#include <iomanip.h>
#include "time.h"

void time::get_time(int& hrs, int& mins, int& secs)
{
    hrs=hours;
    mins=minutes;
    secs=seconds;
}

void time::set_time(unsigned hrs,unsigned mins,
                                        unsigned secs)
{
    hours = hrs%24;
    minutes = mins%60;
    seconds = secs%60;
}

time& time::operator+=(unsigned add_secs)
{
    int add_hrs = (add_secs/3600)%24;
    int add_mins = (add_secs-add_hrs*3600)/60;
    add_secs%=60;

    int min_carry = (seconds+add_secs)/60;
    seconds = (seconds+add_secs)%60;
    int hour_carry = (minutes+add_mins+min_carry)/60;
    minutes = (minutes+add_mins+min_carry)%60;
    hours = (hours+add_hrs+hour_carry)%24;
    return *this;
}

time& time::operator+=(time& add_time)
{
    int min_carry = (seconds+add_time.seconds)/60;

    seconds = (seconds+add_time.seconds)%60;

    int hour_carry =
        (minutes+add_time.minutes+min_carry)/60;

    minutes = (minutes+add_time.minutes+min_carry)%60;
    hours = (hours+add_time.hours+hour_carry)%24;
    return *this;
}

time operator++() //Pre-increment.
{
    time temp_time = *this;
```

```
    (*this)+=1; //Use second += operator.
    return temp_time;
}

boolean operator>(time& time1, time& time2)
{
    if (time1.hours>time2.hours) return TRUE;
    if (time1.hours<time2.hours) return FALSE;

    if (time1.minutes>time2.minutes) return TRUE;
    if (time1.minutes<time2.minutes) return FALSE;

    if (time1.seconds>time2.seconds) return TRUE;
    return FALSE;
}

ostream& operator<<(ostream& ostrm, time& time_out)
{
    ostrm<<dec<<setfill('0')<<setw(2);
    ostrm<<time_out.hours<<':';
    ostrm<<setw(2)<<time_out.minutes<<':';
    ostrm<<setw(2)<<time_out.seconds;
    return ostrm;
}

istream& operator>>(istream& istrm, time& time_in)
{
    istrm>>dec>>setfill('0')>>setw(2);
    istrm>>time_in.hours>>':';
    istrm>>setw(2)>>time_in.minutes>>':';
    istrm>>setw(2)>>time_in.seconds;
    return istrm;
}
-------------------------------------------------------

//bsortdem.cpp
//Uses generic bubble sort function to sort 5 time
//class objects into ascending sequence and then
//displays them, in sorted sequence.

#include <iostream.h>
#include "swap.h"
#include "bubbsort.h"
#include "time.h"

main()
{
    time tim[5] =
```

```
        { time(5,17,39),time(23,14,3),time(17,55,1),
          time(1,1,1), time(0,45,37)};

    bubble_sort(tim,5);

    for (int count=0; count<5; count++)
        cout<<tim[count]<<'\n';
    cout<<"\n\n";
    return 0;
}
```

3.
```
//acctnode.h
//Header file for account nodes.

#include "listtemp.h"
#include <iomanip.h>

#ifndef ACCTNODE_H
#define ACCTNODE_H

struct account_node
{
    unsigned int acct_num;
    float balance;
    account_node* next_node;
    ~account_node();
};

void create_acct_list(list<account_node>&);

#endif
-------------------------------------------------------

//acctnode.cpp
//Implementation file for account nodes.

#include "acctnode.h"
#include <iostream.h>
#include <ctype.h>

account_node::~account_node()
{
    cout<<"\n\nAccount no. :   "<<acct_num;
    cout<<setiosflags(ios::fixed);
    cout<<setprecision(2);
    cout<<"\n\nBalance      :   "<<balance<<'\n';
```

```
}

void create_acct_list(list<account_node>& a_list)
{
    char reply;

    do
    {
        account_node* new_node = new account_node;
        cout<<"\n\nEnter account no.   : ";
        cin>>new_node->acct_num;
        cout<<"\nEnter current balance : ";
        cin>>new_node->balance;
        a_list.add_node(new_node);
        cout<<"\n\nEenter another account?(y/n): ";
        cin>>reply;
    }while(tolower(reply) == 'y');
}
```

```
//examnode.h
//Header file for exam nodes.

#include "listtemp.h"

#ifndef EXAMNODE_H
#define EXAMNODE_H

struct exam_node
{
    char surname[15];
    unsigned short mark;
    exam_node* next_node;
    ~exam_node();
};

void create_exam_list(list<exam_node>&);

#endif
```

```
//examnode.cpp
//Implementation file for exam nodes.

#include "examnode.h"
#include <iostream.h>
#include <ctype.h>

exam_node::~exam_node()
```

```
{
    cout<<"\n\nSurname :   "<<surname;
    cout<<"\n\nMark     :   "<<mark<<'\n';
}

void create_exam_list(list<exam_node>& e_list)
{
    char reply;

    do
    {
        exam_node* new_node = new exam_node;
        cout<<"\n\nEnter surname    :   ";
        cin>>new_node->surname;
        cout<<"\nEnter exam mark :   ";
        cin>>new_node->mark;
        e_list.add_node(new_node);
        cout<<"\n\nEnter another name?(y/n) :    ";
        cin>>reply;
    }while(tolower(reply) == 'y');
}
----------------------------------------------------

//listtemp.h
//Header file for linked list parameterised type.

#ifndef LISTTEMP_H
#define LISTTEMP_H

#include <iostream.h>

template<class T>
class list
{
private:
    T* head;
public:
    list() {head = NULL;}
    ~list();
    void add_node(T*);
};

template <class T>
list<T>::~list()
{
    T* this_node = head;

    while (this_node != NULL)
    {
```

```
        head = head->next_node;
        delete this_node;
        this_node = head;
    }
}

template <class T>
void list<T>::add_node(T* new_node)
{
    new_node->next_node = head;
    head = new_node;
}

#endif
--------------------------------------------------------

//template.cpp
//Creates 2 linked lists with differing structures,
//using same template.

#include "listtemp.h"
#include "examnode.h"
#include "acctnode.h"

main()
{
    list<exam_node> exam_list;
    list<account_node> acct_list;

    create_exam_list(exam_list);
    create_acct_list(acct_list);

    return 0;
}
```

Index

D

E